CANBERRA PAPERS ON
STRATEGY AND DEFENCE NO. 118

THE SEAS UNITE: MARITIME COOPERATION IN THE ASIA PACIFIC REGION

Edited by

Sam Bateman and Stephen Bates

Published by
Strategic and Defence Studies Centre
Research School of Pacific and Asian Studies
The Australian National University
Canberra, Australia
1996

National Library of Australia
Cataloguing-in-Publication entry

The seas unite : maritime cooperation in the Asia Pacific region.

Bibliography.
ISBN 0 7315 2535 3.

1. National security - Pacific Area. 2. Pacific Area cooperation.
3. Marine resources - Pacific Area. 4. Asia - Relations - Pacific
Area. 5. Pacific Area - Relations - Asia. I. Bateman, W.S.G.
(Walter Samuel Grono), 1938-. II. Bates, Stephen, 1952-.
III. Australian National University. Strategic and Defence Studies
Centre. IV. CSCAP Maritime Cooperation Working Group.
Meeting. (2nd: 1996 : Kuala Lumpur). (Series : Canberra papers
on strategy and defence ; no. 118).

337.11823

Series Editor Helen Hookey
Word processing by Elza Sullivan
Cartography by Keith Mitchell and Ian Faulkner, Cartography
    Unit, RSPAS, ANU
Cover design by Roy Blinston Design Studio, photograph by
    Miguel Fortes
Printed by ANU Printing Service
Published and distributed by:
    Strategic and Defence Studies Centre
    Research School of Pacific and Asian Studies
    The Australian National University
    Canberra ACT 0200
    Australia

Telephone (06) 2438555
Fax (06) 2480816

ABSTRACT

This monograph includes the discussion papers presented at the Second Meeting of the CSCAP Maritime Cooperation Working Group held in Kuala Lumpur 16-17 April 1996.

These papers confirmed that maritime issues, and the maritime environment generally, are a rich source of ideas and initiatives for developing the habit of cooperation and dialogue between Asia Pacific countries.

Our choice of title for the proceedings of the second meeting, *The Seas Unite: Maritime Cooperation in the Asia Pacific Region*, reflects the progress made by CSCAP Maritime Cooperation Working Group in defining issues and identifying key areas for further action. The papers presented to the meeting enabled the Working Group to identify a comprehensive way ahead covering a wide range of initiatives that could provide the basis for a possible regional agreement on maritime cooperation, education and training, and the management of regional seas. These initiatives are described in more detail in the last chapter of this book. Preceding chapters cover areas such as regional naval cooperation, shipping and maritime safety, marine scientific research and environmental issues, and the resolution of marine resource and boundary disputes.

The CSCAP Maritime Cooperation Working Group is dealing with issues which are of growing common concern to regional countries. They have immense potential value as a basis for preventive diplomacy and confidence building in the region. This potential has been recognised by the ASEAN Regional Forum but, while progress is being made, there is still a long way to go in implementing practical measures to overcome the tensions and unresolved problems of jurisdiction and sovereignty that exist in the maritime environment of the Asia Pacific region.

Canberra Papers on Strategy and Defence are a series of monograph publications that arise out of the work of the Strategic and Defence Studies Centre at the Australian National University. Previous Canberra Papers have covered topics such as the relationship of the superpowers, arms control at both the superpower and Southeast Asian regional level, regional strategic relationships and major aspects of Australian defence policy. For a list of New Series Canberra Papers please refer to the last pages of this volume.

Unless otherwise stated, publications of the Centre are presented without endorsement as contributions to the public record and debate. Authors are responsible for their own analysis and conclusions.

CONTENTS

FIGURES

TABLES

ACRONYMS AND ABBREVIATIONS

ACRS	Arms Control and Regional Security
ADB	Asian Development Bank
ADCP	Acoustic Doppler Current Profiler
ADEX	Air Defence Exercise
AIT	Asian Institute of Technology
AMIDI	Australian Marine Data Inventory
APEC	Asia Pacific Economic Cooperation
ARF	ASEAN Regional Forum
ARs	Artificial Reefs
ASCOPE	ASEAN Council On Petroleum
ASEAN	Association of Southeast Asian Nations
ASEAN-OSRAP	ASEAN Oil Spill Response and Preparedness
ASOEN	ASEAN Senior Officials for the Environment Network
ASW	Anti-Submarine Warfare
AUS-CSCAP	Australian Committee of CSCAP
AusAID	Australian Agency for International Development
CBM	Confidence-Building Measures
CCOP	Committee for Coordination of Joint Prospecting for Mineral Resources
CDE	Conference on Disarmament in Europe
CIDA	Canadian International Development Agency
CNS	Chief of the Naval Staff
CSBM	Confidence- and Security-Building Measures
CSCAP	Council for Security Cooperation in the Asia Pacific
CSCE	Conference on Security and Cooperation in Europe
CSIRO	Commonwealth Scientific and Industrial Research Organisation
DENR	Department of Environment and Natural Resources (The Philippines)
DMA	Dangerous Military Activities
DOD	(US) Department of Defense
DPRK	Democratic People's Republic of Korea (North Korea)
DSOTs	Daily System Operational Tests
DSTO	(Australian) Defence Science and Technology Organisation

ECSCAP	European CSCAP
EEZ	Exclusive Economic Zone
ESCAP	Economic and Social Commission for Asia and the Pacific
EU	European Union
FAO	Food and Agriculture Organisation
FAWEU	Forces Answerable to the Western European Union
FPDA	Five Power Defence Arrangements
GATT	General Agreement on Tariffs and Trade
GDP	Gross Domestic Product
GIS	Geographic Information System
GOOS	Global Ocean Observing System
GPS	Global Positioning System
GRT	Gross Registered Tonnage
HENs	Heads of European Navies
IADS	Integrated Air Defence Systems
IBRD	International Bank for Reconstruction and Development
ICAO	International Civil Aviation Organisation
ICJ	International Court of Justice
ICLARM	International Centre for Living Aquatic Resources Management
ICSU	International Council of Scientific Unions
IDSA	Institute for Defence Studies and Analyses
IMO	International Maritime Organisation
IMRID	Indonesian Marine Resources Information Database
INCSEA	Incidents at Sea agreement
IOC	Intergovernmental Oceanographic Commission
IODE	International Oceanographic Data Exchange
IPKF	Indian Peace-Keeping Force
ISG	Intersessional Support Group
ISIS	Institute for Strategic and International Studies (Malaysia)
ISM	Intersessional Meeting
ISS	International Seapower Symposium
ITOPF	International Tanker Owners Pollution Federation Ltd
JET	Joint Exercises Trincomalee

JGOFS	Joint Global Ocean Flux Study
JMSDF	Japan Maritime Self-Defense Force
LCDR	Lieutenant-Commander
LCR	Living Coastal Resources
LIPI	Indonesian Institute of Sciences
LNG	Liquefied Natural Gas
LPG	Liquefied Petroleum Gas
LTTE	Liberation Tigers of Tamil Eelam
MCA	Multiple Claim Area
MCM	Mine Countermeasures
MCMAs	Marine Coastal Management Areas
MCSBM	Maritime Confidence- and Security-Building Measure
MEPP	Middle East Peace Process
MIED	Maritime Information Exchange Directory
MIMA	Maritime Institute of Malaysia
MR	Maritime Reconnaissance
MREP	Marine Resource Evaluation and Planning
MRMs	Mutual Reassurance Measures
NATMIS	National Marine Information System
NATO	North Atlantic Treaty Organisation
NGO	Non-Governmental Organisation
NOAA	(US) National Oceanic and Atmospheric Administration
NPT	Non-Proliferation Treaty
OECD	Organisation for Economic Cooperation and Development
OSCE	Organisation for Security and Cooperation in Europe
OSD/ISA	(US) Office of the Secretary of Defense/International Security Affairs
PAFTAD	Pacific Trade and Development Conference
PASOLS	Pacific Area Senior Officers' Logistic Seminar
PASSEX	Passing Exercise
PECC	Pacific Economic Cooperation Conference
PFP	Partnership for Peace
PHP	Philippine Peso
PMC	Post-Ministerial Conference
PRC	People's Republic of China

R&D	Research and Development
RAN	Royal Australian Navy
RAS	Replenishment-At-Sea
REMASSAR	Regional Maritime Surveillance and Safety Regime
RMAF	Royal Malaysian Air Force
RMN	Royal Malaysian Navy
ROK	Republic of Korea (South Korea)
RSN	Republic of Singapore Navy
RTN	Royal Thai Navy
SAARC	South Asian Association for Regional Cooperation
SAIC	Science Applications International Corporation
SAR	Search and Rescue
SAREX	SAR Exercise
SCA	Spratly Coordinating Agency (proposed)
SEANWFZ	Southeast Asian Nuclear Weapon Free Zone
SEAPOL	South-East Programme in Ocean Law, Policy and Management
SIPRI	Stockholm International Peace Research Institute
SLOCs	sea lines of communication
SMA	Spratly Management Authority (proposed)
SMAs	Special Marine Areas
SMIS	Strategic Maritime Information System
SOM	Senior Officials Meeting
STANAVFORPAC	Standing Naval Force in Asia (proposed)
TAC	Treaty of Amity and Cooperation in Southeast Asia
TBMs	Trust-Building Measures
TOGA	Tropical Ocean Global Atmosphere
UN	United Nations
UNCED	United Nations Conference on Environment and Development
UNCLOS	United Nations Convention on the Law of the Sea
UNDP	United Nations Development Programme
UNEP	United Nations Environment Programme
UNESCO	United Nations Educational, Scientific and Cultural Organisation
UNGA	United Nations General Assembly
UNROCA	United Nations Register of Conventional Arms
UNTAC	United Nations Transitional Authority in Cambodia

USN	US Navy
WB	World Bank
WCRP	World Climate Research Programme
WEEO	Weapons Electrical Engineering Officer
WESTPAC	IOC Sub-Commission for the Western Pacific
WEU	Western European Union
WMO	World Meteorological Organisation
WOCE	World Ocean Circulation Experiment
WPFCC	Western Pacific Fisheries Consultative Committee
WPNS	Western Pacific Naval Symposium
WTO	World Trade Organisation
ZOPFAN	Zone of Peace, Freedom and Neutrality

CONTRIBUTORS

Desmond Ball is a Professor in the Strategic and Defence Studies Centre, Australian National University, Canberra. (He was Head of the Centre from 1984 to 1991.) He is author or editor of some 40 books or monographs on nuclear strategy, defence decision-making, Australian defence, and security in the Asia Pacific region. His recent publications include monographs entitled *Building Blocks for Regional Security: An Australian Perspective on Confidence and Security Building Measures (CSBMs) in the Asia-Pacific Region* (Strategic and Defence Studies Centre, Australian National University, Canberra, 1991); *Signals Intelligence in the Post-Cold War Era: Developments in the Asia-Pacific Region* (Institute of Southeast Asian Studies, Singapore, 1993); *The Transformation of Security in the Asia/Pacific Region* (Frank Cass, London, 1996); and *Presumptive Engagement: Australia's Asia-Pacific Security Policy in the 1990s* (Allen & Unwin in assoc. with the Department of International Relations, Australian National University, Sydney and Canberra, 1996); and articles on issues such as the strategic culture in the Asia Pacific region and defence acquisition programmes in the region, published in *Security Dialogue, Security Studies* and *International Security*. Professor Ball is a founding member of the Steering Committee of the Council for Security Cooperation in the Asia Pacific (CSCAP) and Joint Chairman of the Australian Committee of CSCAP (AUS-CSCAP).

Mohd Nizam Basiron is presently a Senior Analyst at the Centre of Coastal Development, Marine Environment and Resources, Maritime Institute of Malaysia. His previous employment was with the World Wide Fund for Nature (Malaysia) as a Scientific Officer for Conservation Policy Development. His area of interest is Post-UNCED Development in Malaysia, particularly in relation to marine pollution from land-based activities.

Sam Bateman retired from the Royal Australian Navy (RAN) in 1993 with the rank of Commodore, and took up a position as Manager (now Executive Director) of the Centre for Maritime Policy at the University of Wollongong in New South Wales. His naval experience included four ship commands, five years' service in Papua New Guinea, and several postings in the force development and strategic policy areas of the Department of Defence in Canberra. He has written extensively on defence and maritime issues in Australia and the Asia Pacific and the Indian Ocean regions, and is a Joint Chairman of the Council for Security Cooperation in the Asia Pacific (CSCAP) Working Group on Maritime Cooperation.

Stephen Bates is the Executive Officer of the Australian Committee of the Council for Security Cooperation in the Asia Pacific (AUS-CSCAP). He has an MA in International Relations from the Australian National University and is completing a doctoral thesis entitled 'The New Regionalism: Comparing Developments in the EC, North America and the Asia Pacific'. His publications include *The South Pacific Island Countries and France: a study in interstate relations* (Department of International Relations, Australian National University, Canberra, 1990).

George R. Cresswell is the leader of the regional oceanography and remote sensing project at the Commonwealth Scientific and Industrial Research Organisation (CSIRO) in Hobart, Tasmania. He has a Bachelor of Science degree from the University of Western Australia and a PhD from the University of Alaska. He was Co-Chief Scientist for the ASEAN-Australian Regional Ocean Dynamics Expedition 1993-95, working with marine scientists and ships from most of the ASEAN countries. His work includes studies of the seas of Australia and Southeast Asia: with D. Quadfasel, 'A note on the seasonal variability of the South Java current', *Journal of Geophysical Research*, Vol.97, 1992; with J. Peterson, 'The Leeuwin Current south of Western Australia', *Australian Journal of Maritime and Freshwater Research*, Vol.44, 1993; with A. Frische, J. Peterson and D. Quadfasel, 'Circulation in the Timor Sea', *Journal of Geophysical Research*, Vol.98, 1993; with S. Blackburn, 'A Coccolithophorid Bloom in Jervis Bay, Australia', *Australian Journal of Marine and Freshwater Research*, Vol.44, 1993; 'Nutrient Enrichment of the Sydney Continental Shelf', *Australian Journal of Marine and Freshwater Research*, Vol.45, 1994; 'The Leeuwin Current near Rottnest Island, Western Australia', *Australian Journal of Marine and Freshwater Research*, in press, 1995; and with Z. Changbao, P. Tildesley and C. Nilsson, 'SAR Observations of Internal Lee and Wake Waves from Sea

Mounts', *Australian Journal of Marine and Freshwater Research*, in press, 1995.

Admiral Sir James Eberle is Director of the UK Japan 2000 Group, having been Director of the Royal Institute of International Affairs from 1984 to 1991. He retired from the Royal Navy in 1983. Between 1976 and 1983 he held the posts of a member of Admiralty Board, Commander-in-Chief UK Fleet, Allied Commander-in-Chief NATO Channel Command, and Commander-in-Chief of the Royal Navy Home Command. He undertook postgraduate education at the Royal Naval College, Greenwich, and attended the Joint Services Staff College and the NATO Defence College. He carried out a Defence Fellowship at University College, Oxford. He holds the Honorary Degree of Doctor of Laws/Letters from the Universities of Bristol and Sussex. Sir James holds the Honorary Appointment to the Royal Household of Vice Admiral of the United Kingdom.

Miguel Fortes is a Professor of Marine Science at the Marine Science Institute of the University of the Philippines. For the past twenty-five years he has worked as a coastal zone biologist doing research and academic studies on coastal and maritime plant ecology and as a Technical Consultant to, among others, USAID, UNEP/UNDP, ADB/WB, CIDA, IDRC and WTO, analysing natural resource policy and development issues, with a focus on marine resource use, land use change, environmental assessment, tourism development and coastal rehabilitation. He is the author of six books, 41 technical articles for international/regional refereed journals and proceedings and 32 articles in national journals. In March 1996 he was awarded the International Biwako Prize for Ecology by the Shiga Prefecture of Japan.

Bates Gill leads the Project on Security and Arms Control in East Asia at the Stockholm International Peace Research Institute (SIPRI) in Sweden, and is a consultant on East Asian affairs to the Center for Nonproliferation Studies in Monterey, California. Formerly he held the Fei Yiming Chair in Comparative Politics at the Johns Hopkins University Center for Chinese and American Studies, Nanjing, China.

His research focuses particularly on arms trade, arms production and regional security in East Asia. He is co-author of the MIMA-SIPRI report entitled *ASEAN Arms Acquisitions: Developing Transparency* which first appeared in August 1995, and co-editor of the forthcoming book, *Arms Trade, Transparency, and Security in Southeast Asia* (Oxford University Press, 1996). Among his publications in the annual *SIPRI Yearbook* are 'Arms Acquisitions in East Asia' (1994) and 'Northeast Asia and Multilateral Security Institutions' and 'The divided nations of China and Korea: discord and dialogue' (1996). His fourth book, *Arming East Asia*, will be published by Oxford University Press in 1997. Other publications include articles in *Asian Survey, China Quarterly, Orbis, Pacific Review, Arms Control Today* and *Nonproliferation Review*.

Eric Grove was a civilian Lecturer at the Britannia Royal Naval College, Dartmouth from 1971 to 1984. Leaving as Deputy Head of Strategic Studies he worked for a year with the Council for Arms Control before becoming a freelance historian, lecturer and defence analyst. During this time he was Visiting Lecturer at the Royal Naval College Greenwich and Cambridge University, and a Research Fellow at the University of Southampton. His monographs include *Vanguard to Trident: British Naval Policy Since World War II* (Bodley Head, London, 1987); *The Future of Sea Power* (Routledge, London, 1990); and *Maritime Strategy and European Security* (Brassey's, London and Washington, 1990). Since 1993 he has been on the staff at the University of Hull, where he is Senior Lecturer in Politics and Deputy Director of the Centre for Security Studies.

Grant J. Hewison is a Fellow at the Centre for Strategic Studies at Victoria University, Wellington, New Zealand and a Senior Lecturer in the School of Integrated Business Studies at the Auckland Institute of Technology. He has a Bachelor of Arts (Political Science), a Bachelor of Laws and a Master of Laws (Honours) from Auckland University. Prior to taking up his current position at the Auckland Institute of Technology, Grant Hewison was a visiting Law Fellow with the Center for International Environmental Law in Washington DC. He also acted as Legal Counsel for Greenpeace New Zealand between 1989 and 1991. As an expert of international standing in the area of trade and the environment, ocean law and policy, and international law generally, he has participated in numerous international conferences on international trade, development and the marine environment. His many articles and publications include a forthcoming edited anthology entitled *Trade, Environment and Sustainable Development - A South Asian Perspective*, edited for the United Nations Conference on Trade and Development; *Guideline on New Zealand's International Obligations Affecting Coastal Environment : Reconciling Trade and the Environment - Issues for New Zealand* (Institute of Policy Studies, Victoria University, Wellington, 1995); 'High Seas Driftnet Fishing in the South Pacific and the Law of the Sea', *Georgetown International Environmental Law Review* (Vol. 5, Issue 2, Spring 1993); and 'Sensitive Aquatic Habitat in the Gulf of Aqaba' (chapter in an Environmental Law Institute publication presented to the Middle East Peace talks, 1993). He is also co-editor of *Freedom For The Seas In The 21st Century: Ocean Governance And Environmental Harmony* (Island Press, Washington DC, 1993).

Rear Admiral (Ret.) Sumihiko Kawamura is currently Senior Adviser to the Aerospace Department of Okura & Co. Ltd and Vice-Senior Adviser to the Machinery and Industries Group of Okura & Co. Ltd in Tokyo. His senior postings in the Japanese Maritime Self-Defense Force (JMSDF) included that of Naval Attaché at the Embassy of Japan in Washington DC and Commander Fleet Air Wings Four and Five. Since retiring from the JMSDF he has been an active contributor to the regional dialogue on maritime issues and has participated in many international maritime conferences.

J.N. Mak is currently Director of Research at the Maritime Institute of Malaysia (MIMA) in Kuala Lumpur. He also heads the Institute's Centre for Maritime Security and Diplomacy. His research interests centre around regional security issues, with special emphasis on defence and naval strategies of the Asia Pacific region, on which he has published extensively. His writings include *ASEAN Defence Reorientation 1975-1992* (Strategic and Defence Studies Centre, Australian National University, Canberra, 1994). His other areas of interest include arms acquisitions and transfers. He is currently focusing on conceptual approaches to confidence building and transparency, and their relevance to Southeast Asia. He is also co-author of the monograph *ASEAN Arms Acquisitions: Developing*

Transparency, published by MIMA and SIPRI in 1995. Forthcoming publications include a chapter on the Malaysian Armed Forces in *Force Modernisation in Southeast Asia*, to be published by the Institute of Southeast Asian Studies, Singapore, and another chapter on 'The ASEAN "Way" and Transparency: Implications for a Regional Arms Register' in a volume on the impact of regional arms registers on confidence and trust building in Southeast Asia, to be published jointly by SIPRI and MIMA.

Colonel Lui Tuck Yew is Head of Naval Operations at the Headquarters of the Republic of Singapore Navy. He has served in a variety of postings, both at sea and ashore in the Singapore Navy, including Head of the Naval Intelligence Department and Squadron Commanding Officer Afloat. He holds a BA (Hons) from Trinity College and an MA (TUFTS).

Rear Admiral Nitz Srisomwong, Superintendent of the Institute of Advanced Naval Studies, has had extensive service in the Royal Thai Navy and has studied abroad at the US Naval War College. His naval postings include that of Naval Attaché in Jakarta and General Director of the Naval Research and Development Department. He has also served as Secretary to the Deputy Minister of the Interior and to the Deputy Minister of Defence and has written articles on maritime, economic and strategic issues.

Jin-Hyun Paik is Professor at the Institute of Foreign Affairs and National Security in the Ministry of Foreign Affairs. Previous positions include Research Associate at The Hague Academy of International Law, Attorney-at-law (Member of New York Bar), Chairman of the Asian Group United Nations Conference on the Law of the Sea, Member of the Presidential Commission on the 21st Century (Korea) and Member of the Commission on External Economic Policy Coordination. Dr Paik's publications include: *Exploring Maritime Cooperation in Northeast Asia: Possibility and Prospects* (ed.); *Nuclear Conundrum: Analysis and Assessment of Two Koreas' Policies Regarding the Nuclear Issues; Rethinking Collective Security in the Post-Cold War, Myth and Reality of the UN's Role in International Peace and Security.*

Lieutenant Commander Razali Md Ali has been in the Royal Malaysian Navy since 1978 and currently serves in the RMN Strategic Wing. He studied strategic studies at the Malaysian National University and maritime studies at the US Coast Guard Training Center in Virginia USA. His naval experience includes two ship commands and several postings in the Ministry of Defence. By profession he is an Anti-Submarine Warfare (ASW) Officer.

Rahul Roy-Chaudhury is a Research Officer at the Institute for Defence Studies and Analyses (IDSA), New Delhi, India, where he specialises in naval and maritime affairs. He was educated in India and Britain, receiving an MLitt degree in International Relations from Oxford University in 1991. He has written extensively on naval and maritime security issues in the Indian Ocean. His first book, *Sea Power and Indian Security* (Brassey's [UK] Ltd., London), was published in 1995. He has also written a number of research articles for academic and defence journals in India and abroad, including *The Asian Strategic Review, Strategic Analysis, Indian Defence Review, Maritime International, Journal of Indian Ocean Studies, Vayu 2000 Aerospace Review* and *Contemporary South Asia.* At IDSA Rahul Roy-Chaudhury has worked on projects and appears for various ministries and agencies of the Indian government. These include a report on 'Post-Cold War Trends in Arms Transfers' for the Prime Minister's Office, and a paper on 'The Changing Face of Defence' for the Ministry of Defence. He is also the Indian representative in the Maritime Cooperation Working Group of CSCAP.

Rear Admiral (Retd) R.M. Sundardi is currently Senior Advisor to the Minister of Defence and Security, Republic of Indonesia. He has a Masters Degree in Physics from the Bandung Institute of Technology, Indonesia, and in Operation Research from the US Postgraduate School, Monterey, California. During his lengthy career in the Armed Forces he held various positions in the Planning Staff of the Headquarters of the Navy and of the Armed Forces. Before assuming his current position he was Director of Strategic Planning in the Ministry of Defence.

Russ Swinnerton is a writer and former naval officer. He has had a number of sea appointments and has served as an operations staff office in strategic, operational and tactical-level headquarters. He commanded the frigate HMAS *Torrens* on deployment in Southeast Asia in 1989-90 and was Australian Defence Adviser to Malaysia 1994-96. He is a recent graduate in Communication from the University of Canberra and was the RAN's visiting fellow at the Strategic and Defence Studies Centre, Australian National University in 1993. He has published a number of journal articles and working papers on regional security issues. He has won two awards for short fiction and has published several short stories. He writes a weekly column on motorcycling for the *Sun* in Kuala Lumpur and has published a novel for children.

Ian Townsend-Gault is Director of the Centre for Asian Legal Studies at the Faculty of Law, University of British Columbia in Vancouver, Canada. He is also the Director of the West Coast Office and a Member of the Board of Directors of the Oceans Institute of Canada. He has worked as teacher, researcher and consultant in law and policy issues applicable to oceans, ocean resources, the environment and the coastal zone for many years. Much of this work has been done in Southeast Asia. In 1989, Ian Townsend-Gault and Ambassador Hasjim Djalal of Indonesia initiated a series of workshops on cooperation between the states of the South China Sea region, with funding from the Canadian International Development Agency (CIDA). More than fourteen meetings have been held in Brunei, China, Indonesia, the Philippines, Singapore, Thailand and Vietnam, on cooperation in subjects such as marine scientific research, marine environmental protection, navigation safety, resource assessment and legal issues arising from cooperation. Townsend-Gault also initiated a programme of technical assistance for Vietnam, also funded by CIDA, on law and policy in marine environmental protection, petroleum management, fisheries and transportation. He has published widely in his areas of specialisation, and has addressed the annual Asia-Pacific Roundtable organised by ISIS Malaysia for the past three years. He is also a regular contributor to conferences organised by the International

Boundaries Research Unit at the University of Durham, England. He is a member of the board of Canadian CSCAP.

Mark J. Valencia is a Senior Fellow with the Program on International Economics and Politics at the East-West Center in Honolulu. He has a Masters of Marine Affairs from the University of Rhode Island and a PhD in Oceanography from the University of Hawaii. Before joining the Center in 1977, Dr Valencia was a lecturer at the Universiti Sains Malaysia and a Technical Expert with the UNDP Regional Project on Offshore Prospecting based in Bangkok. He has published over 100 articles and books, including: *A Maritime Regime for Northeast Asia* (Oxford University Press, 1996); *China and the South China Sea Disputes* (Adelphi Paper, Oxford University Press for the Institute for International and Strategic Studies, Oxford, 1995); *Pacific Ocean Boundary Problems: Status and Solutions* (with Douglas Johnson, Martinus Nijhoff, Dordrecht, 1991); *Atlas for Marine Policy in East Asian Seas* (with Joseph Morgan, University of California Press, Berkeley, 1992); *Southeast Asian Seas: Oil Under Troubled Waters* (Oxford University Press, Singapore and Oxford, 1985); and *Atlas for Marine Policy in Southeast Asian Seas* (with Joseph Morgan, University of California Press, Berkeley, 1983). He is also a frequent contributor to the mass media on Asian maritime affairs and has written several articles for the *Asian Wall Street Journal Weekly, Far Eastern Economic Review, International Herald Tribune,* and *Trends* (Singapore).

Jon M. van Dyke has been a Professor of Law at the William S. Richardson School of Law, University of Hawaii at Manoa, since 1976 and served as Associate Dean between 1980 and 1982. From 1988 to 1990 he was Director of the University's Spark M. Matsunaga Institute for Peace. He previously taught at the University of California's Hastings College of Law in San Francisco (1970-76) and at Catholic University Law School in Washington DC (1967-69). Professor van Dyke has written or edited six books on constitutional law and international law topics and has authored and co-authored many articles in these fields, focusing particularly on international human rights and ocean law and international and environmental law. His most recent book, *Freedom for the Seas in the 21st Century: Ocean Governance and Environmental Harmony* (Island Press, Washington DC,

1993), co-edited with Durwood Zaelke and Grant Hewison, was co-winner of the Harold and Margaret Sprout Award for the best book on international environmental policy for 1994. He is a member of the editorial boards of *Marine Policy* and the *International Journal of Marine and Coastal Law*.

Stanley Weeks is Senior Scientist in the Programs and Policy Division of Science Applications International Corporation (SAIC) in the United States. He has a BS in Foreign Affairs from the US Naval Academy and a PhD in International Studies from the American University. Dr Weeks has over 25 years' experience in international policy and security issues. Recent work at the SAIC has included support for the Office of the Secretary of Defense in developing Pacific multilateral security cooperation and US policy alternatives for Korea, and support for Navy Staff in strategy development, force structure analysis and naval forward presence. His prior background includes leadership in arms control and international negotiations, key strategic planning roles, and extensive operational experience at sea, including command of the *Spruance*-class destroyer flagship for NATO's multilateral Standing Naval Force Atlantic. Dr Weeks' experience in the State Department included US and NATO nuclear and conventional force and policy planning responsibility, as well as responsibility for the Stockholm CDE Agreement on Confidence Building Measures. As a member of the National War College Strategy Department faculty, Dr Weeks developed and led the core course on Strategic Planning and Resource Allocation. Dr Weeks has also served as a member of the United Nations Experts group on Maritime Security and is a member of the Board of Directors of the US Committee of CSCAP. His most recent publications include 'Maritime Risk Reduction and Maritime Cooperation in the Pacific' (for OSD/ISA [EAPR]), August 1996; and 'Naval Forward Presence in the Cold War: Forces for Crisis Response and Deterrence' (for US Navy Staff), August 1996.

PREFACE

This book includes papers presented at the second meeting of the Working Group on Maritime Cooperation established by the Council for Security Cooperation in Asia Pacific (CSCAP). The meeting was held at the Maritime Institute of Malaysia (MIMA) in Kuala Lumpur on 16-17 April 1996. The papers have been published under the auspices of the Australian Committee for CSCAP (AUS-CSCAP).

The objectives of the Maritime Cooperation Working Group are to:

- foster maritime cooperation and dialogue among the states of the Asia Pacific region and enhance their ability to manage and use the maritime environment without prejudicing the interests of each other;

- develop an understanding of regional maritime issues and the scope they provide for cooperation and dialogue;

- contribute to a stable maritime regime in the Asia Pacific region which will reduce the risk of regional conflict;

- . undertake policy-oriented studies on specific regional maritime security problems;

- promote particular maritime confidence- and security-building measures (MCSBMs); and

- promote adherence to the principles of the 1982 UN Convention on the Law of the Sea (UNCLOS).

Two meetings of the Working Group have been held in pursuance of these objectives. We published the proceedings of the first meeting earlier this year under the title *Calming the Waters: Initiatives for Asia Pacific Maritime Cooperation*.[1] Our choice of title for the proceedings of the second meeting, *The Seas Unite: Maritime Cooperation in the Asia Pacific Region*, reflects the progress made in defining issues and identifying key areas for further action.

---

[1]   Sam Bateman and Stephen Bates (eds), *Calming the Waters: Initiatives for Asia Pacific Maritime Cooperation* (Strategic and Defence Studies Centre, Australian National University, Canberra, 1996).

The meetings of the Working Group have confirmed that maritime issues, and the maritime environment generally, are a rich source of ideas and initiatives for developing the habit of cooperation and dialogue between Asia Pacific countries. Scope for cooperation exists in terms both of regional *naval* cooperation with, for example, agreed arrangements for information exchange and standard operating procedures under the auspices of the Western Pacific Naval Symposium (WPNS), as well as the possibility of joint maritime exercises and other cooperative naval operations; and with regional *maritime* cooperation, including agreed regional arrangements for shipping safety, search and rescue, the control of marine pollution, cooperative marine scientific research, and resource management regimes.

The second meeting of the Working Group concentrated on specific proposals, including in the fields of naval cooperation, resource management regimes, marine information data exchange, and education and training. The papers presented to the meeting enabled the Working Group to identify a comprehensive way ahead covering a wide range of initiatives that could provide the basis for a possible regional agreement on maritime cooperation, education and training, and the management of regional seas. These initiatives are described in more detail in the last chapter of this book. Preceding chapters comprise the papers presented at the meeting, grouped as far as possible according to their subject content.

The papers in this volume provide a record of progress with maritime cooperation in the Asia Pacific region. The CSCAP Maritime Cooperation Working Group is dealing with issues which are of growing common concern to regional countries. They have immense potential value as a basis for preventive diplomacy and confidence building in the region. This potential has been recognised by the ASEAN Regional Forum but, while progress is being made, there is still a long way to go in implementing practical measures to overcome the tensions and unresolved problems of jurisdiction and sovereignty that exist in the maritime environment of the Asia Pacific region.

Sam Bateman
Stephen Bates

CHAPTER 1

MARITIME COOPERATION, CSCAP AND THE ARF

Desmond Ball

Over the past half-decade, there has been extraordinary progress with the institutionalisation of security cooperation in the Asia Pacific region. A wide variety of confidence- and security-building measures (CSBMs) have been accepted and are in various stages of implementation, particularly with regard to *transparency* (as compared to *constraint*) CSBMs. Numerous forums and arrangements for multilateral security dialogue have been established. These include arrangements for regular discussion by officials of particular security issues (such as the annual *Workshops on Managing Potential Conflict in the South China Sea*, sponsored by the Indonesian government), as well as regular meetings of officials from particular sectors of the respective national security communities, such as the annual meeting of senior officials from the various intelligence agencies of the ASEAN countries to exchange intelligence assessments on regional security developments, and the mechanisms that have been instituted for regular dialogue among navies in the Western Pacific. Across the region as a whole, the most important developments with respect to regional security cooperation have been the establishment of the ASEAN Regional Forum (ARF), and, at the second-track level, the Council for Cooperation in the Asia Pacific (CSCAP).[1]

Imperatives for Regional Security Cooperation

As late as the early 1990s, it was generally accepted that the prospects for multilateral security cooperation in the Asia Pacific region were very bleak. The United States, and indeed most of the Asia Pacific countries, were firmly committed to bilateral approaches to security issues; multilateral endeavours were represented as being

---

[1]   See Desmond Ball, 'A New Era in Confidence Building: The Second Track Process in the Asia/Pacific Region', *Security Dialogue*, Vol.25, No.2, June 1994, pp.157-76.

incompatible with fundamental aspects of Asia Pacific strategic cultures, and even as damaging to the architecture of bilateral arrangements which had arguably served the region well during the previous decades. The Asia Pacific region was simply too large and diverse, in terms of the sizes, strengths, cultures, interests and threat perceptions of the constituent states, to support any meaningful region-wide security architecture. It has turned out, however, that these 'realities' were not immutable, at least insofar as they ruled out the institutionalisation of an active, purposeful and productive regional security cooperation process.

What accounts for the remarkable progress with the institutionalisation of regional security cooperation over the past half-decade? There are several significant aspects of the evolving architecture of Asia Pacific security that must figure in any explanation.[2] The end of the Cold War and East-West conflict has enhanced the salience of regional conflicts. The Asia Pacific region has its fair share of competing sovereignty claims, challenges to government legitimacy, and territorial disputes, which are now more important as potential threats to regional cooperation and security. Economic growth and technological modernisation throughout much of East and Southeast Asia has permitted a strategic modernisation process which has fundamentally transformed defence capabilities and postures in the region - and has made defence planners much more concerned about the capabilities and policies of their neighbours than with internal security matters. The end of the Cold War has produced greater uncertainty in the region; security planners need to determine the appropriate mixes of national defence capabilities and regional cooperative and confidence-building arrangements for addressing this greater uncertainty. Further, the end of the Cold War and the search for new security modalities has provided an opportunity for increasing the role of cooperation and peaceful settlement of disputes in whatever regional security architecture eventually prevails. Regional leaders are not entirely oblivious to this opportunity.

---

[2] For a more comprehensive discussion of the evolving security architecture of the Asia Pacific region, see Desmond Ball (ed.), *The Transformation of Security in the Asia/Pacific Region* (Frank Cass, London, 1996).

Maritime Issues

Maritime issues are at the forefront of current regional security concerns.[3] The 1982 UN Convention on the Law of the Sea (UNCLOS III) has introduced new uncertainties into the region, particularly in connection with the EEZ and archipelagic state regimes. Of the 30 or so conflict points in the region, more than a third involve disputes over islands, continental shelf claims, EEZ boundaries and other offshore issues. Many emerging regional security concerns, such as piracy, pollution from oil spills, safety of SLOCs, illegal fishing and exploitation of other offshore resources, and other important elements of economic security are essentially maritime. These concerns, together with the requirements for defence self-reliance and force modernisation, are reflected in the significant maritime dimension of the current arms acquisition programmes in the region - for example, the maritime surveillance and intelligence collection systems, multi-role fighter aircraft with maritime attack capabilities, modern surface combatants, submarines, anti-ship missiles, naval electronic warfare systems, and mine warfare capabilities. Unfortunately, some of these new capabilities tend to be more offensive, inflammatory and, in conflict situations, potentially prone to the possibilities of inadvertent escalation. It is therefore important that regional mechanisms be instituted to address these maritime issues.

Maritime Cooperation

In fact, the salience of maritime concerns is well reflected in current regional CSBM proposals - as evident in Table 1.1, where about a third of the proposals are intended to directly address maritime matters, while others have a significant maritime dimension. For example, maritime strike capabilities not only comprise a large proportion of the new acquisitions in the region, but these capabilities are also the ones that are more likely to generate offsetting acquisitions elsewhere in the region and hence to trigger unanticipated and undesired arms races. It is therefore particularly necessary that these acquisitions be accompanied by transparency and dialogue. Many of the new maritime weapons systems, such as submarine warfare

---

[3]   See Desmond Ball, 'The Post Cold War Maritime Strategic Environment in East Asia' in Dick Sherwood (ed.), *Maritime Power in the China Seas* (Australian Defence Studies Centre, Australian Defence Force Academy, Canberra, 1994), chapter 2.

Table 1.1: Proposals for Confidence Building and Security Cooperation in the Asia Pacific Region

---

- Mechanisms for enhancing transparency - publication of White Papers, Capability Reviews, Doctrine Manuals, etc.

- Establishment of a Regional Arms Register, as proposed by the Malaysian Defence Minister, Dato Seri Mohd Najib Tun Razak.

- Intelligence exchanges.

- Strengthening and expanding bilateral cooperative arrangements.

- Sharing concepts and methodologies for defence planning and force structure developments.

- 'Hot lines' for communications between various capitals and headquarters' (e.g. Seoul and Pyongyang).

- Workshops and Working Groups to address particular security issues, e.g. the Indonesian-sponsored Workshops on Managing Potential Conflicts in the South China Sea, and workshops on security of SLOCs.

- CSBMs concerning military exercises, including the notification of exercises to neighbouring countries, invitations to neighbours to attend exercises, and prohibitions on the conduct of exercises in strategic approaches or other sensitive areas.

- The establishment of a regional training centre for peacekeeping operations.

- Cooperation in the maintenance and production of defence hardware required for national and regional resilience.

- Building on the ASEAN PMC process, e.g. establishment of the ASEAN Regional Forum (ARF).

- Establishment of a forum for regional defence dialogue, as also proposed by the Malaysian Defence Minister (the 'Najib talks').

- A forum for security dialogue in Northeast Asia.

- The establishment of Zones of Cooperation, e.g. the Timor Sea Zone of Cooperation and proposals for a South China Sea Zone of Cooperation.

- A Regional Maritime Surveillance of Safety Regime.

- Regional Avoidance of Incidents at Sea Regimes.

- A Regional Airspace Surveillance and Control Regime.

- A Southwest Pacific Sovereignty Surveillance Regime, and the recently announced Regional Maritime Surveillance Communications Network.

- Proposals for a Regional Security Assessment Centre in the Southwest Pacific.

- CSBM proposals concerning the Korean peninsula.

- Proposals for naval arms control in the Pacific.

- A Regional Technology Monitoring Regime.

- The Australian chemical weapons initiative.

- Proposals concerning economic security.

- An Environmental Security Regime.

- Strengthening the networks of non-governmental organisations and the so-called 'second-track' process.

---

systems and long-range anti-ship missiles requiring over-the-horizon targeting, happen to be more prone to accidents and miscalculations; hence the desirability of instituting some avoidance of incidents at sea regime in the region. Other concerns, such as piracy and illegal activities throughout many of the EEZs in the region, can best be addressed through cooperative surveillance and/or information-sharing efforts and arrangements.

Some of the foundations for building confidence and security in the maritime dimension have already been instituted in the region. For example, the Western Pacific Naval Symposium (WPNS), a biennial conference initiated by the Royal Australian Navy (RAN) in

1988, brings together representatives of the navies of the ASEAN states, the United States, Japan, the Republic of Korea, the People's Republic of China, Papua New Guinea, Australia and New Zealand for a frank exchange of views on a wide range of issues, including the law of the sea and SLOC protection. It is a unique forum and a significant step towards better understanding between regional navies. Some of the important conclusions reached during the recent naval dialogues are that the focus of cooperative activities should be on operational matters, directed to very particular concerns (perhaps mostly non-military in nature), and beginning with basic modes and procedures for information exchange rather than the erection of new structures for multilateral maritime surveillance efforts. For example, it was agreed at a Western Pacific Naval Symposium Workshop in Sydney in July 1992 to jointly develop a 'Maritime Information Exchange Directory' (MIED), whereby information on certain maritime activities would be shared by the participating navies.[4] A suggested list of activities which require 'time-critical' reporting includes 'maritime pollution/environment concerns'; high seas robbery/piracy; fisheries infringements; search and rescue; suspicious activity indicating possible narcotics trafficking; [and] humanitarian concerns'.[5] The Directory will include formatting styles, addresses for reporting information, and the agreed means of communication (such as specific radio frequencies). The development of common procedures for communication between regional navies and vessels provides a capability, the significance of which for regional confidence building obviously far transcends the particular purposes of the Directory itself. Similarly, the process of reaching agreement between naval staffs on the priority areas for information reporting will enhance regional appreciation of particular national concerns and interests as well as increase the 'understanding of navies at the working level'.[6]

More structured maritime surveillance regimes are already possible in some particular circumstances, such as particular subregions where commonality of interests is high or situations where

---

[4]   See Vice Admiral I.D.G. MacDougall, Chief of Naval Staff (CNS), 'CNS presentation to WPNS III on the Inaugural Western Pacific Naval Symposium Workshop', Sydney, 9-10 July 1992, p.8.

[5]   ibid., pp.8-9.

[6]   ibid., p.9.

issues can best be addressed multilaterally. In November 1991, the Australian Minister for Defence Science and Personnel, Gordon Bilney, announced plans for the establishment of a Regional Maritime Surveillance Communications Network in the South Pacific, which is 'designed to collect, collate and disseminate maritime surveillance information' throughout that region.[7] Under the plan, each participating country is to receive 'a stand alone communications system' which will be linked to a Maritime Surveillance Centre at the headquarters of the Forum Fisheries Agency in Honiara, and all ship sightings by 'all major surveillance assets - both public and private' are to be reported to the Centre and thence to individual country agencies.[8] Although it would be misleading to generalise too much from initiatives in the South Pacific, where security concerns are almost *sui generis* and the capabilities for independent surveillance activities are extremely limited, some aspects of the Regional Maritime Surveillance Communications Network are nevertheless informative for CSBM processes elsewhere in the Asia Pacific region. For example, the role of defence establishments has been minimised in the reporting network, while the role of military assets has been under-played in discussions of the surveillance arrangements; the focus of concern has been almost entirely on non-military issues (such as protection of fish stocks, and enforcement of immigration, quarantine and customs regulations); and maximum use has been made of existing multilateral institutions, especially the Forum Fisheries Agency and its regional infrastructure.

The establishment of the Zone of Cooperation in the Timor Sea between Australia and Indonesia in 1991 also involves surveillance cooperation activities which are not only suggestive for other such possible zones but which themselves contribute directly to confidence building between the parties. In the case of the Timor Gap, agreement on joint surveillance activities was an integral part of the agreement to establish the Zone of Cooperation, but it has also served as a catalyst for more general arrangements for coordinating surveillance operations between Australia and Indonesia in the broader area of the Timor and Arafura seas. These include the exchange of information on the programming of surveillance units, occasional joint exercises

---

7   The Hon. Gordon Bilney, Minister for Defence Science and Personnel, 'Address at the Regional Defence Cooperation Conference', Sydney, 4 November 1991, p.8.
8   ibid., pp.8-9.

between these units, the establishment of routine communications links between ships, aircraft and shore authorities, and the development of standardised reporting procedures.[9]

In other cases, multilateral maritime surveillance regimes are under consideration for dealing with particular problems and issues, such as piracy and oil spills in international waterways. In early 1992, for example, Malaysia, Singapore and Indonesia agreed to cooperative efforts to combat the increasing threat of piracy in the Strait of Malacca and the Phillip Channel south-west of Singapore. The navies and police forces of the three countries have begun to compile and share information on the areas where piracy is most rampant, to establish communications links between them to coordinate patrols against pirates, to organise joint sweeps against pirate strongholds, and to establish an anti-piracy centre in Kuala Lumpur to provide information on pirate activities for the use of both shipowners and police forces in the region.[10] The three countries are now discussing the establishment of a common surveillance system over the Straits, to provide shared radar coverage of all traffic through the waterway.[11] While there is little enthusiasm in the region for proceeding with the establishment of a full-blown Regional Maritime Surveillance and Safety Regime (REMASSAR) at this stage, the combination of the development of a regional 'Maritime Information Exchange Directory', the establishment of specific-purpose multilateral surveillance regimes in areas of particular concern, and the strengthening of the myriad of bilateral maritime surveillance arrangements in the region will go far to address the requirements of a REMASSAR anyway.

The ASEAN Regional Forum (ARF)

The most fundamental building block for regional arms control regimes is the institutionalisation of regional security dialogue.

---

9   See Desmond Ball and Commodore Sam Bateman, RAN, *An Australian Perspective on Maritime CSBMs in the Asia-Pacific Region*, Working Paper No.234 (Strategic and Defence Studies Centre, Australian National University, Canberra, August 1991), pp.18-21.

10 See 'Joint Force to Fight Pirates', *Asian Defence Journal*, March 1992, p.88; Lindsay Murdoch, 'Jakarta Mounts Crackdown on Asian Pirates', *Age*, 9 July 1992, p.7; and 'Anti-Piracy Centre "To Be Set Up in Malaysia"', *Straits Times*, 28 February 1992, p.20.

11 'KL, Singapore, Jakarta Study Surveillance System in Strait', *Asian Defence Journal*, April 1993, p.80.

Such dialogue should lead to better appreciation of the concerns, interests and perceptions of the participating countries, enhancing mutual understanding and trust, and preventing misinterpretations, misunderstandings and suspicions likely to cause tensions and even conflict. More generally, institutionalised dialogue would serve as a mechanism for managing some of the uncertainty which presently confounds regional security planners and analysts. However, too much should not be expected from the dialogue process in terms of agreed solutions to regional security problems, at least through the rest of the 1990s. The task for the near term, as Mahathir bin Mohamad stated more than a decade ago with respect to regional dialogue on economic cooperation, is 'the tedious one of getting to know each other'.[12] It could well take more than a decade for the developing dialogue processes within the region to produce sufficient mutual understanding, confidence and trust for resolving or managing substantive regional security issues.

There have been some very significant developments in this area over the past few years. The most important of these is the ASEAN Post-Ministerial Conference (PMC) and ASEAN Regional Forum (ARF) process.[13] In July 1991, the Twenty-fourth ASEAN Ministerial Meeting in Kuala Lumpur agreed that the ASEAN PMC was an 'appropriate base' for addressing regional peace and security issues.[14] This was endorsed at the Fourth ASEAN Summit in Singapore in January 1992, and the first discussions on regional security issues took place at the Twenty-fifth ASEAN Ministerial Meeting in July 1992.

Several attendant developments worked to transform the ASEAN PMC process into an institutionalised regional security dialogue mechanism. To begin with, the PMC arrangements became much more multilateralised both in membership, to include the so-called 'non-like-minded' (China, Russia, Vietnam and Laos) and, in agenda preparation, to broaden the purview beyond essentially ASEAN concerns. It was agreed at the Twenty-sixth ASEAN

---

12 Mahathir bin Mohamad, '"Tak Kenal Maka Tak Cinta"' in *Asia-Pacific in the 1980s: Toward Greater Symmetry in Economic Independence* (Centre for Strategic and International Studies, Jakarta, May 1980), p.18.

13 See Ball, 'A New Era in Confidence Building', pp.157-76.

14 *Joint Communique of the Twenty-Fourth ASEAN Ministerial Meeting, Kuala Lumpur, 19-20 July 1991*, p.5.

Ministerial Meeting in Singapore on 23-24 July 1993 that henceforth the security component of the PMC dialogue would be known as the ASEAN Regional Forum (ARF), with 18 members - the six ASEAN countries (Malaysia, Indonesia, Thailand, Singapore, the Philippines and Brunei), their seven major trading partners (the United States, Japan, Canada, South Korea, Australia, New Zealand and the European Community), and the five 'guests' and 'observers' at the ASEAN meeting (Russia, China, Vietnam, Laos and Papua New Guinea).[15]

The first ARF meeting was held in Bangkok in July 1994. To begin with, the ARF agenda was quite modest. Though, as Singapore's Defence Minister, Dr Yeo Ning Hong noted, the fact that 18 countries 'at different levels of development and with different views on how to achieve regional stability and resolve security issues' could meet to discuss sensitive security matters 'is by itself a significant achievement'.[16] The first meeting was exploratory in nature and concerned as much with getting the mechanics and the process of dialogue right as with substantive issues.

The second ARF meeting was held in Bandar Seri Begawan in Brunei Darussalam on 1 August 1995. The ministers considered and endorsed the Report of the Chairman of the ARF Senior Officials Meeting (SOM) prepared in May 1995, and adopted 'a gradual evolutionary approach' to security cooperation as set out in a Concept Paper prepared by the ASEAN senior officials for the ARF SOM in Bandar Seri Begawan in May.[17] This evolution is to take place in three stages:

Stage 1: Promotion of Confidence-Building Measures

Stage 2: Development of Preventive Diplomacy Mechanisms

---

15   *Joint Communique of the Twenty-Sixth ASEAN Ministerial Meeting, Singapore, 23-24 July 1993* (Press Release, 26th ASEAN Ministerial Meeting/Post Ministerial Conferences, Singapore, 23-28 July 1993), para.8. See also 'Ministers Endorse Security Forum', *Canberra Times*, 24 July 1993, p.7; and Michael Vatikiotis, 'Uncharted Waters', *Far Eastern Economic Review*, 5 August 1993, pp.10-11.

16   'The Jane's Interview', *Jane's Defence Weekly*, 19 February 1994, p.52.

17   'Chairman's Statement of the Second ASEAN Regional Forum (ARF), 1 August 1995, Bandar Seri Begawan', p.1. See also ASEAN Senior Officials, 'The ASEAN Regional Forum: A Concept Paper', May 1995 in Desmond Ball and Pauline Kerr, *Presumptive Engagement: Australia's Asia-Pacific Security Policy in the 1990s* (Allen & Unwin, Sydney, 1996), pp.111-19.

Stage 3: Development of Conflict-Resolution Mechanisms.[18]

The Concept Paper included two lists of confidence-building measures and other cooperative activities (see Table 1.2). The first list 'spells out measures which can be explored and implemented by ARF participants in the immediate future', that is, over the next couple of years, such as publications of statements of defence policy, participation in the UN Conventional Arms Register and reciprocal high-level personnel exchanges. The second list is 'an indicative list of other proposals which can be explored over the medium and long-term by ARF participants and also considered in the immediate future by the Track Two process', such as cooperative approaches to SLOCs, the establishment of zones of cooperation in areas such as the South China Sea and maritime information databases.[19]

Table 1.2: The ARF Process

STAGE I: IMMEDIATE (1995-96)

I CONFIDENCE-BUILDING MEASURES

Principles

1   The development of a set of basic principles to ensure a common understanding and approach to interstate relations in the region; and

2   Adoption of comprehensive approaches to security.

Transparency

3   Dialogue on security perceptions, including voluntary statements of defence policy positions;

4   Defence Publications such as Defence White Papers or equivalent documents as considered necessary by respective governments;

5   Participation in UN Conventional Arms Register;

---

18   ibid., p.112.
19   ibid., pp.116-19.

6   Enhanced contacts, including high level visits and recreational activities;

7   Exchanges between military academies, staff colleges and training;

8   Observers at military exercises, on a voluntary basis; and

9   Annual seminar for defence officials and military officers on selected international security issues.

II PREVENTIVE DIPLOMACY

1   Develop a set of guidelines for the peaceful settlement of disputes, taking into account the principles in the UN Charter and the TAC;

2   Promote the recognition and acceptance of the purposes and principles of the TAC and its provisions for the pacific settlement of disputes, as endorsed by the UNGA in Resolution 47/53 (B) on 9 December 1992; and

3   Seek the endorsement of other countries for the ASEAN Declaration on the South China Sea in order to strengthen its political and moral effect (as endorsed by the Programme of Action for ZOPFAN).

III NON-PROLIFERATION AND ARMS CONTROL
Southeast Asia Nuclear Weapons-Free Zone (SEANWFZ).

IV PEACEKEEPING

1   Seminars/Workshops on peacekeeping issues; and

2   Exchange of information and experience relating to UN Peacekeeping Operations.

V MARITIME SECURITY COOPERATION
Disaster Prevention

STAGE II: MEDIUM AND LONG TERM

I CONFIDENCE-BUILDING MEASURES

1   Further exploration of a Regional Arms Register;

2   Regional security studies centre/coordination of existing security studies activities;

3   Maritime information data bases;

4.   Cooperative approaches to sea lines of communication, beginning with exchanges of information and training in such areas as search and rescue, piracy and drug control;

5   Mechanism to mobilise relief assistance in the event of natural disasters;

6   Establishment of zones of cooperation in areas such as the South China Sea;

7   Systems of prior notification of major military deployments that have region-wide application; and

8   Encourage arms manufacturers and suppliers to disclose the destination of their arms exports.

II PREVENTIVE DIPLOMACY

1   Explore and devise ways and means to prevent conflict;

2   Explore the idea of appointing Special Representatives, in consultation with ARF members, to undertake fact-finding missions, at the request of the parties involved in an issue, and to offer their good offices, as necessary; and

3   Explore the idea of establishing a Regional Risk Reduction Centre as suggested by the UN Secretary-General in his Agenda For Peace and as commended by UNGA Resolution 47/120 (see section IV, operative para 4). Such a centre could serve as a data base for the exchange of information.

III NON-PROLIFERATION AND ARMS CONTROL

A regional or sub-regional arrangement agreeing not to acquire or deploy ballistic missiles.

IV PEACEKEEPING

Explore the possibility of establishing a peacekeeping centre.

V MARITIME SECURITY COOPERATION

1   A multilateral agreement on the avoidance of naval incidents that apply to both local and external navies;

2   Sea Level/Climate Monitoring System;

3   Establishment of an ASEAN Relief and Assistance Force and a Maritime Safety (or Surveillance) Unit to look after the safety of the waters in the region;

4   Conventions on the Marine Environment

- Dumping of Toxic Wastes

- Land-based Sources of Marine Pollution;

5   Maritime surveillance; and

6   Explore the idea of joint marine scientific research.

The ARF SOMs, ISMs, and ISG

It was recognised that the PMC/ARF process must be supported by the development of some institutionalised infrastructure at both the official and the non-governmental levels. At the official level, a process of senior officials' meetings has been instituted to support the PMC process, with matters such as the preparation of agenda and meeting arrangements. The first of the SOMs was held in Singapore in May 1993 and involved extensive discussion of multilateral approaches to regional peace and security, including such subjects as preventive diplomacy and conflict management, non-proliferation (both nuclear and non-nuclear), UN peacekeeping activities, the UN Conventional Arms Transfer Register, the extension of the Non-Proliferation Treaty (NPT), exchanges of information among defence planners, prior notification of military exercises, and the concepts of the Zone of Peace, Freedom and Neutrality (ZOPFAN) and the Southeast Asia Nuclear Weapon Free Zone (SEANWFZ). The SOMs agreed to undertake further research of four particular measures:

i   non-proliferation regimes and their application at the regional level;

ii   conflict prevention and management, including peacekeeping;

iii   possibilities for security cooperation in Northeast Asia; and

iv   confidence-building measures applicable to the region.[20]

The first ARF SOM was held in Bangkok in May 1994, preparatory to the ARF meeting in July. Various proposals for CSBMs were tabled at the SOM,[21] but these received only perfunctory consideration, as most of the meeting was taken up with the protocol and organisational aspects of the first ARF. The second ARF SOM was held in Brunei in May 1995, two months prior to the second ARF. This meeting was much more productive. It received for consideration the Concept Paper prepared by the ASEAN senior officials, as well as the products of three other 'intersessional' meetings (on trustbuilding, peacekeeping, and preventive diplomacy). In addition to endorsing the Concept Paper, the ARF SOM also recommended the establishment of an Intersessional Support Group (ISG) on Confidence Building and of Intersessional Meetings (ISMs) on Cooperative Activities (including Peacekeeping) to assist the Chairman of the ARF SOMs.[22] These intersessional mechanisms are likely to become the most important mechanism for the development and implementation of regional CSBMs.

The 'Second-Track' Process

At the same time as the ASEAN PMC process developed into a more fully multilateralised and institutionalised Regional Security Forum, there has been a burgeoning of non-governmental activities

---

20   *Chairman's Statement, ASEAN Post-Ministerial Conferences, Senior Officials Meeting, Singapore, 20-21 May 1993*, paras. 8,10.

21   See CSCAP Pro-tem Committee, *The Security of the Asia Pacific Region*, Memorandum No.1 (Council for Security Cooperation in the Asia Pacific, April 1994); and Gareth Evans and Paul Dibb, *Australian Paper on Practical Proposals for Security Cooperation in the Asia Pacific Region* (Paper commissioned by the 1993 ASEAN PMC SOM and submitted to the ARF SOM, Bangkok, April 1994, and published by the Strategic and Defence Studies Centre, Australian National University, Canberra, January 1995).

22   See 'Chairman's Statement of the Second ASEAN Regional Forum (ARF), 1 August 1995, Bandar Seri Begawan', p.4.

and institutional linkages, now generally referred to as the 'second-track' process. According to a recent compilation, these second-track meetings now exceed one per week.[23] Some of these are small workshops, sometimes involving less than two dozen participants, and designed to address specific issues (such as security of the sea lanes through the region or territorial disputes in the South China Sea).

The Council for Security Cooperation in the Asia Pacific (CSCAP)

At the second-track level, the most structured and ambitious initiative has been the establishment of the Council for Security Cooperation in the Asia Pacific (CSCAP). The essential purpose of CSCAP is to provide 'a more structured regional process of a non-governmental nature ... to contribute to the efforts towards regional confidence building and enhancing regional security through dialogues, consultation and co-operation'.[24]

Three essential themes permeated the discussions that attended the establishment of CSCAP. The first was that the Council should be a non-governmental institution but that it should involve government officials, albeit in their private capacities. Although it was considered essential that the institution be independent from official control in order to take full advantage of the extraordinary vitality and fecundity of non-governmental organisations (NGOs) engaged in the second-track process, as well as to allow relatively free discussion of diplomatically sensitive issues that could not be brought up in official forums, it was also recognised that official involvement was necessary in order to attract government resources and to ensure that the value and practicability of the NGO efforts secured official appreciation. In other words, the prospects for implementation should count for as much as the intrinsic worth of any ideas generated in the second-track process. It was considered important that the official involvement

---

23 See *Regional Security Dialogue: A Calendar of Asia Pacific Events, July 1995-June 1996* (Prepared jointly by the Regional Security Section, Department of Foreign Affairs and Trade, Canberra, and the Strategic and Defence Studies Centre, Australian National University, Canberra, 5th edn, July 1995).

24 Desmond Ball, 'CSCAP: Its Future Place in the Regional Security Architecture' in Bunn Nagara and Cheah Siew Ean (eds), *Managing Security and Peace in the Asia-Pacific* (Institute for Strategic and International Studies (ISIS) Malaysia, Kuala Lumpur, 1996), p.301.

include senior military personnel as well as defence civilians and foreign affairs officers.

The second theme derived from the experience of NGOs such as the Pacific Trade and Development Conference (PAFTAD) and the Pacific Economic Cooperation Conference (PECC) in the promotion of Asia Pacific economic cooperation through the 1970s and 1980s. These NGOs have contributed to the regional economic cooperation process in several important ways. They have, to begin with, developed and disseminated the ideas and stimulated the discussion that engendered the process. They have conducted the technical economic studies and analyses which sowed the benefits of liberalisation of trade in the region, either through formal free trade arrangements or, more recently, the concept of 'open regionalism'. They have demonstrated to government officials that meaningful and productive dialogue on complex and important policy matters is possible notwithstanding the extraordinary disparity in the sizes and interests of the numerous parties involved. Indeed, some of them, and most especially PECC, have explicitly been structured to involve officials themselves in this dialogue - albeit in their 'unofficial' capacities. PECC has even engaged in negotiation with respect to the resolution of differences between states which have arisen during the dialogue process.[25] By providing forums for official but 'unofficial' dialogue, the NGOs have contributed to greater official interaction and enhanced mutual confidence, as well as providing a sound 'building block' for supporting cooperative arrangements at the governmental level itself.

Many of the participants in the foundation of CSCAP were also actively involved in the PAFTAD and PECC processes. Indeed, several of the institutions were also the coordinators of their national PECC committees. In a sense, CSCAP was loosely modelled on the PECC experience and practice. It was intended that CSCAP should support official forums concerned with regional security dialogue and cooperation, such as the ASEAN PMC and the SOMs, in much the same way that PECC supports the Asia Pacific Economic Cooperation (APEC) process. More particularly, the establishment of CSCAP

---

25   See Lawrence T. Woods, 'Non-governmental Organizations and Pacific Cooperation: Back to the Future?', *The Pacific Review*, Vol.4, No.4, 1991, pp.312-21; and Lawrence T. Woods, *Asia-Pacific Diplomacy: Nongovernmental Organizations and International Relations* (University of British Columbia Press, Vancouver, 1993), chapter 8.

Member Committees and Working Groups closely reflects those established in the PECC programme in terms of their general rationales and operational activities.

The third theme in the foundation of CSCAP was the acceptance of the need to build on extant arrangements in the region wherever possible rather than construct new structures and processes. In practice, this meant building upon the arrangements and processes developed by the ASEAN ISIS association, and particularly ISIS Malaysia, which are the most advanced in the region in terms of both their infrastructure and their cooperative arrangements and practices.

The progress that CSCAP has made over the past three years has been quite remarkable. In addition to the founding ten members of the Council (Australia, Canada, Indonesia, Japan, South Korea, Malaysia, the Philippines, Singapore, Thailand and the United States), four other countries have joined (New Zealand, Russia, North Korea and Mongolia), as well as three Associate Members (European CSCAP, India, and the United Nations). Seventeen member committees have been established, as well as a CSCAP Secretariat in Kuala Lumpur.

Four Working Groups, which are intended to be the primary mechanism for CSCAP activity, have also been established. These are a Working Group on CSBMs, which has held three meetings; a Working Group on Concepts of Comprehensive and Cooperative Security, which has held two meetings; another on Security in Northeast Asia, which has held one meeting; and the Working Group on Maritime Cooperation, which has held two meetings.

However, CSCAP still faces some difficult issues which must be resolved before it can become an effective and viable institution. The most important of these are, first, determination of the proper balance between conceptual and policy-oriented activities, and of the appropriate working relationship between CSCAP and official forums such as the ASEAN PMC/ARF; and, second, membership issues, such as the incorporation of China and Taiwan into CSCAP activity. On the one hand, Taiwan is an increasingly important player on the regional security stage in its own right, while the CSCAP principle of inclusiveness demands its involvement in CSCAP activity. On the other hand, however, China remains adamant that Taiwan should be excluded, and the participation of China is so critical that many believe that its conditions should be accepted.

Figure 1.1: CSCAP Structure

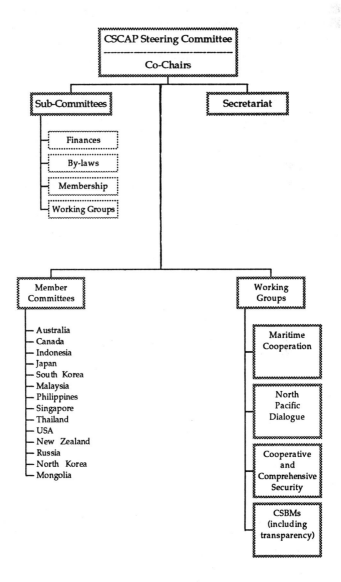

Without China's involvement in CSCAP, any work that the Council does for official forums like the ARF with respect to issues such as maritime cooperation will lack validity. But to include China on its own conditions could well reduce the ability of the Council to contribute constructively to the resolution of regional security issues.

The CSCAP Working Group on Maritime Cooperation

The CSCAP Working Group on Maritime Cooperation is one of the most important second-track activities in the region. Under the leadership of Indonesian and Australian co-chairs, Rear Admiral R.M. Sunardi (Retd) and Commodore Sam Bateman (Retd), this Group has been well structured, efficiently organised, conscious of its objectives, and has a perspective plan designed to achieve those objectives.[26] Its membership includes serving and retired naval officers, marine scientists, international lawyers, ocean and coastal management authorities, and scholars from various disciplines. A broad view of security has been adopted, encompassing such issues as maritime safety, resources conservation, coastal zone management and unlawful activities at sea (for example, drug smuggling, illegal population movements and piracy), as well as more conventional maritime security issues. The papers produced at the first meeting of the Group in Kuala Lumpur in June 1995 provide a strong, broad and inspiring foundation for future proceedings.

This Group is especially well placed to directly serve the CSCAP objective of enhancing regional security through the development of policy-relevant measures for dialogue, cooperation and confidence building. Maritime issues are at the forefront of regional security concerns; the need for enhanced maritime security cooperation is well appreciated by regional security officials and policy makers; and this Group has the expertise to address many of the issues involved.

The interest of the ARF in maritime cooperation is explicated in the ARF Concept Paper which specifies, for implementation over the medium and long term, both maritime confidence-building

---

[26] See Sam Bateman and Stephen Bates, 'Introduction' in Sam Bateman and Stephen Bates (eds), *Calming the Waters: Initiatives for Asia Pacific Maritime Cooperation*, Canberra Papers on Strategy and Defence No.114 (Strategic and Defence Studies Centre, Australian National University, Canberra, 1996), pp.1-7.

measures (that is maritime information databases; cooperative approaches to sea lines of communication, beginning with exchanges of information and training in such areas as search and rescue, piracy and drug control; mechanisms to mobilise relief assistance in the event of natural disasters; and the establishment of zones of cooperation in areas such as the South China Sea) and maritime cooperation measures. These latter measures include 'a multilateral agreement on the avoidance of naval incidents that apply to both local and external navies', and various mechanisms involving 'oceans governance' (for example, conventions on the marine environment, joint marine scientific research, a regional sea level/climate monitoring system, search and rescue measures, and maritime surveillance).[27]

Insofar as an important purpose of CSCAP is to support the ARF process, this provides a broad but sufficiently articulated agenda for consideration by this Group.

Conclusions

Extraordinary progress has been made over the past decade with the institutionalisation of confidence- and security-building measures in the Asia Pacific region. As compared to the situation in the early 1990s (and as evinced in a comparison of Tables 1.1 and 1.2), the process is now much more structured and focused. The ARF has been established and has endorsed a schedule for implementation of a wide variety of CSBMs; and a second-track process, of which CSCAP is the premier institution, has been developed to support the ARF.

The CSCAP Working Groups are intended to produce studies and memoranda of direct relevance to the policy makers and senior officials involved in the ARF process. In the case of the Working Group on Maritime Cooperation, an agenda has been articulated by the ARF in the ARF Concept Paper. The Group is not obliged to cover all the disparate matters listed in the Concept Paper, but neither should it limit its activities to those matters. It may well believe that there are other significant maritime issues which also warrant consideration.

---

[27]   ASEAN Senior Officials, 'The ASEAN Regional Forum: A Concept Paper' in Desmond Ball and Pauline Kerr, *Presumptive Engagement*, pp.118-19.

Moreover, insofar as an important function of the second-track process is to serve as a path-breaker for official processes, it is important that the Group explore issues which are currently not sufficiently appreciated by officials, or remain too sensitive for official consideration, or require novel approaches to implementation. On the one hand, the Group should be guided by the ARF agenda. Here, the question of a regional agreement on the avoidance of risks at sea and various issues of 'oceans governance' should be expeditiously addressed by the Group. On the other hand, the Group has a licence to go beyond the official agenda. The maritime issues in the region are not only very important, they are also difficult, and would benefit greatly from new ideas. This Group has extraordinary expertise. Its imagination should not be inhibited.

CHAPTER 2

MARITIME SECURITY IN EAST ASIA: EUROPE'S MARITIME INTERESTS

James Eberle

This chapter sets out briefly to address the questions, What legitimate 'European interests' in the state of maritime security in the East Asian region does Europe have? And how might these best be served?

It is written from the standpoint of a British member of the European Union, as a contribution from European CSCAP (ECSCAP) to the development of a multilateral security dialogue within East Asia under the auspices of the ASEAN Regional Forum (ARF) and the Council for Security and Cooperation in the Asia Pacific (CSCAP).

Background

The twentieth century, in global terms, can be widely described as the 'Atlantic Century'. In its final years, we see the United States as the undisputed single global superpower. Nevertheless, as the millennium approaches, the rapid economic growth of many of the East Asian economies, the evolution of APEC and its thrust towards growing free trade, and the growth of multilateralism (within the ARF) in the field of security, as an adjunct to existing bilateral security arrangements, have all begun to heighten the perception within informed European circles of the importance of East Asia. This importance is not only measured in terms of a valued trading partner - many leading European companies expect that, by the end of the century, the Asia Pacific region will account for between 20 to 30 per cent of their turnover - but also as a partner in the fields of economic and social development, global environmental issues, cultural exchange, the practice of good government and the recognition of human rights. This importance has been underlined by the recent European/Asian Heads of Government meeting. Thus there is recognition that the future century could well be the 'Pacific Century'.

However, at less well-informed levels of public opinion in Europe, there is little awareness of the great social and economic developments that are underway in Asia. China is seen as something of a 'dinosaur' of the communist age, whilst there there is also a vaguely perceived threat to European prosperity from the 'low-wage' economies of the East. In Asia too, the post-Second World War withdrawal of European powers from their imperial past, the all-pervading influence of the United States, and the economic dominance achieved by Japan have, in general terms, all led to a public perception that European interest in the region continues to decline. The recent French nuclear tests have revived much deep-felt resentment of the legacies of European colonialism.

The fundamentals of European economic cooperation with Japan, the leading East Asian economy, were set out in the 1991 European Community/Japan Declaration. There has been disappointment in some quarters about the practical results of this declaration. Nevertheless, the European Council has recently endorsed the priorities of the European Commission in respect of a wider Asian policy, which are set out as follows:

- to continue to strengthen the Union's bilateral relations with individual countries and regions in Asia;

- to raise the profile of Europe in Asia;

- to support efforts by Asian countries to cooperate at the regional and subregional level, such as the ASEAN Regional Forum, with a view to enhancing peace and security in the region, and generally to strengthen the Union's relations with regional groups such as ASEAN and the South Asian Association for Regional Cooperation (SAARC);

- to work with Asian countries in the management of international affairs with a view to sustaining international peace and security;

- to strengthen links with Asian countries in multilateral forums, and further encourage Asian participation in multilateral organisations;

- to open markets and maintain a nondiscriminatory business environment conducive to an expansion of European-Asian trade and investments;

- to integrate into the world trading system those Asian countries which are moving from state control to market-orientated economies;

- to contribute to sustainable development and to poverty alleviation in the least prosperous countries of Asia.

The inclusion, at a high priority, of support of efforts by Asian countries to enhance peace and security in the region is of particular importance in relation to the role that can be played by the European Union at governmental level through its membership of ARF; and, at the non-governmental level, by the associate status of the European Union in CSCAP.

The particular problems of maritime security relate firstly to the overall concept of stability in the area, and secondly to the more particular issues of the security of maritime trade.

Stability in East Asia

There will be many and varied perceptions within Europe of stability in East Asia. There will, however, be widespread agreement that there are two fundamental uncertainties that cast the widest shadows over the region's future. The first is uncertainty with regard to the extent of the longer term United States' commitment to maintaining a strong forward military presence in East Asia. Such a military presence has, since the Second World War, been a major stabilising influence in the area. The second is uncertainty as to the future direction of China's external policy, which will itself be greatly influenced by internal political and economic developments. China now has the ability to be a major influence in four important areas of maritime trade - oil, ore, coal and grain. The 'knock on' effects of such changing freight markets also greatly affect the shipbuilding industry, where there is a current surplus of capacity, and not least in South Korea. In security terms, the great sensitivity of the Taiwan dispute, and Chinese actions in respect of Tibet, together with moves to assert its claimed sovereignty in the South China Sea, are the cause of widespread concern. The behaviour of the Beijing government in the handover of Hong Kong to Chinese rule is also being closely watched as a harbinger of China's future behaviour on the world stage.

There are other situations where the future is difficult to foresee. Japanese politics are in the process of major change. Indonesia, a country which is rapidly becoming a major player in Southeast Asia, faces a major problem in succession. In Northeast Asia, there are the seeds of a major conflict on the Korean peninsula, which have nuclear overtones. Japan's relations with Russia will continue to be ambivalent whilst the issue of the Northern Islands remains unresolved. The prospective opening of the Arctic sea route from Asia to Europe could have significant economic and security implications. Nevertheless, the generally perceived remoteness of the Asia Pacific region from Europe and its major Atlantic trade routes tend to produce a somewhat muted sense of concern in Europe.

Europe recognises a growing self-confidence amongst people in Southeast Asia, a region where per capita GDP is expanding at an annual rate which is approximately twice that of the developed OECD countries. Furthermore, it has been estimated that the number of Asians with an average disposal income equal to, or greater than, the average European disposable income will exceed the number of Europeans who are so endowed by early in the next century. It is reassuring that, for the present at least, this new-found self-confidence is being channelled into growing regional cooperation rather than into national self-assertiveness. Nevertheless, the future internal cohesion of states in the area, which in some cases is already fragile, may well depend on their success in spreading the benefits of economic success fairly throughout the community. Internal instabilities would inevitably have repercussions on external relations.

Maritime Issues

There are few Asian-Pacific states that do not have significant maritime frontiers and strong maritime interests. The region also encompasses a number of strategic straits, some of which lie across the vital oil supply routes from the Persian Gulf (oil exports from the Middle East to the Asia Pacific region, which at present total some 70 per cent of consumption, are expected to double in the next ten years). As the economies of the region have prospered and extra-regional influences have declined, so have governments turned their attention more closely to the security of their own maritime interests. The result has been a period of considerable growth in the size and capabilities of regional navies.

Maritime issues can conveniently be divided into four categories: disputes about the sovereignty of small offshore islands; the protection of seaborne trade; issues of maritime boundaries adjacent to undisputed sovereign territory; and the maintenance of law and order at sea.

Disputes over sovereignty are related primarily either to underlying political issues (Japan's Northern Islands) or to underlying economic issues concerning their possible future value in terms of natural offshore resources (the Spratly Islands). With regard to politically driven issues, any European involvement is likely to be confined to the support of former colonial territories where the legally established order is seen to be under threat. Such support could involve the presence of European forces of law and order and might involve the presence of warships. In the case of economic resource disputes, it needs to be remembered that the processes of successful exploration and extraction of offshore oil and gas involve expertise and costs that are likely only to be available in major international companies. Such companies are unlikely to make the necessary capital investments if the ownership of those resources is in dispute; and particularly if the resources are under threat of armed intervention. Such disputes can thus only sensibly be settled by negotiation. The recent agreement between the British and Argentine governments with regard to the prospective seabed oil resources in the vicinity of the Falklands/Malvinas Islands sets a useful precedent.

The protection of sea lanes of communication has long been a prime task of naval forces. The free movement of people across the sea and the free flow of seaborne trade can be threatened by the use of naval force for economic blockade, by sinking merchant shipping on the high seas and by the closure, perhaps by mining, of international straits or narrow seaways. Such 'freedom of the high seas' has, during much of the eighteenth and nineteenth centuries, been seen as a vital interest of maritime nations, not only as a means of maintaining economic prosperity and of exerting global influence, but also in some extreme cases as a means of national survival. However, the seaways are no longer the 'great highway' for human travel. Sea travel has been superseded by air travel. This has brought about a certain 'sea blindness' amongst people who otherwise have no direct connection with the sea, a sea blindness which obscures the continuing vital part that the seaborne carriage of raw materials and manufactured goods plays in the totality of global trade.

Nevertheless, the maritime community has been slow to recognise the degree to which times have changed. No longer is maritime trade the sole lifeblood of the global economic system. It is the transfer of money, services, information and ideas that pass round the world by almost instantaneous global communication networks, supported by the transfers of human capital, that dominates the international economic scene. This in turn is one of the factors that has reduced the vulnerability of maritime trade to military action as a means of applying political pressure. There are numerous examples in the last forty years where economic sanctions, including maritime blockade, have failed to produce the political result for which they were imposed.

Another factor reducing the impact of military action against merchant shipping as a means of coercion against a nation-state is the degree to which the shipping industry is now amongst the most international of any of the components of the global economy. Ships are built in one country, owned in another, insured in a third, registered in a fourth, crewed by nationals of yet another, operated under multinational companies for their commercial and technical management and carry cargoes of a truly international character.

The coming into force of the United Nations Convention on the Law of the Sea, after negotiations which have spanned more than twenty-five years, is an event of major importance in the field of international cooperation. However, the regime has the effect of enclosing very large areas of the previous 'maritime global commons' within national jurisdiction. The exact delineation of the new boundaries of the Exclusive Economic Zone, the Continental Shelf and the 12-mile territorial sea will inevitably be the cause of local disputes and tensions.

The maintenance of law and order at sea has in recent years become a significant international issue, not least in the field of the environment and resource management. The potential for conflict of fishery disputes has been all too well illustrated worldwide by issues of whaling, in the Pacific and the Atlantic over the catching of tunafish, on the Newfoundland Banks over cod and in European waters, where the Common Fishing Policy has raised strong national resentment and where, despite a high degree of regulation, overfishing is endangering the survival of several species.

Piracy in a number of areas of the world has become an issue of international importance and concern. During the first half of 1995, some 60 attacks on shipping were reported, with a particularly notable rise in potentially serious incidents in the area of the South China Sea. In July 1995, the Secretary General of the International Maritime Organisation (IMO) reported that he was 'worried, in particular, about the navigational hazards to ships often carrying dangerous cargoes, and the potential danger to navigation and the marine environment these ships may pose if left unattended, while steaming at full speed and under attack by pirates in confined waters'. The final total of piracy incidents reported to the International Maritime Bureau in 1995 represented an 85 per cent increase over the previous year.

The fight against the international drug trade now has substantial international maritime dimensions - as has the problem of the passage of illegal migrant peoples. Insurance frauds involving both ships and cargoes are a continuing source of major concern in the growing field of international crime. The safe carriage of dangerous cargoes such as nuclear materials and liquified natural gas is also an emotive and controversial environmental issue of particular importance to the European and Asian scene. In the former case, the declarations of nuclear-free zones may also raise difficult issues through inconsistency with commitments made under the UN Convention on the Law of the Sea (UNCLOS).

European Interests

Europe's principal interest lies in the maintenance of a free, fair and open global trading system under the World Trade Organisation (WTO). European trade with the Asia Pacific now exceeds Europe's trade with the United States. European trade with Asia has grown by an average of more than 10 per cent per year over the last five years. However, in the 1980s, East Asia accounted for only some 1 per cent of the cumulative Foreign Direct Investment from EU countries (OECD figures) compared with 18 per cent which went to the United States. But investment in Asia is now growing rapidly. For instance, between 1987 and 1994, the net book value of UK investments in Japan doubled. As Asian prosperity grows, there is clearly much further potential for growth of both trade and investment.

The British Chamber of Shipping forecast of world seaborne trade during the next fifteen years (tonne/miles) suggests an annual growth rate of some 4.5 per cent. However, for the Asian region, a higher growth rate of some 7 per cent to 8 per cent can be expected. It is notable that during the early 1990s, South and East Asia (includes India) maintained a healthy seaborne trade growth rate, in contrast to a reduction in other parts of the world, including many OECD countries. The significant programme of expansion of port facilities within the region reflects regional confidence in a continuing high rate of growth of maritime trade, both within and from without the region. The availability of adequate onward land communication may, however, be a limiting factor.

Britain's particular interest with regard to trading in and through Hong Kong, her massive investments there, and her continuing political obligations, will remain after the handover of sovereignty to China in 1997. The expanding nature of Britain's trade links within the Commonwealth, and with other Asian countries including Taiwan, is also likely to underpin traditional British trading and financial interests within the Pacific region. Britain's 'special partnership' with Japan, a widely based partnership which is still broadening and deepening, has special importance both for the Pacific region and for Europe itself as other European countries turn increasingly to the rapidly growing Asian market.

Britain also retains regional security obligations under the Five Power Defence Arrangements with Australia, Malaysia, New Zealand and Singapore. France also retains significant residual defence, political and economic ties within the region.

There is some measure of concern, not only in Europe, at the expansion of military capabilities in the region, as the expanding economies permit greater expenditure on arms, and particularly naval arms. It cannot be denied, however, that such expansion is not unwelcome to European arms suppliers. It is, however, sometimes described as a 'naval arms race', although this is likely to prove largely a misperception. The creation under UNCLOS of the 200 Mile Exclusive Economic Zone (EEZ) has given rise to a valid requirement for ships larger than the customary small craft suitable for control of the 12-mile territorial sea. The arming of such larger ships with the more sophisticated surveillance equipment and command, control and communication facilities appropriate to the much larger sea area of the EEZ, and the ready availability of effective missile systems that are both easy to fit and easy to use, has created elements of naval force that are appropriate to warfighting as well as to their designated constabulary tasks. In the case of the Chinese Navy, however, there appears to be a concerted effort to move from a force dedicated primarily to the coastal defence task towards a balanced 'blue-water' fleet with a power-projection capability. Europeans are mindful of the adage that nations do not mistrust each other because they are armed;

but arm themselves because they do not trust each other. A race for superiority in armed force would inevitably increase the likelihood of conflict.

The extent to which European powers should, and might, become involved in regional conflict within the Asia Pacific region is strongly influenced by two general factors. First, that Britain and France are the only two countries of the European Union that have global military reach, albeit of modest size, and effectiveness in major conflict. Second, that European countries are at present deeply involved in their own problems of establishing a new structure for European security, which would embrace the central and east European countries of the former Warsaw Pact. Furthermore, the maintenance of the vital American commitment to European security through NATO may in future conceivably involve a new trans-Atlantic 'bargain' in which the continuation of the US commitment in Europe would be matched by an implied European commitment to the worldwide support of the United States in maintaining international peace and security.

The Military Dimension

The maintenance of a free, fair and open global trading system demands a free, fair and open structure for seaborne trade. Such issues of principle with regard to maritime services are still being negotiated in the follow-up to the Uruguay Round of GATT and the establishment of the WTO. Whatever the outcome, there will remain the potential threat of the use of naval force at sea to achieve political ends. However, the internationalisation of the shipping industry, as has been briefly described, has greatly reduced the political effectiveness of such action against merchant trade. Even in the Iran-Iraq war, and despite significant tanker losses in the Gulf, oil continued to flow by sea without any major hike in oil prices. As in the case of the Middle East, naval operations of a warlike nature on the high seas that pose a significant threat to international shipping are likely to lead to a response by the international community and the United Nations. Whilst it should be expected that there would be a strong natural reluctance of European governments to become involved militarily in disputes in Asia, the extent to which the dispute involved issues of principle affecting international order would largely determine the European response. The commitment of appropriate

European naval forces to a peace support operation should not be ruled out. European involvement in the UN operations in Cambodia (UNTAC) illustrates Europe's willingness to share the burden of international security. It also reflects the special responsibilities of the Permanent Members of the UN Security Council.

How Europe's Maritime Interests Might Best Be Secured

Europe's maritime interests in Asia can best be secured by the support of measures to reduce, and eliminate where possible, the causes of conflict within the region. The movement towards regional economic cooperation and free trade under the auspices of APEC, as well as other subregional agreements, are much to be welcomed, as is also the movement towards the ideas of cooperative security and the establishment of multilateral structures for regional and subregional security cooperation, for example within the ARF.

Europe is also likely to be strongly supportive of measures to improve the effectiveness of the appropriate international agencies and regional structures for maritime cooperation in the maintenance of law, order and safety at sea. The role of the IMO in assisting the combating of piracy worldwide is an important example. While it is upon national governments and shipowners that the responsibility for effective action to counter piracy lies in concerting such action, the International Maritime Bureau (whose regional piracy centre is based in Kuala Lumpur) has played a useful role. In wider issues, the role of the Indonesian-led Workshop on Conflict Resolution in the South China Sea and the Western Pacific Naval Leaders Conference in acting as forums for the discussion of regional maritime issues are models that deserve attention.

The establishment of a complex series of confidence- and security-building measures (CSBMs) under the regime of the Conference on Security and Cooperation in Europe (CSCE) undoubtedly played a significant part in the process that ended with the collapse of the 'iron curtain'. These CSBMs were almost entirely related to non-maritime issues, for it was argued forcefully by the United States that maritime CSBMs would impact unfavourably on the principle of the Freedom of the High Seas and would limit the freedom of action of US naval forces unfavourably compared with the naval forces of the Soviet Union. The one outstanding and successful maritime CSBM was the Incidents at Sea Agreement (INCSEA) between the US Navy and the Soviet Navy. This was subsequently copied in a number of similar bilateral agreements. Pressure to multilateralise these agreements has declined following the end of East-West confrontation.

The European CSBMs were related to a situation in which there were two declared hostile blocs - NATO and the Warsaw Pact. Such a situation does not exist in the Pacific region and it is less than clear how relevant European experience in this field may be to the Asian situation. There can, however, be no doubt that measures to promote cooperation in matters of security policy, to increase transparency (in military programmes and budgets; in the structure, equipment and purpose of armed forces; and in the import and export of military equipment), to improve safety at sea, and to contribute to disaster prevention, all have a global as well as a very important regional impact. They are thus particularly to be encouraged.

Conclusion

Europe's interests in the Pacific region are founded on the need for confidence in a stable political, economic and social order in Asia, the rule of law, and a business framework that is conducive to foreign investment. These are interests of major and increasing importance, an importance that is not perhaps fully recognised in Europe or Asia. The maintenance of a stable order, within an essentially ocean-based community, is strongly influenced by maritime affairs.

The establishment of a free, fair and open trading system, which is also a prime European concern, depends on the maintenance of a free, fair and open structure for seaborne trade and for the freedom of navigation. This introduces many issues of a security nature which directly affect European interests. The continued membership of Europe in CSCAP is important in this respect.

Europe's maritime interests are best met by measures to assist in reducing the causes of conflict in the region, promoting trade, supporting regional and subregional cooperation on security issues, contributing to measures to combat international crime, and in continuing to provide the means to support international peace operations under the United Nations.

CHAPTER 3

REGIONAL NAVAL COOPERATION

I THE EUROPEAN EXPERIENCE

Eric Grove

It is dangerous to apply the experience of one part of the world to another. Historical, cultural and political differences must always be taken into account. What works well in one context may not be appropriate in another. Nevertheless, in a more general sense it is probably useful to examine what is possible among one set of sovereign states in order to decide what, in a general sense, is practical and might be useful for more general application. The following brief account of the scope and nature of naval cooperation in Europe is offered in this latter sense. In no sense is it put forward prescriptively or in any way to imply that we in Europe have found some magic 'answer'. Our not inconsiderable progress in this area is clearly highly scenario-dependent. Nevertheless, given the fact that just over a half a century ago each of Western Europe's four greatest navies was in hostilities against at least one other - and often two or three of the others - one should not take too much for granted the benign international environment of today's Europe.

European security is structured around a number of overlapping organisations, some of which provide the framework for naval cooperation. In parallel there are bilateral and multilateral arrangements outside overarching security structures, although often these gain considerable - perhaps primary - impetus from the general process of 'European construction'.

Any discussion of European naval cooperation must begin with NATO. This has provided the primary framework for both the development of three effective combined standing forces, composed in the main of European assets, and the remarkably advanced mechanisms of inter-operability that allow Western European navies to operate together in any political framework required. Indeed, I would argue that NATO procedures are now the global 'industrial standard' for combined naval operations. Of course, the United States has played the major role in the development of these standards - and their promulgation outside the Alliance - but the European dimension of the NATO maritime enterprise should not be underestimated, especially in a context where France is adopting a more positive attitude to NATO. In order to enhance the European naval pillar of the Alliance, the custom has been established of regular twice-yearly meetings of the professional heads of the naval services of the European members of the Alliance, the so-called Heads of European Navies (HENs) meetings. At their meeting in Rome in 1992 the HENs commissioned meetings of their nations' operational staffs at which fleet schedules are compared and opportunities for cooperation identified. The process now involves a pre-HENs Captains-level meeting to resolve agenda issues, a plenary meeting of the HENs themselves, and the subsequent fleet-scheduling staff meeting. The informality of this framework needs to be stressed. HENs have no NATO (or Western European Union - see below) status; the cooperation they arrange is driven by opportunity rather than by policy and depends on the coincidence of scheduling.[1] Nevertheless, the European navies find the process useful and productive. A similar process might be possible in other frameworks in other parts of the world - ASEAN perhaps.

The chosen formal vehicle for providing the European Union with a defence dimension is the Western European Union, an alliance that pre-dates NATO but which has been overshadowed by it. Nevertheless, the Western European Union (WEU) provided cover for the informal 'concertation' arrangements for European naval operations in the Gulf during the Iran-Iraq war and for coordinated embargo operations carried out by Western European navies before and during the Gulf War. A WEU monitoring operation in the Adriatic pre-dated the NATO operation and parallelled it as both escalated to sanctions enforcement. Although this parallelism had negative operational effects, WEU political cover eventually allowed French participation in the combined NATO/WEU Operation Sharp Guard

---

[1]   This discussion of HENs and much else in this paper owes a great deal to Commander Mike Codnor RN (Rtd), now of the Royal United Services Institute of Strategic Studies (RUSI) in London, who has done much original work, both within and without the service, on European naval cooperation. His contribution is gratefully acknowledged by the author.

that saw a totally integrated set of task groups carrying out a highly effective embargo.

The small WEU Planning Cell in Brussels has developed an operational plan called Combined Endeavour that provides for the generation of maritime contingency forces from 'Forces Answerable to the Western European Union' (FAWEU) for those tasks defined in the WEU's Petersberg Declaration: crisis management, peace support and humanitarian operations. The political background to this process has been far from easy, given the differing views of WEU members on the desirability of separate European defence plans, which may give this tentative but still useful process a wider relevance in other circumstances where political problems prevent greater integration.

Outside the formal WEU framework is EUROMARFOR, a force of French, Italian, Spanish and Portuguese ships operating periodically in the Mediterranean. This is but one initiative by ad hoc groups of Western European states to come closer together. Another notable initiative is the Admiral Benelux organisation that effectively makes the Dutch and Belgian navies a single operational organisation under a bi-national integrated operational headquarters. As one observer recently put it: 'The new command, said to be unique, is responsible for the planning and execution of all operational and training activities by Belgian and Dutch naval forces not assigned overseas'.[2]

Bilateral and multilateral training and exercising is well established in Europe. HENs have commissioned a compendium of national training facilities and sea training facilities in the United Kingdom, France and Belgium that are often used by other European nations. NATO has a well-established exercise programme with which WEU activities are being coordinated and national exercises are used to provide opportunities for combined activities at both a command post and maritime operational level. The NATO Partnership for Peace initiative has been used to cast the net of cooperative exercising and training to cover former Warsaw Pact states (most of which have WEU partnership status) and the trilateral RUKUS (Russia-UK-US) forum has been used to develop detailed modalities of cooperation (such as draft Rules of Engagement) between the erstwhile Cold War enemies.

---

2   J.J. Lok, 'Partnership With Potential', *Jane's Navy International*, Vol.101, No.3, April 1996.

At the procurement level European cooperation is fostered by both NATO's Conference of National Armaments Directors and WEU's Western European Armaments Group. Although the road has been a somewhat stormy one, there have been successful common European warship projects (for example, the Benelux-French Tripartite mine countermeasures vessel). Currently, the United Kingdom, France and Italy are cooperating on a common air defence frigate, 'Project Horizon', with an advanced European anti-air missile system, and Germany and the Netherlands on another frigate design.

The essence of all this is the potential for cooperation in whatever 'variable geometries' and at whatever levels seem appropriate. Although the road to the current level of cooperation and inter-operability has been far from trouble-free and there are many contemporary problems still to be solved, the fact that this record of achievement has been achieved against a background of considerable controversy as to the detailed architecture of European security demonstrates what can be done to bring navies together in an uncertain political environment. In turn, naval cooperation has often interacted with the political context to validate further cooperative initiatives. Navies inherently lend themselves to cooperative action and this quality is being fully exploited in the European context. We Europeans offer this experience as a possible source of inspiration - certainly not a formula - for similar progress elsewhere.

II ALTERNATE PERSPECTIVES
FROM SINGAPORE

Lui Tuck Yew

The end of the Cold War has brought about tremendous changes in the Asia Pacific region. Foremost among these changes is the shift in paradigm from ideological concerns to economic interests. States in the region now place increasing importance on the promotion of sustained economic growth. To achieve this growth, there is a need for continued stability in the region. An important avenue to maintaining stability is to increase maritime cooperation between naval forces at sea, as many of the Pacific nations are archipelagic or coastal states sharing common borders. Such cooperation increases interaction between states, is an effective confidence-building measure and also holds potential benefits for the maritime community as a whole.

Naval cooperation can be broadly conceptualised into two echelons. The first echelon is the supporting framework or foundation. This framework consists of measures which improve the feasibility of conducting cooperative operations and includes the means to facilitate information exchange, inter-operability and logistics cooperation. In recent years, some progress has been made at the Western Pacific Naval Symposium (WPNS) in these areas and I shall elaborate on some of them.

The first such area is that of information exchange. The concept for the Maritime Information Exchange Directory (MIED) was first raised at the WPNS Workshop in July 1993. This concept was endorsed in November 1993 for further development and the directory was eventually promulgated in November 1994.

The MIED is a directory that provides guidance in the form of a 'ready reference' book. It gives a naval ship transiting another country's waters an idea of the particular concerns of that country and points of contact for time-critical information. These concerns include marine accidents and oil pollution incidents. The directory would initially be a navy-to-navy document and any reporting made through the directory would be from one navy to another. From there, the information could then be further disseminated to the appropriate internal agency of the littoral nation for action. Reporting is entirely voluntary but, judging from the keen response of member states, I am sure that we will see greater use of the MIED in future.

The second area is to increase inter-operability among navies. The problem of inter-operability is a critical one faced by navies attempting to cooperate at sea. Different communications and operational procedures often hinder effective cooperation. On the other hand, complete interoperability is an ambitious goal and unlikely to be achieved given the sometimes sensitive nature of operational procedures. However, substantial progress can be made on non-sensitive inter-operability issues through appropriate forums such as the WPNS.

An example of such a development is the compilation of the WPNS Replenishment-At-Sea (RAS) Handbook, which was endorsed in November 1994. This publication details ships' layouts and RAS procedures for the WPNS Fleets' reference, and is a good example of how a common standard can be achieved.

Building on this, I am sure more progress can and will be made in the area of inter-operability, particularly in improving communications and standardising operating procedures. For example, a publication listing basic common communications protocol and tactical procedures can be promulgated. Likewise, we will need to shift the focus from ship-to-ship communications to include communications with maritime patrol aircraft as well as other airborne assets, which will, for example, facilitate search and rescue operations.

Training exchanges should also be promoted to enhance inter-operability. A suggestion was mooted at the last WPNS Workshop in Jakarta that member countries look toward the further opening up of training courses to personnel from other WPNS member countries. To facilitate this, the workshop proposed that a list should be compiled by member countries listing the types of courses and capacity that can be made available for foreign participation.

The third area is cooperation in logistics aspects such as maintenance and production of parts and components, and in hardware supply and acquisition. This can be broadly classified into two levels of cooperation.

The first, and possibly highest, level is one where we jointly develop or acquire a new capability. A good example of such recent cooperation in defence equipment acquisition and development is the ANZAC Frigate programme, under which ten 'Meko 200' class frigates will be built in Australia and commissioned between 1995 and 2004 - eight of them by the Royal Australian Navy and the other two by the Royal New Zealand Navy. However, cooperation at this level is often difficult due to differences in the procurement time frame and in operational requirements.

The second level of logistics cooperation is one which, I think, is more achievable in this region. This is in the area related to the maintenance aspect of the defence equipment which we already have in our inventories. A cursory examination of the systems on board our various classes of ships in each of the navies represented in CSCAP will indicate that we share many systems in common.

There is some potential for us to cooperate in the production of parts and components and in the maintenance aspect of the equipment that we have in common. But for such cooperative efforts to work, they must be commercially viable. There are several advantages in such cooperation. First, we diversify the sources for the logistics support of our systems. Second, we can expect to experience a shorter acquisition time for parts and a quicker turn-around time for the repairs. Countries are more likely to support one another and release spares, or even ammunition, from their own inventories in aid of a partner's request for assistance when they themselves have a capability to manufacture such spares and ammunition and can effectively determine the time required to replenish their own inventories. A quicker turn-around time in repairs can be achieved not only through the reduced transportation time due to the shorter distances involved, but also because we can build into the system a series of mechanisms to accord higher priority to the repairs involving regional countries.

The second echelon of naval cooperation involves operation at sea. As was the case with the first echelon, the prudent and practical approach would be to firstly identify areas where we can embark on basic levels of cooperation. From such cooperation, we can acquire the necessary confidence and experience in the procedures to progress into more complex areas of cooperation. A good starting point would be in the areas where there is already international expectation and structures in place for naval cooperation. These areas are enunciated in the 1982 United Nations Convention on the Law of the Sea (UNCLOS), whose provisions generally constitute international law and practice and balance fairly the interests of all states. I shall elaborate on some examples which show greatest potential for naval cooperation and highlight Singapore's experiences in some of them.

The first such area is environmental protection. Article 192 provides that all states have the obligation to protect and preserve the marine environment. Article 194 also provides that states shall take all measures to prevent, reduce and control pollution of the marine environment from any source.

The second possibility is in anti-piracy operations. Article 100 of the Convention requires all states to cooperate to the fullest extent possible in the repression of piracy on the high seas.

The third area is in search and rescue operations. Article 98 requires every coastal state to promote the establishment, operation and maintenance of an effective search and rescue service regarding safety over the sea, and to cooperate where necessary with neighbouring states for this purpose.

The fourth area concerns illicit drug trafficking. Article 108 provides that all states shall cooperate in the suppression of illicit traffic in narcotic drugs engaged in by ships on the high seas. It further provides that any state which believes upon reasonable grounds that a ship flying its flag is engaged in illicit traffic in narcotic drugs may request the cooperation of other states to suppress such traffic.

Thus we see that, in these areas, regional states share common obligations as provided for under UNCLOS. There is, therefore, incentive and motivation to embark on cooperative programmes to fulfil these obligations, especially as experiences and information can be pooled for the benefit of all participants. Singapore, in particular, has experiences in some areas of cooperative efforts.

Since 1993, Singapore and Indonesia have cooperated in coordinated anti-sea robbery patrols. These exercises are scheduled on three-monthly cycles and consist of a tactical gaming exercise and two months of coordinated patrols. The exercises are hosted in turn by our two countries and we are very pleased with the success of the programme, as evidenced by the virtual elimination of sea robberies within the Singapore Strait and its immediate approaches since its inception in 1992.

Singapore is also part of a larger regional search and rescue organisation established under the provision of the convention on International Civil Aviation Organisation (ICAO) and is responsible for the overall coordination of all search and rescue activities within the Singapore Search and Rescue (SAR) region. To improve the inter-operability amongst the national SAR set-ups and to ensure that joint SAR operations can be mounted swiftly and efficiently when the need arises, Singapore has been participating, on a regular basis, in bilateral SAR exercises (SAREX) with both Malaysia and Indonesia under the Joint Malaysia-Singapore SAREX and Indopura SAREX series of exercises.

The ASEAN Regional Forum (ARF) is already looking into enhancing cooperation amongst ARF participants in SAR. The recently concluded ARF Intersessional Meeting on SAR chaired by the United States and Singapore saw ARF participants agreeing to the publication of a directory of regional SAR contact points. They also agreed to look into various areas of SAR cooperation.

In the area of environmental protection, there has been close cooperation among the six governments in ASEAN. The ASEAN Oil Spill Response Action Plan serves as a prime example of regional cooperation to limit the consequences of oil spillage resulting from accidents at sea. The action plan provides a tiered response procedure to enhance the ability of a country to respond to a spill which may be beyond the country's national capability. Periodic testing of the action plan has since been implemented to ensure its effectiveness and readiness.

In all these areas, there is scope for wider regional cooperation. This will serve to complement the on-scene naval exchanges we currently have in the form of bilateral and multilateral training exercises.

In conclusion, naval cooperation is an important avenue for states in the region to forge closer ties and to work together for mutual benefit. The two echelons that I have spoken of provide a conceptual framework that not only summarises the budding developments which have taken place, but that also shows how we can build on these developments in the future.

III A THAI PERSPECTIVE

Nitz Srisomwong

The post-Cold War era has profoundly changed the global security environment. It also presents a unique opportunity for states in the Asia Pacific region to seize the initiative and actively determine their own security destiny. The regional sea lines of communication are vital to the national security interests of all the regional states and to those of several major external states. Therefore, the need for regional naval cooperation is paramount. However, naval cooperation can take many other forms, including port visits, command post exercises, navy-to-navy talks, data exchanges, technology transfers, technology exchanges, and cross-servicing agreements. All of these facilitate cooperation at sea through training, planning and greater technological compatibility.

During the past two decades, Thailand has been engaged each year in a number of different instances of naval cooperation across all inter-operability areas of responsibility and it is clear this kind of cooperation is increasing. Such cooperation enhances the inter-operability and proficiency of foreign navies, thereby improving their capacity to conduct coalition operations. Neighbouring countries can gain the most benefits by fully participating in cooperative activities in particular circumstances. In the post Cold-War era, there was a fundamental change in threat perceptions and, therefore, a decline in the sense of common purpose that had provided cohesion among the countries of the Asia Pacific region. I believe that it is still possible for problems to occur at sea and that such problems will not be solved without some transparent policy guidelines from central government. If we can establish trust and understanding at the highest level, then the policy guidelines that are agreed upon can be passed down to the lower level.

An absence of, or perceived decline in, major power interest could stimulate naval competition and increase concern about China's intentions - for example, with respect to disputed islands. This problem may only be solved when we find our common purpose again.

The Royal Thai Navy has been tasked with missions of regional security such as the protection of sea lines of communications, the prevention of drug trafficking at sea, the suppression of piracy acts at sea, the conservation of natural resources, and disaster relief. These missions require regional cooperation, especially among ASEAN countries. Such cooperation takes the form of the combined patrolling of the adjoining maritime zone. The combined exercises that Thailand conducts with neighbouring states also facilitate the maintenance of cooperation and understanding that are necessary for peace and stability in the region. Such exercises include 'Cobra Gold', 'Sea Eagle' and 'Carat' with the US Navy; 'Austhai' and 'Kakadu' with the Royal Australian Navy - and I would like to mention here that 'Kakadu' is one of the most outstanding exercises; 'Thalay Laut' and 'Seaex Thamal' with the Malaysian Navy; 'Sing Siam' with the Singapore Navy; and 'Sea Garuda' with the Indonesian Navy. We have also conducted combined exercises with other allied countries such as the Philippines and New Zealand, whenever the opportunity to do so has presented itself. (Such exercises have as their objective the strengthening of bilateral relationships and the promotion of mutual understanding as well as the development of tactical knowledge and the accumulation of experience.) Most combined exercises with allied forces will be conducted in the form of PASSEX (Passing Exercises).

Thailand's regional role in the security and safety of the sea lines of communication is an important issue which demands cooperation with our neighbours. With the rapid growth in the international economy in general and in international trade in particular, Southeast Asia has become a passageway for the tankers transporting the oil that is needed to power expanding industries. The congestion of maritime traffic in the Malacca Straits has increased the possibility of an oil spill or oil slick from off-shore drilling and accidents. Such problems have caused enormous damage to maritime and coastal resources, marine life and the ecological system. The Royal Thai Navy has started a plan for dealing with oil spill disasters, with forces in readiness to clean up immediately any oil spill once an accident occurs. But given that the Royal Thai Government has reduced each year the Royal Thai Navy's budget allocation, any expansion of the Royal Thai Navy's role is not possible.

However we plan to maintain our role in the conservation of natural resources, in disaster relief both in the coastal area and in the high seas, and in the enforcement of maritime law.

I believe that the opportunity for large-scale missions in the region will decline just as major power interest in the region has declined. But future coalition opportunities will inevitably arise when specific interests coincide, perhaps more often at the lower end of the mission spectrum in areas such as environmental monitoring, humanitarian assistance and water space management. Most of the benefits of naval cooperation afloat are political, although occasionally specialised help from particular partners is useful. Naval cooperation may not build firm coalitions, but it can make coalitions possible and improve their efficiency. Finally, I do hope we can consolidate trust and mutual understanding and re-establish our sense of common purpose so as to provide a basis for naval cooperation in the Asia Pacific region.

IV THE MALAYSIAN PERSPECTIVE

Razali Md Ali

The Asia Pacific is primarily a maritime region and our economic survival is linked to the sea lines of strategic approach. Over 40 littoral nations depend on the sea for commerce and defence. As the seas of this region are a maritime theatre both economically and militarily, there is a complementary requirement for cooperation by partners of the region. This cooperation will in turn nurture the uninterrupted seaborne trade that is vital to our prosperity and that enables the pursuit of maritime interests and the control of the national maritime resources in an ordered and non-confrontational manner.

Given these geostrategic considerations, it is very important for nations to work together to explore the various alternatives for establishing maritime security cooperation. One fundamental avenue is through naval cooperation. I will discuss here some of the Royal Malaysian Navy (RMN) activities that serve as alternative forms of maritime cooperation. Then I will make some suggestions as to how closer cooperation in the maritime security field could be fostered.

Enhancement of Naval Cooperation

Currently, naval cooperation in this region is conducted either bilaterally or multilaterally. Existing bilateral cooperation takes the form of joint operations and training, exercises and the provision of training facilities. As for the Royal Malaysian Navy (RMN), current bilateral naval cooperation includes:

•   joint exercises with countries such as the United States, Thailand, Indonesia, Singapore, Brunei and Australia; and

•   joint operations with countries such as Indonesia, Thailand and the Philippines.

In the area of non-military maritime cooperation, some ad hoc joint operations have been shown to be feasible, particularly in the case of search and rescue and on environmental matters. Malaysia has even established the joint Maritime Action Programmes with Indonesia and the Philippines (OPTIMA and PHIMAL) to deal with criminal activities along their common sea boundaries.

On a multilateral plane, Malaysia's commitment under the Five Power Defence Arrangements (FPDA) with Singapore, Britain, Australia and New Zealand can be seen as an important naval linkage between member countries. At this juncture, this type of naval cooperation has successfully removed some elements of mistrust that could hinder the establishment of more cordial relations among member countries.

'Meeting of Minds' amongst the Asia Pacific Countries

As we have seen, maritime confidence-building measures (CBMs) have proven to be the most successful means of promoting naval cooperation. The International Seapower Symposium (ISS) and the Western Pacific Naval Symposium (WPNS), which have CBMs at the top of their agenda, are the two most important forums for the enhancement of ties amongst Asia Pacific navies. Here, high-ranking naval attendees discuss the ways and means of promoting maritime understanding and naval cooperation.[1] Most important of all, these forums provide naval leaders with the opportunity for personal contact and repeated opportunities to get to know each other better. This would appear to augur well for the future of the region.

Suggestions

Based on our previous experience, we would like to suggest the following means enhancing naval cooperation:

- *Establishment of a maritime peace regime in the Asia Pacific.* The conflicting and overlapping claims in the region need to be resolved by political means. At the same time some form of peace regime needs to be established to manage any possible crisis that could develop into military flare-up.

- *Need for a multilateral INCSEA (Incidents at Sea) agreement.* This type of agreement is considered as one of the ways to prevent accidents and miscalculations at sea. INCSEA establishes an

---

[1] The popularity of the Western Pacific Naval Symposium can be seen in the fact that the number of participating countries has increased to 17.

obligation for all parties at sea to avoid any manoeuvres which could endanger ships of other parties under surveillance.

- *Need for senior naval representatives in the ARF*. Many methods of developing CBMs have been adopted in this region through WPNS and ISS. These forums need to be considered more seriously as platforms where actions can be initiated and objectives advanced further, rather than being regarded as only occasions for a formal naval get-together. The discussions at the WPNS and ISS seem to have no end and involve no political commitment on the part of those taking part. It is time now to consider the participation of naval representatives in the ARF to enable their views to be registered and taken into consideration.

- *Need for a common operational doctrine*. To enhance better understanding and trust at the operational level, there is a need for a certain degree of inter-operability amongst naval vessels at sea. This doctrine could be used to facilitate common operational procedures for Asia Pacific navies including non-traditional partners.

Conclusion

Though we have experienced numerous forms of naval cooperation we feel that they have not been given due recognition in higher decision-making forums.

V AN (UNOFFICIAL) AUSTRALIAN PERSPECTIVE ON COLLABORATIVE GUNNERY EXERCISES

Russ Swinnerton

Introduction

Why would we wish to cooperate? In general, our interests in fostering maritime cooperation are three-fold. First, cooperation helps build confidence and trust between maritime forces. Second, cooperative structures can be used to maintain communication when tensions are heightened. Third, it can create an environment where maritime forces can combine to do real work on the high seas or within national jurisdiction, to achieve what Michael Leifer called a stable maritime regime.[1] Cooperation also serves to prepare the ground for inter-operability and harder edged collaborative operations if the shooting starts.

Now that we have put naval gunfire on the table, we might usefully employ the concept to illuminate the question of cooperation. When we are determined to satisfy ourselves that the gun mounted on the bow of our ship is serviceable, we fire it. Our daily checks of systems, turret, ammunition and crew are not sufficient to satisfy us. If we wish to be sure that the weapon is not only going to go bang when we say shoot, but to also hit the target, then we fire it.

It occurs to me that our recent first-track endeavours in the maritime cooperative field in Southeast Asia are very much like our daily system checks. They are fine, when the sea room is too restrictive for a firing practice, but inadequate if we are after a confidence-building result. Recent reporting of Western Pacific Naval Symposium (WPNS) meetings, and the ASEAN Regional Forum (ARF) intersessional meetings on CBMs and, more particularly, on search and rescue, are reminiscent of what one feels when the Weapons Electrical

---

1   Michael Leifer, 'The Maritime Regime and Regional Security in East Asia', *The Pacific Review*, Vol.4, No.2, 1992, pp.126-36, cited in Sam Bateman, 'Maritime Cooperation and Dialogue' in Dick Sherwood (ed.), *Maritime Power in the China Seas: Capability and Rationale* (Australian Defence Studies Centre, Canberra, 1994), pp.143-55.

Engineering Officer (WEEO) presents himself on the bridge after Daily System Operational Tests (DSOTs) and reports the system serviceable without a shot being fired: 'well, he would say that, wouldn't he?'.

This short paper suggests that cooperation for its own sake is serving very limited aims. If we wish our cooperation to hit the target of building confidence and of providing a vehicle for easing tensions when tensions rise, then our habits of cooperation should be to meaningful ends. If they are, then they will also facilitate the work of building the stable maritime regime.

The Meetings

Before dwelling on some of the specifics of naval cooperation (or, more properly, of maritime cooperation, since we still have a few recalcitrant air forces in the region with maritime assets and aspirations), it might be helpful to briefly review the enabling processes of cooperation, the meetings such as the ARF and WPNS. The last Malaysian Defence Minister, the Hon. Dato' Sri Mohd Najib bin Tun Haji Abdul Razak, while delivering the keynote address at a maritime CBM seminar in Kuala Lumpur in August 1994, publicly welcomed the ARF as 'beginning the process of institutionalising CBMs'.[2]

ARF Intersessionals

Several first-track ARF meetings and intersessional conferences have now been held, the two most notable in the field of maritime cooperation dealing with confidence-building measures (CBMs) and search and rescue (SAR). Participating countries attended with a mixture of experts and policy officers. Those from outside the narrow professional subject field who have attended profess great admiration and interest in the way the experts are able to cooperate in the intersessional context (particularly so in the case of the SAR meeting).

---

[2] Dato' Sri Mohd Najib bin Tun Haji Abdul Razak, Keynote Address at MIMA seminar: *CBMs At Sea in the Asia Pacific Region: Meeting the Challenges of the 21st Century*, Kuala Lumpur, 2-3 August 1994.

But this should not surprise us: SAR specialists are already directed by a number of international agreements, overseen by the International Maritime Organisation (IMO) and International Civil Aviation Organisation (ICAO), to cooperate. That the cooperation is imperfect at a number of interfaces is irrelevant - the forums for international cooperation in SAR already exist, and the ARF is unnecessary as a vehicle to bring these specialists together.

We need to be wary, therefore, of seeing too much significance from this kind of process- rather than substance-driven meeting. Let us not draw too much comfort from the fact that SAR specialists can talk together. They talk together on an almost daily basis, and when the unforeseen disaster occurs, all (or almost all) of the niceties of diplomatic behaviour and precedent are subordinated in the interests of saving life at sea or in the air: in practice, SAR works pretty well.

The ARF might alternatively be able to offer a forum for consideration of security issues that might stimulate maritime cooperation, for which there are no other effective international forums. The tricky bit is in deciding which areas. At the distant, difficult end of the continuum, we have the following possible areas of intersessional consideration:

- A mechanism for resolving political maritime claims such as claimed archipelagic sea lanes, rather than through the IMO's Safety Committee.

- A mechanism for resolving disputed territorial claims of the Spratly variety.

It is, of course, hoped that the ARF will ultimately offer an avenue for a solution to the Spratly issue, and it may only be possible to reach that level of consideration after passing through a number of less-contentious (process-driven) stages. Certainly, it is not possible now to address such issues. At the softer, more consensual end of the spectrum, we might consider:

- Distant-water fishing operations. Although other forums do exist to address fishing in the Western Pacific, they do not place fishing into a regional security context, and yet in the region fishing is a regular cause of shots being fired and ships being sunk.

- Maritime fraud with effects across borders - phantom ships - drawing together the insurers, cargo owners, enforcement agencies and flag state registries who deal with or are victims of phantom ships.

- Cross-border pollution issues, such as transfer of 'hazardous' wastes, debating such issues as whether tank-cleaning sludge should be treated as covered by the Basel Convention (notifiable, requiring prior informed consent for its acceptance), or regarded as a by-product of sea transport.

All these issues, except perhaps fishing, may be too 'soft' to generate sensible first-track consideration. It still seems important, however, to prove the mechanism by addressing a substantive issue before we have to fire in the face of a real threat to security. Perhaps the ARF could hold an intersessional meeting on regional naval cooperation, and invite the WPNS to conduct it. This would offer at least one significant advantage, in providing for broader understanding and recognition of the benefits that WPNS has already generated.

WPNS

WPNS is a gathering of professionals without political or policy intervention - it is almost invisible in policy terms. Whilst WPNS has achieved significant progress, particularly in disseminating information to assist inter-operability, it is to some extent limited by its first-track nature. It is inherently conservative, tending to enshrine national rather than regional positions, and tends to demand consensus of the entire group before accepting concepts for development. And it does not advertise.

In general, there seem to be no proponents of the regional view. No one suggests, for example, the importance of recording in proceedings or otherwise publishing the extent of existing bilateral or multilateral cooperation actually underway in the region as an expression of the possible for other regions. There seems no endorsement of the principle of members moving at their own pace to adopt multilateral activity, regarding resolutions as recommended or advisory, and not immediately binding.

It would seem to be helpful for WPNS to inform and be informed by the parallel processes concerned with maritime and broader regional security cooperation.

The Infrastructure

WPNS exists, has credibility and a substantial track record. Its strengths should be built on, in a way that maximises its advantages whilst recognising the importance of progress in areas of substance.

WPNS' lack of regional advocacy can be contrasted with PASOLS, the Pacific Area Senior Officers' Logistic Seminar. PASOLS (perhaps because of the importance, for logistic support, of achieving significant progress in operationalising its concepts for cooperation) has a standing secretariat able to focus outcomes, preserve corporate memory and manage the flow of documentation that sustains the organisation between meetings. PASOLS has been running for over twenty years, and its example of a standing secretariat offers an insight into how WPNS might be improved.

A standing secretariat for WPNS would offer the following advantages:

- It would provide a staff to coordinate and schedule meetings, and contribute effort and experience to assist the host navy in mounting and conducting meetings. With a sufficiently senior chief of staff in the secretariat, it could also contribute to encouraging appropriate attendance.

- It could provide editorship, custody and maintenance of documents covering WPNS doctrine and procedures.

- It would provide a central reservoir of experience, both in terms of WPNS itself, and the cooperative activities of its members.

- A secretariat could begin the process of developing the regional advocacy and voice that is necessary to gain maximum benefit from such an organisation.

- It could schedule exercises and provide a nucleus for and oversight of planning of specific WPNS exercises or activities.

The resource cost of a secretariat would also require resolution. A small staff only is envisaged, preferably representing several navies, and preferably located centrally in the region. Creative solutions are called for, where existing arrangements are used wherever possible to offset costs. One navy might donate office space, and another space-available air transport. An existing regional security arrangement (which offers a mechanism for sharing operating costs and which represents at least four WPNS members) might also be approached for support.

Countering the STANAVFORPAC Argument

Before considering some initiatives that might succeed as vehicles for cooperation, it is worth describing why a Standing Naval Force in Asia (STANAVFORPAC) is unlikely to be accepted:

- The long passage distances imposed by the geography of the Pacific Ocean makes this kind of cooperation less attractive in resource terms, compared to the eastern Atlantic and North Sea.

- The politics of international cooperation in the Western Pacific tend away from formal multilateralism and institutional solutions to problems of this nature. Even proposing a standing naval force sends unattractive messages of European solutions to Asian problems.

- The region has no underlying command, logistic or organisational structure analogous to NATO from which to establish and manage such a force. At the least, a STANAVFORPAC would require a shore operational and logistic headquarters that would impose a significant overhead.

Sharing Training Opportunities

Southeast Asian states, while not comfortable with multilateral exercises or more overt military cooperation, might be attracted to some low-key cooperative training activities programmed by WPNS. They could be structured, objective-driven training activities without any political scenario, concentrating target services and other exercise resources in a way which would allow very cost-effective training. This is a model that several regional navies already use, usually unilaterally, to maximise training benefits.

Using the cooperative framework of WPNS, it would be possible to schedule a number of these training activities in a way that would allow sequential participation by a number of regional navies. Direct training benefits would be achieved, in addition to the collateral benefits of association. Such activities, shorn of the wool of ceremonial and scenario, would allow cost-effective training and significant collateral benefits.

Such an exercise schedule would also offer the opportunity for rapid progress in developing inter-operability, initially in areas of non-sensitive cooperation, such as SAR, disaster relief and cooperative high seas surveillance. Depending on ASEAN's collective threat assessment, it would be possible in future to extend such an arrangement to include defensive activity such as mine countermeasures (MCM), even to the higher order sea lines of communication (SLOC) protection activity of anti-submarine, anti-surface and anti-air warfare.[3]

Australian Maritime Operations in Southeast Asia

Using cooperation with Malaysia as an example, let me briefly describe how practical maritime cooperation with Australian ships and aircraft works at present.

Malaysia and Australia share a maritime surveillance operation through 'deployments of P3C maritime patrol aircraft to the Royal Malaysian Air Force (RMAF) base at Butterworth, Malaysia, to conduct surveillance missions in South-East Asian waters'.[4] These operations cover mutually agreed patrol lines to satisfy mutually derived military surveillance objectives. In the course of patrols, the aircraft of course obtain information of direct use to Malaysia in enforcing the regulations of its EEZ - we are continuing to improve our

---

3   These notes are extracted from a paper prepared for a MIMA/SIPRI project on Regional Arms Control.

4   *Defending Australia*, Defence White Paper 1994 (Australian Government Publishing Service, Canberra, 1994), pp.89-90.

efficiency in passing sortie information to RMAF authorities ashore in near-real time.

Royal Australian Navy (RAN) ships also cooperate with the Royal Malaysian Navy (RMN) and RMAF assets in the conduct of military surveillance exercises and operations. These activities (except the P-3C operations) are replicated with most other countries in ASEAN.

There were thirty-three RAN ship visits to Malaysian ports in 1995. The ships conduct Five Power Defence Arrangement (FPDA) Exercise 'Starfish' every year, and this is an activity that can be increasingly classed as a high-level exercise opportunity. Air-defence-capable ships also participate in the FPDA Integrated Air Defence Systems (IADS) Major Air Defence Exercises (ADEX) at least once per year (twice in 1996). A substantial bilateral exercise programme is also maintained, both in the LUMUTEX series (a harbour period followed by a sea phase) and in less-formal Passing Exercises (PASSEXs). Some of these PASSEXs involve submarine and P-3C involvement.

Conclusion

The ARF has achieved much. WPNS, too, has made significant progress in a number of areas, albeit without gaining much regional recognition of the benefits obtained. Both organisations are praised for their work in setting forward a framework within which future cooperative activities might take place.

Real work needs to be done, however, to address real problems in the maritime environment. There are issues now for which these international cooperative frameworks might be usefully employed to improve the security environment. If work of substance and not just process is achieved, the effectiveness (and the perception of effectiveness) of the ARF and WPNS will be significantly enhanced. The confidence of the participants in them will increase confidence, something which will prove invaluable should those organisations need to undertake urgent work in future to sustain the security environment.

At present, the emerging regional security environment offers conditions that are particularly suitable for cooperation. It is a time for advancing ideas and opportunities unencumbered by over-concentration on traditional difficulties and impediments. There are of course risks with too dramatic a pace of development, but if these are recognised and allowed for, then they do not need to hinder the fall of shot.

VI INDIA AND THE INDIAN OCEAN

Rahul Roy-Chaudhury

In a manner similar to navies of certain shapes and sizes worldwide, the Indian Navy is ideally suited to the conduct of operations in support of political objectives. This is due to the inherent characteristics of its forces, including their flexibility, visibility, and mobility, as well as the unique nature of the medium upon which they traverse.[1] In addition, the large and interconnected water bodies which dominate the Earth provide considerable access worldwide. Major issues such as the freedom of navigation, shipping, environmental pollution, and the changes in the Law of the Sea, are therefore international by nature and the responsibility of all littoral and island states in the world.

In view of these factors, the navy has taken the lead amongst the three Indian armed services in demonstrating its political roles in peacetime. Over the years, its perspective on cooperation has traditionally focused on visits to foreign ports, the hosting of foreign warships, disaster relief and bilateral naval assistance. In a recent development, it has begun to focus on the conduct of joint naval exercises with foreign navies.

India's Perspective

In a major shift in policy in late 1991, the Indian government accepted the navy's proposal to resume what were considered to be high-profile interactions with foreign navies. These were to take place in the form of joint exercises with selected littoral and extra-regional navies of the Indian Ocean. This was a particularly important decision as it brought to an end over twenty-five years of self-imposed isolation on the part of the Indian Navy, during which time virtually no joint naval exercises were conducted.

---

1   See Hedley Bull, 'Sea Power and Political Influence' in Jonathan Alford (ed.), *Sea Power and Influence: Old Issues and New Challenges* (Gower, Farnborough, 1980), p.8.

It was no coincidence that this move came when it did. A dramatic transformation of the global strategic environment had just taken place. The Cold War had come to an end, the Gulf War had ended in victory for the multinational forces, and the erstwhile Soviet naval presence in the Indian Ocean was expected to be negligible in the near future. In view of these developments, prospects for multi-dimensional maritime and naval cooperation in the region appeared most opportune.

The nature and scope of the joint naval exercises envisaged, however, were quite different from those which had taken place a quarter of a century earlier. These were joint multilateral naval exercises, organised in the 1950s and the 1960s by the British, and held annually amongst the navies of India, Pakistan and Sri Lanka, with the participation of the Royal Navy, and, at times, the Australian and New Zealand navies as well. Held for a three-week period in August, off the north-eastern Sri Lankan port of Trincomalee, they came to be known by the acronym JET (Joint Exercises Trincomalee). JET provided the navies the opportunity to carry out advanced tactical exercises, especially crucial anti-submarine training exercises, which were really not possible due to the absence of submarines in virtually all Indian Ocean navies at the time.[2] These tasks were somewhat simplified as all the navies then operated on Allied Tactical Publications (ATP) and Common Signal Publications (CSP).[3] In 1964 JET came to an abrupt end, in view of the increasingly antagonistic relations between India and Pakistan. Just over a year later, India was involved in a war against Pakistan.

For over twelve years after the end of JET, the Indian Navy did not carry out any exercise with a foreign navy. This was due primarily to the increased level of Cold War tensions and the onset of superpower naval rivalry in the Indian Ocean. In these circumstances, India's non-aligned foreign policy did not allow any joint naval exercise to take place with the two major protagonists or their allies. This was clearly a blow to the erstwhile Soviet Union, which was interested in carrying out exercises of this nature. It is important to

---

2   Rahul Roy-Chaudhury, 'Indian Naval Diplomacy', *Indian Defence Review*, January-March 1995, p.53.

3   Lt Cdr B.M.Dimri, 'Naval Diplomacy and UNCLOS III', *Strategic Analysis*, April 1994, p.66.

note, however, that this did not affect the important warship supplier/recipient relationship between the two countries. As for the non-aligned group of countries, it was, unfortunately, considered that joint bilateral naval exercises did not constitute an important dimension of India's diplomatic relationship.

The first of only two exceptions to the policy of not carrying out joint naval exercises took place during the brief period of the Janata Party rule in New Delhi in the late 1970s. On this occasion, the Indian Navy carried out a single joint multilateral naval exercise with Australian and New Zealand naval forces. Both the Indian and Australian naval forces participating in these exercises were led by aircraft carriers.[4] This was followed twelve years later in 1989 with a single joint bilateral naval exercise with warships of the Indonesian Navy off Surabaya.

The government's determined new policy of encouraging the conduct of joint bilateral naval exercises, amidst the uncertainties of the global and regional security environment, aims to achieve three things:

• *To dispel concern over India's naval build-up programme and expansion of power-projection capabilities.* Such concerns had been made known to India from about the mid-1980s by some of the littoral states of the Indian Ocean, including Australia. They essentially related to the Indian Navy's purchase of a second aircraft carrier in 1986 and to the three-year lease of a nuclear-powered submarine from the erstwhile Soviet Union in 1988. Moreover, the rationale for Indian naval expansion was also questioned and simplistically and erroneously perceived to be due to the desire of the country to be the dominant power in the region. The absence of a clear-cut policy statement from the Indian government, as to the reasons for the modernisation and expansion of the navy, along with the isolation of the service, clearly added to these concerns.

Joint naval exercises are seen by the Indian government as a means to dispel these concerns and build confidence and trust

---

4   Vice-Admiral S.Mookerjee (Retd), 'Joint Naval Exercises: Overdue Change of Course', *United Services Institute of India Journal*, April-June 1992, p.160.

in the relationship amongst the littoral states of the Indian Ocean. It is expected that the nature of interactions the joint exercises provide, both at sea and port, will generate greater transparency as to Indian naval activities and responsibilities. In this respect, sensitive naval bases, such as the naval air establishment at Port Blair in the Andaman Islands and the submarine base at Vishakapatnam, have also been opened up to warships of a selective few countries. Since 1991, naval ships from Malaysia, Indonesia, Australia, Singapore and France have visited Port Blair. Singapore Navy warships also visited Vishakapatnam for the first time in 1996.

- *To improve the nature of bilateral relations with the littoral states of the Indian Ocean, as well as others.* Joint naval exercises are increasingly being seen as an important aspect of the country's foreign policy. In this endeavour, they help instil, as well as build upon, a military dimension to bilateral political relationships.

  For countries of the Indian Ocean littoral which previously did not have a military relationship with India, joint naval exercises could also lead to the promotion of Indian defence products and services in the short term. For the others, joint naval exercises are seen as improving the totality of the political relationship, as well as signifying India's interest in peace and stability in the Indian Ocean. In the case of the United States, for example, the continued naval interactions, amidst serious political differences, signify the desire of both countries to keep their relations on an even keel.

- *To improve the Indian Navy's tactics and strategy.* Interactions with foreign navies, especially those which are highly professional and technologically advanced, enable the Indian Navy to learn valuable lessons for warfighting and peacetime operations. They also provide opportunities to assess the skill and combat capabilities of foreign navies at sea. There is, however, some dispute as to the value of the lessons to be learnt from the limited nature of the joint naval exercises carried out so far.[5]

Experiences

Over the years, the Indian Navy has gained considerable experience in a number of forms of naval cooperation. These largely remain limited to the Indian Ocean and are essentially bilateral by nature, and relatively modest in scope.

Visits to Foreign Ports

Since the mid-1980s, the Indian Navy has increased the frequency of goodwill visits to those countries in the Indian Ocean which expressed concern over the nature and extent of its expansion. For the past ten years, for example, the Indian Navy has visited ports in Indonesia and Malaysia virtually every year. This included the visit of two warships to Penang in 1990-91, to take part in the international fleet review that marked the fiftieth anniversary of the Royal Malaysian Navy. The most recent visit to Malaysia of two Indian warships took place in January 1995. Since 1985, Indian naval ships have also visited Australian ports three times. During 1991-94, the Indian Navy visited 22 countries and approximately 25 ports. In contrast, during the same period, the South African Navy visited 35 countries and 54 ports.[6]

Hosting Foreign Warships

Indian ports continue to host visits by foreign warships, including those from Malaysia, Indonesia, Australia, and the United States. As mentioned earlier, sensitive naval establishments have also been opened up to warships of foreign countries on a selective basis. In view of its 'gunboat diplomacy' during the 1971 Indo-Pakistani war, the entry of American warships to Indian ports had been refused till the mid-1980s. During the 1990-91 Gulf War, however, US ships on

---

5   ibid., p.163.
6   Wayne Abrahamse, 'Developing Countries and Naval Diplomacy' in Greg Mills (ed.), *Maritime Policy for Developing Nations* (South African Institute of International Affairs, Johannesburg, 1995), p.131.

their way to the war zone were allowed refuelling stops.[7] In November 1993, the first visit in very many years of a Chinese warship, a destroyer-size training ship, took place at Bombay. On the earlier Chinese naval visit to the Indian Ocean in the mid-1980s, no Indian port had been visited. In March 1995, the first visit (in a very long time) of a South African naval ship, a combat support vessel, took place in response to the visit, three months earlier, of two Indian warships to South Africa.

Disaster Relief

On a few occasions, the Indian Navy has responded to requests from foreign governments to provide aid and disaster relief. A recent example, Operation 'Madad' (Help), was the Maldivian request for relief supplies, when a massive tidal wave struck some of its islands in July 1991.[8]

Bilateral Naval Assistance[9]

a) Sri Lanka 1971: The first major role of the Indian Navy in cooperation with a foreign government took place in 1971 during the insurgency in Sri Lanka. In April that year, the Indian government provided military assistance to Sri Lanka in order to counter the Janatha Vimukthi Peramuna (JVP) or People's Liberation Front, a terrorist organisation of Maoist origin. This followed a formal request by the government of Sri Lanka to several countries, including India, Pakistan and Britain. In the event, India was the first country to provide the required military assistance, in the form of naval and air units.

Five Indian frigates transported military supplies to Colombo and carried out surveillance duties off the Sri Lankan coast (in association with the Sri Lankan Navy). The main task of the Indian naval force lay in preventing the seaborne supply of arms and ammunition to the terrorist movement. This was carried out

---

7   Rahul Roy-Chaudhury, 'Showing the Flag', *Maritime International*, February 1996, p.17.
8   Dimri, 'Naval Diplomacy and UNCLOS III', p.69.
9   For further details on this section, see Rahul Roy-Chaudhury, *Sea Power and Indian Security* (Brassey's, London, 1995).

successfully. By the end of June 1971, the JVP had suffered major losses as a result of the Sri Lankan military and paramilitary forces. The Indian naval force was consequently withdrawn.

b) Sri Lanka 1987-90: In view of the Indo-Sri Lankan Agreement of July 29, 1987, units of the Indian Peace-Keeping Force (IPKF) deployed in northern and eastern Sri Lanka came into conflict with the Liberation Tigers of Tamil Eelam (LTTE), the most powerful Tamil militant organisation on the island. The Indian Navy played an important, and fairly successful, role in these operations.

The terms of the Indo-Sri Lankan Agreement provided a specific role for the Indian Navy and Coast Guard, in contrast to that of the IPKF. While the latter was given a general task to 'guarantee and enforce the cessation of hostilities', paragraph 2.16 (B) of the agreement specifically stated:

> The Indian Navy/Coast Guard will cooperate with the Sri Lankan Navy in preventing Tamil militant activities from affecting Sri Lanka.[10]

This did not mean that the Navy was restricted to active surveillance and engagement missions alone, but that they were considered the most important in terms of the agreement. The prevention of the flow of arms to Sri Lanka would not only weaken the morale of the LTTE, but greatly assist Indian military operations on land.

The extent of cooperation with the Sri Lankan Navy, however, remained minimal. This was partly due to its limited capacity and to its reluctance to engage forcibly in any sort of military action. It appeared to be following the precedent set by the army, which had been confined to barracks by the terms of the agreement. Nonetheless, the Sri Lankan Navy's knowledge of the coastal areas was of much benefit to the Indian Navy. Other roles of the Indian Navy included transportation and logistical support missions, as well as active military support to forces on the ground. All Indian military forces, including the navy, were withdrawn by the end of March 1990, on the explicit orders of the then Sri Lankan president.

---

[10] For the text of the Indo-Sri Lankan Agreement, see Satish Kumar (ed.), *Yearbook on India's Foreign Policy 1987-1988* (Tata McGraw-Hill, New Delhi, 1988), pp.233-8.

c) The Maldives 1988: In November 1988, the Indian Navy played a crucial role in ensuring the security of the Maldive Islands and in bringing about the capture of the mercenaries involved in a coup attempt. Soon after the decision was taken by the Indian Cabinet to intervene, on the request of the Maldives government, a naval Tu-142 maritime reconnaissance (MR) plane was sent to ensure that the runway at Hulule airport was not blocked. While Indian Air Force transport aircraft were landing in the Maldives, a group of 46 mercenaries commandeered a 5,000 tonne merchant ship, and set sail with twenty-seven hostages aboard. The next morning, a naval Il-38 MR plane spotted the ship, and a Tu-142 MR aircraft determined its course. Two Indian frigates in the area were promptly sent in pursuit. When negotiations with the mercenaries proved futile, the warships shelled and dropped depth charges near the merchant ship. In the early hours of November 6, the mercenaries finally surrendered and their ship was boarded by Indian naval personnel.

d) Sri Lanka at present: Since 1993, the Indian Navy and Coast Guard have been cooperating with the Sri Lankan Navy in conducting surveillance and patrol operations in the Palk Straits, in an attempt to prevent the supply of arms/ammunition to Tamil militants from the Indian coast or elsewhere. There have been a few successes during these operations, although they have not been conducted jointly.

Participation in United Nations Operations

For the first time, in the early 1990s, Indian naval ships actively participated in a United Nations peacekeeping effort off the Somalian coast, with both the Unified Task Force-Somalia (UNITAF) and the United Nations Operation in Somalia (UNOSOM II).[11] For just over two years from December 1992, two ships of the Indian Navy provided humanitarian aid to Mogadishu from Mombasa. During these operations, low-level joint multilateral exercises were also carried out with warships of the American, Canadian, Italian and French navies.[12] Although Indian naval vessels did not assist the

---

11   Rear-Admiral K.R.Menon, 'Maritime Developments and Opportunities in South Asia' in Sam Bateman and Dick Sherwood (eds), *Australia's Maritime Bridge Into Asia* (Allen & Unwin, Sydney, 1995), p.41.

12   Rear-Admiral Sampath Pillai, 'Somalia-Indian Navy in the Land of Punt', *Quarter Deck*, 94, 1994, p.65.

induction of the Indian military contingent of about 5,000 people, three warships were deployed off the southern Somalian port of Kismayu to help in their de-induction and in the transportation of their equipment to India.

Provision of Advanced Notice of Naval Exercises

In an important but little noticed development, both India and Pakistan reached, and signed, an agreement on 6 April 1991 on the provision of 'Advanced Notice of Military Exercises, Manoeuvres, and Troop Movements'.[13] The agreement was ratified by both countries, and came into force with the exchange of the Instruments of Ratification in August 1992.[14] This was a crucial naval confidence-building measure, in view of the limited distance between the two major Indian and Pakistani naval bases and the shape of the coastline.[15]

The governments of both India and Pakistan reached this agreement in order to prevent any crisis situation arising from a misreading of the other side's intentions. The major aspects of the naval dimension of the agreement are as follows:

• If a major naval exercise is held, involving six or more ships of destroyer/frigate size and above, exercising in company and crossing into the other's Exclusive Economic Zone (EEZ), the schedule of the exercise is to be transmitted in writing to the other side through diplomatic channels 30 days in advance (from the commencement of movement of warships from their locations).

• This would comprise information on the type and level of the exercise, and the planned duration of the activity.

---

13   For the text of the agreement, see Rear-Admiral K.R.Menon (Retd), 'Maritime Conflict Resolution and Confidence-Building in South Asia', *Indian Defence Review*, October-December 1995, pp.39-41.

14   J.N.Dixit, *Anatomy of a Flawed Inheritance: Indo-Pakistan Relations: 1970-1994* (Konark Publishers, Delhi, 1995),pp.315-16.

15   Menon, 'Maritime Conflict Resolution and Confidence-Building in South Asia', p.30.

• In case of some change in exercise area/grouping of warships, details of the change are to be brought to the notice of the other country at least 15 days in advance.

• Naval ships and submarines of the two countries are not to come less than three nautical miles from each other, in order to avoid any accident while operating in international waters.

In addition, during the meetings held between the Indian and Pakistani armed forces in 1991, some progress was made on both the establishment of communication links between units at sea and measures to prevent mutual interference.[16] On 24 January 1994, India sent six non-papers to Pakistan; one of these related to additional confidence-building measures between the two countries, including the setting up of an institutional mechanism to resolve ambiguities to enable a more effective implementation of the agreement on 'Advanced Notice of Military Exercises, Manoeuvres, and Troop Movements'.[17] These were rejected by Pakistan. The subsequent round of Foreign Secretary level talks, where these proposals could have been discussed, is yet to take place.

The Conduct of Joint Bilateral Naval and Coast Guard Exercises

In view of the dramatic shift in the Indian government's policy in 1991, a number of joint bilateral exercises have been held with thirteen littoral as well as extra-regional navies of the Indian Ocean (Tables 3(VI).1 and 3(VI).2).

In terms of the littoral states of the Indian Ocean, the Indian Navy's emphasis continues to be placed on the Bay of Bengal/Eastern Indian Ocean, with joint naval and coast guard exercises being conducted with five countries so far. Significantly, four of them are members of the Association of Southeast Asian Nations (ASEAN). Although the present series of joint naval exercises began with an Australian warship off the Andamans in 1991, the momentum with Australia has not been maintained. Indeed, the Indian Navy has conducted the largest number of joint naval exercises with the Republic of Singapore Navy (RSN); the fourth such exercise concluded

---

16   ibid., pp.31-2.
17   Dixit, *Anatomy of a Flawed Inheritance*, p.316.

in March 1996. Joint naval exercises have also been carried out with two countries of the Arabian Sea/western Indian Ocean, Oman and the United Arab Emirates (UAE). More are expected to follow soon. Most of these exercises have been relatively modest in scope, being conducted with about one or two warships on each side, for about a day or two.

Amongst the extra-regional navies of the Indian Ocean, the most significant, and the largest, joint naval exercises have been conducted with the United States. Notwithstanding the emotional outburst in protest in the Indian Parliament on the eve of the first such exercises ('Malabar 92') off Goa in May 1992, they took place in March 1996. However, the second round of exercises to be planned had to be postponed continuously for about three years, till they were finally conducted off Cochin in May 1995 ('Malabar 95'). The third Indo-US joint naval exercises took place less than a month ago, despite serious differences on nuclear and ballistic missile issues between the two countries.

In marked contrast to the 'passing exercises' of 'Malabar 92', 'Malabar 95' involved the most important dimension of naval warfare in the present day, that of anti-submarine warfare (ASW). These involved ASW tactics and communication, including the detection and mock destruction of submarines, and encompassed the participation of all three dimensions of naval power - air, surface and subsurface. Moreover, these exercises were carried out for a period of four days, and, in addition to the participation of destroyers and frigates (two on each side) involved, for the first time, nuclear-powered submarines and the P-3C Orion MR aircraft on the American side, and Kilo-class submarines on the Indian side. The selection of the forces employed was particularly beneficial to both navies. In September 1994, a ten-day exercise was also held in India between the special forces of the two services. The first ever joint naval exercises with the erstwhile Soviet Union/Russia were carried out only in 1993.

Over the years, the frequency of joint naval/coast guard exercises has not altered considerably, averaging at nearly five a year. In all, the Indian Navy and Coast Guard have carried out 24 joint bilateral naval/coast guard exercises since October 1991 (Table 3(VI).3).

Table 3(VI).1: Joint Bilateral Naval and Coast Guard Exercises with Littoral States of the Indian Ocean since 1991

Country	Year
Bay of Bengal/Eastern Indian Ocean	
Australia	1991
	1992
	1996
Indonesia	1994
Malaysia	1994
Singapore	1993
	1994
	1995
	1996
Thailand	1995
Arabian Sea/Western Indian Ocean	
Oman	1993
United Arab Emirates (UAE)	199S
Maldive Islands (Coast Guard Exercises)	1991
	1992
	1994

Table 3(VI).2: Joint Bilateral Naval Exercises with Extra-Regional Navies of the Indian Ocean since 1991

Country	Year
France	1992
New Zealand	1993
Russia	1993 1994
UK	1992 1993
USA	1992 1995 1996

Table 3(VI).3: Frequency of Joint Naval and Coast Guard Exercises

Year	Frequency
1991 (October-December)	2
1992	5
1993	5
1994	5
1995	4
1996	3
October	
Total	**24**

Suggestions

The broad areas of naval cooperation identified and suggested since the early 1990s by naval personnel (both serving and retired), commentators and analysts, include the following - greater transparency in procurement plans and the future shape and size of naval forces and the rationale for naval deployment; cooperation against transnational threats such as narco-terrorism and piracy; multilateral agreement on the prevention of incidents at sea; cooperation in hydrography and the training of personnel; joint multilateral naval exercises; and a multilateral symposium on the Indian Ocean.[18] The most fruitful areas of naval cooperation for India are warship maintenance and construction and naval hydrographic training and operations.

Warship Maintenance and Construction

India's status as a maritime nation, with considerable economic, political and military interests in the Indian Ocean, is emphasised by its large and highly developed shipbuilding industry. This consists of over 40 shipyards, both large and small, located in the public as well as the private sector. In addition, over 300 small-scale and ancillary industries supply crucial items and equipment to the three largest shipyards in the country, which are administered by the Ministry of Defence (Department of Defence Production).

In view of the Indian government's determined policy to attain a sufficiently high degree of self-reliance in warship production, the three defence shipyards have successfully built a number of sophisticated warships. These include submarines, destroyers, frigates

---

[18]   See, for example, Vice-Admiral Mihir Roy (Retd), 'Maritime Cooperation in the Indian Ocean' in Mills (ed.), *Maritime Policy for Developing Nations*, and 'From Confrontation to Cooperation: A New Agenda for the Indian Navy', *United Services Institute of India Journal*, January-March 1993; Capt. C. Uday Bhaskar, 'Regional Naval Cooperation', *Strategic Analysis*, November 1992; Commodore Sam Bateman, 'Confidence and Security Building: An Australian View', and Admiral M.W.Hudson (Retd), 'Australia's Naval Policy in the Twenty-first Century' in Jasjit Singh (ed.), *Maritime Security* (Institute for Defence Studies and Analyses, New Delhi, 1993); Admiral Sir James Eberle (Retd), 'Prospects for Regional Cooperation in Maritime Affairs', and Brigadier General Soedibyo (Retd), 'Regional Security and Military Cooperation: An Indonesian Perception' in *The Indian Ocean: Challenges and Opportunities* (Navy Foundation, Delhi, 1992).

and corvettes, along with patrol boats, minor coastal combatants and auxiliary ships, which are presently in service with the Indian Navy.[19]

The spare capacities in Indian defence shipyards could be utilised for the maintenance and repair, as well as the construction, of ships of littoral as well as extra-regional navies. This could be undertaken on a bilateral basis in a planned and efficient manner. This would enable the economical and effective construction and repair of warships in the Indian Ocean region.

Naval Hydrographic Training and Operations

The Indian Navy has been fortunate in gradually developing a hydrographic capability which is possibly the fourth largest today.[20] It is also the first navy in the world to have had a hydrographer as chief.[21] The Indian Navy's fleet of six indigenously built survey ships is to expand to ten by the end of the decade, and then to sixteen soon afterwards.[22] The Indian naval hydrographic centre at Dehradun could organise and conduct training programmes on a regular basis for naval officers of Indian Ocean littoral countries. The spare capacity of the service can be utilised to undertake surveys for other countries in the Arabian Sea and the Bay of Bengal. For the first time, the Indian Navy undertook, and successfully completed, the survey of Oman's coastline last year, in a $5 million contract.

The conduct of naval hydrographic training and operations in a bilateral manner would enable establishment of hydrographic departments with navies of the Indian Ocean littoral which do not have them already, as well as enable the survey of large areas of the seabed in a joint and coordinated manner. This would facilitate the production of nautical charts; the exploration of the sea bed for oil, natural gas, and minerals; and the development of fisheries.

---

19 See Rahul Roy-Chaudhury, 'India's Defence Shipyards', *Maritime International*, March 1995, pp.7-8.
20 Menon, 'Maritime Conflict Resolution and Confidence-Building in South Asia', pp.37-8.
21 This rare distinction goes to the late Admiral Jal Cursetji, who was the Chief of Naval Staff from March 1976 to March 1979.
22 'Naval Hydrography Charting New Courses' (Interview with Commodore K.R. Srinivasan, the Chief Hydrographer of the Indian Navy), *Times of India*, 4 October 1995, p.5.

Naval Training

The Indian Navy continues to be the largest indigenous naval force in the Indian Ocean littoral, with a balanced and mixed fleet structure and a strength of about 55,000 personnel. In view of these factors, its training requirements are varied and multidimensional, necessitating the establishment of a number of basic and specialised training academies and institutions throughout the country. A number of them regularly train personnel from selected foreign navies. They accounted for 114 officers and 98 sailors in 1992-93.[23]

The training provided at these facilities could be channelled more effectively through coordination with other training establishments in the Indian Ocean littoral on a bilateral basis. This would provide selected naval officers and sailors with international exposure and specialised training in areas such as helicopter conversion courses and operations on helicopters and MR aircraft, in the field of naval aviation alone.

Increased Emphasis on Ship Visits

The value of ship visits, to foreign ports as well as the hosting of foreign warships, has often been underestimated. This is a crucial aspect of naval cooperation and needs to be emphasised. This could take the form of visits by different types of warships, longer calls at port and, more importantly, coordination with the visit of a Head of State or Government to the host country. The success of systematic naval ship visits can go a long way in building confidence amongst states in the Indian Ocean.

Annual Conference on Naval Cooperation in the Indian Ocean

At this stage of interaction amongst navies, it would make considerable sense to convene a conference, on an annual basis, that could discuss the positive aspects as well as the problems and difficulties of enhanced naval cooperation in the Indian Ocean. Naval officers, as well as members of the strategic community and academics

---

23   Menon, 'Maritime Developments and Opportunities in South Asia', p.43.

of individual countries, could take part in these deliberations. This would be a crucial confidence-building measure, as it could bring out the perceptions and/or the misperceptions of countries in the region. This could prevent misperceptions of the arms (especially naval) build-up amongst ASEAN states in the late 1990s, as was the case concerning the Indian Navy in the mid-1980s.

Conclusion

In terms of regional naval cooperation, two major related trends are discernible in the policies of the Indian government and the Indian Navy in the near future - an overwhelming emphasis on trilateral, as opposed to multilateral, forms of cooperation in sensitive activities such as joint naval exercises, and stress on the Indian Ocean as a whole, rather than any constituent part.

The Indian Navy's emphasis on bilateral forms of cooperation can be seen from its experiences in terms of naval assistance and agreements, and even the rationale for the current series of joint naval exercises. Joint multilateral naval exercises were carried out only in the 1950s and 1960s when the global strategic environment was quite different, on one occasion in 1977-78, and for a limited period of time during Indian naval operations off the Somalian coast as part of UN peacekeeping activities.

The only proposal for joint multilateral naval exercises emanating from Naval Headquarters in the early 1990s came from Admiral L. Ramdas, the Chief of Naval Staff (1991-93). Ramdas envisaged the conduct of joint naval exercises with some of the ASEAN states in 1993. This proposal was finally reduced to a gathering (appropriately called 'Milan') of navies from six countries, including Thailand, Indonesia and Singapore, at Port Blair in February 1995, with the president of India present at the inaugural function.

The problems with joint multilateral naval exercises, whether by conception or extension of bilateral exercises, are not difficult to see. Not only is there an absence of an agreed upon single common threat perception, but the defence of the Sea Lines of Communication (SLOCs) in the Indian Ocean does not necessarily require the conduct of formal joint multilateral naval exercises.[24] Any such exercise, by definition, would necessitate the inclusion of some countries and the exclusion of others. This could be misperceived as the beginning of a military alliance of sorts, targeted against specific country/countries, and would increase tensions in the area, rather than decrease them.

This would be particularly insensitive *vis-à-vis* India's relations with the People's Republic of China (PRC).[25] Although the modernisation of the Chinese Navy and its presence in the Indian Ocean in the future is a source of concern to the Indian Navy, it would be foolhardy to engage the navies of the ASEAN countries for joint multilateral naval exercises. Instead, the first visit of a Chinese naval warship to India in very many years in 1993 was followed by the visit of two Indian ships to Shanghai in 1995 and the first visit of an Indian Chief of Naval Staff to Beijing earlier this year.

The absence of a multilateral forum for the whole of the Indian Ocean, as opposed to any constituent part, complicates matters further, as there is no organisation under which truly multilateral naval exercises could satisfactorily be conducted. This is important from India's point of view, as it has vital economic and political interests in the western part of the Indian Ocean as well, including its dependence on the supply of oil from the Persian Gulf. The development of an Indian Ocean rim community is also some time away. Moreover, a regional multilateral organisation like the South Asian Association for Regional Cooperation (SAARC), of which India is a member, is totally ineffective in this respect, in view of the differing security perceptions of its members.

In effect, although regional naval cooperation in the Indian Ocean on sensitive issues such as joint multilateral naval exercises could be an effective 'building block' for regional security, India is not

---

24 Charles A. Meconis and Commander Stanley B. Weeks (Retd), *Cooperative Maritime Security in the Asia-Pacific Region: A Strategic and Arms Control Assessment* (Institute for Global Security Studies, Seattle, 1995), pp.63-5.

25 See Captain C. Uday Bhaskar, 'India and the Indian Ocean: Post-Cold War Possibilities' in Major General Dipankar Banerjee (ed.), *Towards an Era of Cooperation: An Indo-Australian Dialogue* (Institue for Defence Studies and Analyses, New Delhi, 1995), pp.321-2.

likely to take part in such activities in the near future.[26] In this respect, it would be far more fruitful to concentrate on other aspects of naval cooperation, such as warship maintenance and construction, naval hydrographic training and operations, naval training, increased emphasis on ship visits, and the organisation of an annual conference on the Indian Ocean.

---

[26] See Sam Bateman and Anthony Bergin, 'Building Blocks for Maritime Security in the Indian Ocean: An Australian Perspective' in Banerjee (ed.), *Towards an Era of Cooperation*, p.328.

CHAPTER 4

INCIDENTS AT SEA AGREEMENTS AND MARITIME CONFIDENCE-BUILDING MEASURES

Stanley B. Weeks

Introduction

Maritime confidence-building measures (CBMs)[1] have an increasing potential role in contributing to regional stability. The principal maritime CBM to date has been bilateral Incidents at Sea (INCSEA) agreements, which have focused on avoiding dangerous actions by naval forces on the high seas outside of territorial waters. As indicated below, INCSEA agreements still have considerable utility in both bilateral and, increasingly, multilateral regional or subregional contexts.

But the post-Cold War maritime security environment will also require going beyond INCSEA agreements to include a variety of measures to increase openness and transparency, and to foster cooperation in a broad range of maritime issues. While the end of the Cold War has eliminated the most serious previous single maritime risk of conflict (between the US and Soviet navies), it has given rise to new maritime security concerns, as regional powers (most notably in the Asia Pacific region) increasingly shift to more extended and capable offshore maritime defence capabilities. This naval modernisation has been spurred by several factors: concerns about the drawdown and potential withdrawal of a stabilising US naval presence; worries about the future naval potential of other large potential regional powers (such as Japan, China and India); a reduced focus in many smaller countries (for example, in Southeast Asia) on internal counter-insurgency issues; and, perhaps most importantly, by

---

[1]   CBMs are defined here as 'measures that tend to make military intentions more explicit by increasing transparency and predictability, thus reducing the risk of war by accident or miscalculation'. Others have used the terms confidence- and security-building measures (CSBMs), trust-building measures (TBMs), and mutual reassurance measures (MRMs).

the November 1994 entry into effect of the 1982 UN Convention on the Law of the Sea (UNCLOS III). The new Law of the Sea provisions, including extending Exclusive Economic Zones (EEZs) to two hundred miles offshore, have greatly increased demands for maritime policing and resource management. Finally, the phenomenal recent growth of global trade and economic development both enables greater expenditures on maritime security and generally increases the importance of the security of sea lanes and ocean resources.

The Maritime Strategic Context

An assessment of the potential post-Cold War role of maritime CBMs must consider the specific regional (and often subregional) strategic contexts for such measures.

US/Europe: The US and most of its Western European allies now have in place bilateral INCSEA agreements with Russia. Additionally, some of the existing Organisation for Security and Cooperation in Europe (OSCE)[2] accords (the Stockholm Conference on Disarmament in Europe (CDE) of 1986 and subsequent Vienna accords) require advance notification of very large exercises and provide for observation of those naval forces specifically employed to affect the land battle (for example, amphibious forces). In general, the maritime security environment in Europe is stable and naval forces in the region continue the process of post-Cold War reductions.

Latin America: In Latin America, naval forces have also been reduced in recent years. Although there are not maritime CBMs in place, this is understandable given that most regional navies have long-standing cooperative arrangements (including developed common exercise and communication procedures) through their annual UNITAS naval exercises with the United States.

Middle East: The Middle East, on the other hand, has a long history of Arab-Israeli conflict and continuing arms build-ups. As a result of the Middle East Peace Process (MEPP), there has been significant, though relatively unpublicised, recent progress in maritime CBMs. As part of the multilateral part of the MEPP, a working group was established on Arms Control and Regional Security (ACRS). Within this working

---

2   In 1995 the Conference on Security and Cooperation in Europe (CSCE) became the OSCE.

group, Canada agreed to serve as 'mentor' in developing maritime CBMs, specifically pursuing two initiatives: (1) a regional INCSEA agreement; and (2) a maritime search and rescue (SAR) arrangement for the region.

Progress began in September 1993 with a workshop that was facilitated by the Canadian mentors, under MEPP co-sponsors, the United States and Russia, at the Canadian Coast Guard College in Sydney, Nova Scotia, and attended by Arab, Israeli and Palestinian maritime personnel. There was consensus that both an INCSEA Agreement and a regional SAR arrangement would be desirable and achievable. A second workshop was held in Antalya, Turkey, in March 1994, followed by an INCSEA and SAR at-sea demonstration for naval officers from the region, conducted by US, Canadian and Italian naval forces in July 1994 in Venice, Italy. Canada then sponsored the first Senior Officers' Symposium for Middle East naval leaders, from 29 August to 1 September 1994 in Halifax, Nova Scotia. Each delegation spoke on its perception of maritime security in the region. After further intensive discussions at a meeting in November 1994 on the Jordanian shore of the Dead Sea, the text (less a formal implementing/accession article) of a regional multilateral INCSEA Text, and a SAR Framework, were agreed. The MEPP Multilateral Plenary Meeting in Tunis in December 1994 approved the INCSEA text and SAR framework for regional implementation, which is now in process, with continuing Canadian mentorship. Despite the continuing vulnerability of any MEPP accords to the turbulent political ups-and-downs of the Arab-Israeli conflict, the establishment of a framework for maritime cooperation across the vast region from Morocco to Kuwait is quite a remarkable achievement.[3]

The Asia Pacific Region

The most challenging region for future maritime CBM development is the Asia Pacific region, which overall has a minimal structure of maritime CBMs, and maritime forces and interests which

---

[3]   For an excellent account of the MEPP maritime process history, see Peter Jones, 'Maritime Confidence-Building Measures in the Middle East', unpublished paper prepared for the University of British Columbia Conference, *From Cooperative Security to Multinational Peacekeeping: The Role of Medium Power Navies in the New Century*, 23-25 February 1995.

are rapidly growing. This more complex new maritime security context in the Asia Pacific region requires a new assessment of potential maritime risk reduction and CBMs in the region. In assessing the specific relevance of these maritime CBMs, the unique characteristics of the Asia Pacific region must be noted. As a recent survey of CBMs noted:

> The region is more geographically, politically, and culturally diverse than any other in which confidence building efforts have been pursued. Perhaps most importantly, while troubled with some of the world's most explosive hotspots, the Asia Pacific as a whole is characterised less by actively adversarial relationships than by the potential for conflict. Territorial disputes, competing economic and resource interests and lingering domestic insecurities suggest the need for measures aimed at averting the rise of tension and conflict.[4]

This is not to suggest that previous maritime CBM experience, more oriented to actively confrontational situations, is not relevant to the Asia Pacific region, but rather to argue for careful adaptation of each experience. Moreover, the geographic disparities in the Asia Pacific region suggest the need for varying subregional approaches in some CBM areas between Northeast Asia, Southeast Asia, the South Pacific and the Indian Ocean. In Northeast Asia, the maritime interests and forces of four major powers (the United States, Russia, Japan, and China) intersect, while the continuing standoff on the Korean peninsula implies that confidence building, in the absence of political preconditions of normal relations, may be best limited to Cold War-type conflict-avoidance measures. In Southeast Asia, there is a long history of informal ASEAN maritime cooperation, supplemented by a more recent web of bilateral and multilateral confidence-building and cooperative maritime measures. In the South Pacific, broad cooperative maritime regimes have developed between Australia, New Zealand and the Pacific island states, focused on non-military maritime concerns of EEZ surveillance and control of fishing

---

4   Susan Pederson and Stanley Weeks, 'A Survey of Confidence Building Measures' in Ralph Cossa (ed.), *Asia Pacific Confidence and Security Building Measures*, CSIS Significant Issues Series (Center for Strategic and International Studies, Washington DC, 1995).

resources.[5] The Indian Ocean has been less examined as a focus of localised maritime CBMs or cooperation. It is noteworthy that in both Northeast and Southeast Asia, the main territorial disputes are maritime in nature (for example, Russia-Japan (Kuril Islands/Northern Territories), Korea-Japan (Dok-Do/Takeshima Island), China-Japan (Diaoyutai-Senkaku Island), as well as Taiwan and, in the South China Sea, the Paracel Islands (Vietnam-China) and the Spratly/Nansha Islands (China, Vietnam, Malaysia, Taiwan, Philippines, Brunei). CBMs cannot substitute for formal diplomatic/legal negotiations to settle territorial disputes, but maritime CBMs may be particularly valuable in minimising the risk of conflict in such circumstances.

Maritime Confidence-Building Measures

There are a variety of maritime CBMs, in addition to INCSEA agreements (to be discussed separately below), which should be considered as a menu for various regional and/or subregional applications. In reviewing these maritime CBMs, it might be helpful to consider them in a broader theoretical construct of three general categories of CBMs: declaratory measures, transparency measures and constraint measures.

I   *Declaratory Measures* (Figure 4.1).[6]   Although not strictly maritime in nature, statements of intent or general principles such as the ASEAN Treaty of Amity and Concord of 1976 may establish regional principles of conflict-avoidance that can, over time, be developed through concrete CBM measures. Precedents in Europe include the CSCE Helsinki Final Act of 1975. More recently, in the Middle East, the 'conceptual' working group of the ACRS process has been discussing broad agreed principles of relations among regional states. In the specific maritime context, global acceptance of the Law of the Sea principles of UNCLOS III would probably be the most appropriate CBM of this type. Broader bilateral non-attack

---

5   Commander Dick Sherwood, RAN, 'The Australian Experience with Regional Maritime Cooperation', paper delivered to the *Anatalya Round of the Middle East Peace Process Multilateral Working Group on Arms Control and Regional Security*, Anatalya, Turkey, 21 March 1994.

6   Figures 4.1, 4.2, and 4.3 are from Pederson and Weeks, 'A Survey of Confidence Building Measures'.

pledges such as the Indo-Pakistani Simla Accord of 1971 and the December 1991 ROK-DPRK Agreement also have obvious positive implications for maritime security. One of the most useful specific maritime declaratory measures might be for China and other nuclear-capable nations to join the United States, Russia, the United Kingdom and France in unilaterally renouncing normal deployment of nuclear weapons on ships and maritime aircraft.

Figure 4.1: Declaratory Measures

* Brian-Kellogg Pact renouncing war (1928)

* Soviet nuclear no-first-use pledges

* Indo-Pakistani Simla Accord (1971), renouncing force

* Helsinki Final Act (1975), acceptance of existing borders

* Helsinki Final Act (1975), acceptance of existing borders

* December 1991 ROK-DPRK Agreements, non-attack and nuclear-free peninsula pledges

* Negative Security Assurance (NSA), pledging no nuclear attack on non-nuclear powers

II   *Transparency Measures* (Figure 4.2). A second general category of CBMs, transparency measures, encompasses information exchange, communication, notification, and observation and inspection measures.

* *Information Exchange.* In the current context of strategic uncertainty and maritime force development in the post-Cold War world, information measures may be the most valuable CBMs applicable in the various regional strategic contexts. Such measures include dialogue, the publications of defence white papers, the establishment of arms registry and military-to-military contacts, seminars and personal exchanges.

Dialogue: The value of maritime aspects of broader security dialogue within regions (and subregions) is particularly noteworthy. There exists now a well-developed US-Russian INCSEA-related naval dialogue, and an ongoing European dialogue through NATO, the Partnership for Peace (PFP), and the OSCE. In the less-formed maritime CBM context of the vast Asia Pacific region, such dialogue is particularly important. In addition to the annual United Nations conferences on regional security and confidence building in Kathmandu, and the official ASEAN Regional Forum security discussions, inaugurated in 1994, a host of unofficial or 'track-two' conferences and workshops dealing with Asia Pacific maritime security and confidence building have been conducted in recent years. The Western Pacific Naval Symposium, and its associated workshops, have led the way in operationalising maritime cooperation since the inception of the WPNS in 1988. All security dialogue meetings are particularly valuable to establish contacts and as sources of ideas for future office addressal, when political conditions have ripened. Most importantly, even unofficial dialogue and contacts may help establish expectations of routine cooperation and legitimise the concept of openness regarding maritime activities.

Defence White Papers: Increasingly detailed defence white papers have been published by many nations in recent years. The obvious next step is for other nations that have not yet done so to publish such white papers, including details of their current maritime force structure and perhaps a five-year force and shipbuilding projection. In this regard, development (perhaps by appropriate regional forums such as OSCE in Europe and the ASEAN Regional Forum in the Pacific) of common minimum standards or outlines for defence white papers would be helpful.

Arms Registry: The current UN regime provides, among others, for reports of imports or exports of vessels or submarines of over 750 metric tons. Standardisation and development of further regional reporting requirements might usefully be undertaken by appropriate regional forums, pending further UN development of the Arms Registry regime. For example, the Malaysian Minister for Defence proposed in 1992 that a 'regional register' be established to support the UN Arms Registry regime in the Asia Pacific region. Obviously, the first priority should be for those nations which are not yet doing so, in all regions, to provide full reporting to the United Nations.[7]

Military-to-Military Contacts/Seminars and Personal Exchanges: Recent trends in the many regions have been very positive in this area. This is a centrepiece of the PFP between NATO and former Eastern bloc states. Even in the Asia Pacific region, there have been US-Russian exchanges, increased Korea-Japan maritime contact, the China-Japan strategic dialogue and the web of interactions in the ASEAN/Australian area. This is an important area for further developing, and making routine, professional contacts and exchanges. The February 1995 Indian-sponsored naval meeting of ships and leaders from both the Indian Ocean and Southeast Asia also indicates how such exchanges can link regions or subregions.[8]

- *Communications Measures.* As noted earlier, Latin American navies have developed common communications procedures in the course of their annual UNITAS naval exercises with the US Navy. The US and other NATO navies likewise have long-developed common procedures. In the Asia Pacific region, the Western Pacific Naval Symposium workshops have developed a regional Maritime Information Exchange Directory and are now developing a common Tactical Communications Manual.[9] In addition to wide adoption of these practical maritime communication measures by all Asia Pacific maritime nations, any eventual INCSEA agreements (see below) in this or other regions or

---

7   See, 'The United Nations Register of Conventional Arms-Whence? Whether? ... and Why?', *Disarmament*, Vol.XVII, No.1, 1994.
8   'Passage to India', *Far Eastern Economic Review*, 19 January 1995, p.12.
9   Sherwood, 'The Australian Experience with Regional Maritime Cooperation', p.8.

subregions would include provisions for communication/consultation on unusual or dangerous maritime activities.

- *Notification Measures.* Experience to date with notification CBMs has primarily been with ground force manoeuvres. Tailoring of such measures to the varied maritime force structures and practices of such broad regions as Europe, the Middle East and the Asia Pacific would require very difficult negotiations, more characteristic of formal arms control than CBMs. Nations have tended to resist notifying the movement of air and naval units to avoid limiting the inherent flexibility and mobility of such units. Accordingly, such measures are unlikely to be among the first CBMs to be undertaken for the regional maritime environments of the post-Cold War world, although they would be welcome as unilateral voluntary measures.

- *Observation/Inspection Measures.* CBMs in this category which are of potential applicability to the maritime environment include observation of naval exercises and manoeuvres, inspection of naval facilities and surveillance regimes and control zones. Voluntary invitation of observers to naval exercises, and voluntary invitations of inspectors to naval facilities, would be noteworthy assurances of openness and should be considered by maritime nations. However, as with notification measures, attempts to formally negotiate such measures between disparate maritime force structures would have the complexity of formal arms control and might engender less, not more, trust.

A particularly promising CBM for various regions and subregions is maritime cooperation on ocean resources surveillance. This type of surveillance regime has precedents in the Asia Pacific region, including both multilateral measures such as fisheries surveillance cooperation in the South Pacific Forum and bilateral measures such as Australian-Indonesian Timor Gap

Figure 4.2: Transparency Measures

Information Measures	Communications Measures	Notification Measures	Observation/ Inspection Measures
Defence White Paper	Crisis Management (Hotlines)	Military manoeuvres/ Movements	Invitation of Observers
Publications	Conflict Prevention Centers (CPC)	Military alerts	Surveillance and Control zones
Calendar of military activities	Multilateral Communications Network	Increase in personnel (ground/air)	Open skies
Arms registry	Mandatory consultation on unusual/dangerous activities	Call-up of Reserves	Troop separation and monitoring
Exchanges of military data	Communication for unexplained nuclear incidents	Test missile launches	Sensors/Early Warning Stations
Military-to-military Contacts	Obligatory consultations in situations with increased nuclear war risk	Nuclear accidents	Nuclear missile factories
Doctrine/defence planning seminars			Nuclear missile destruction
Military personnel/student exchanges			Chemical facilities
NBCM material inventories			
NBCM facilities			

Figure 4.3: Constraint Measures

Risk Reduction Measures	Exclusion/Separation Measures	Constraints on Personnel, Equipment, Activities
Agreement to Reduce Risk of Nuclear War (71) Incidents at Sea Agreement (72) Russo-Japanese Air Traffic Safety Agreement (85) Nuclear Risk Reduction Center Agreement (87) Dangerous Military Activities Agreement (89)	Demilitarized Zones Disengagement Zones Keep-out Zones (Air/Sea) NBCM-Free Zones	Personnel: • National limits • Category limits • Zone limits Equipment: • Deployment limits (by geographic area or numbers) • Category/type limits • Storage/monitoring limits • Nuclear missile types/deployment Activities: • Maneuvres/movements limits, by size or geographic area • Advance notification for movements, exercises, alerts • Limits on readiness • Bans on simultaneous exercises/alerts and/or certain force/unit types • NBCM testing • Nuclear fissile material production constraints

surveillance and Malaysian-Indonesian pollution monitoring.[10]

III   *Constraint Measures* (Figure 4.3). There are three such constraint measures: risk reduction measures, exclusion or separation measures and constraints on personnel, equipment and activities.

- *Risk Reduction Agreements.* These agreements, such as Incidents at Sea agreements, are designed to prohibit or contain the consequences of inherently dangerous or inadvertent military activities, through articulating codes of conduct for military forces and mandating crisis consultation and communication. Because they tend to address the consequences of mutually undesirable activities without unduly constraining operational forces, risk reduction measures have figured prominently in the early stages of the political relaxation of tensions.

  As more navies (particularly in the Asia Pacific region) grow in reach and capability in the post-Cold War environment, both bilateral and tailored multilateral/subregional Incidents at Sea (INCSEA) agreements are potentially valuable CBMs. By way of background, the 1972 Navy-to-Navy US-Soviet (INCSEA) Agreement was a product of initial Cold War *détente* and a landmark tension-reduction and confidence-building measure between the major-power navies.[11]

  Establishing special rules to minimise ship manoeuvres that create dangers of collisions, to prohibit actions such as simulated attacks that might be interpreted as hostile or harassment, and to establish special communications procedures, the US-Soviet INCSEA Agreement has been remarkably successful in minimising incidents between

---

10   Sherwood, 'The Australian Experience with Regional Maritime Cooperation', p.4.
11   For more on the US-Soviet INCSEA agreement, see S. Weeks, 'Measures to Prevent Major Incidents at Sea' in J. Goldblat (ed.), *Maritime Security: The Building of Confidence* (United Nations, New York, 1992); R.P. Hilton, 'A Confidence-Building Measure at Work: The 1972 United States-USSR Incidents At Sea Agreement', *Disarmament Topical Papers 4: Naval Confidence Building Measures* (United Nations, New York, 1990); and S.M. Lynn-Jones, 'A Quiet Success for Arms Control: Preventing Incidents at Sea', *International Security*, Vol.9, No.4, Spring 1985.

the two navies - despite their more frequent global interaction in the first two decades after the agreement. The 1972 agreements have also served as a model for over a dozen more recent similar bilateral INCSEA agreements, as well as for the broader 1989 US-Soviet agreement at the Joint/General Staff level on prevention of Dangerous Military Activities (DMA). *However, the 'high seas' coverage limits of the INCSEA Agreement do not address boundaries and operations in territorial waters, nor do the INCSEA provisions cover the inherently stealthy submerged submarine.* The experience of the 1972 US-Soviet Incidents at Sea Agreement (and the 1989 US-Soviet Dangerous Military Activities Agreement) suggests several supplementary approaches to minimise incidents at sea in the post-Cold War maritime strategic context. Existing bilateral agreements (US-Russia, Russia-Western European nations, Russia-Japan, Russia-ROK) and potential additional bilateral agreements (Japan-China, ROK-China, Russia-China, DPRK-ROK, China-Taiwan, US-China, China-India) still provide a sound technical and political basis to avoid particular bilateral incidents between naval powers at sea.

As a complement to these bilateral INCSEA agreements - or, perhaps, as a substitute for bilateral agreements not yet reached, serious consideration should be given to tailored INCSEA or 'Safety at Sea' multilateral subregional agreements for Northeast Asia, Southeast Asia, the Baltic Sea, the Black Sea and perhaps the Indian Ocean.[12] Such multilateral agreements might be negotiated by naval

---

[12]   See, for further discussion, Peter Jones, 'Maritime Security Cooperation and CBMs in the Asia-Pacific: Applying Maritime CBMs in Regional Contexts', paper prepared for the *Fourth Asia-Pacific Dialogue on Maritime Security*, Nakorn Pathom, Thailand, 8-9 August 1994; S.M. Lynn-Jones, 'Agreements to Prevent Incidents at Sea and Dangerous Military Activities: Potential Applications in the Asia-Pacific Region' in A. Mack (ed.), *A Peaceful Ocean? Maritime Security in the Pacific in the Post Cold War Era* (Allen & Unwin, Sydney, 1993); C.A. Meconis, 'Naval Arms Control in the Asia-Pacific Region after the Cold War' in Elisabeth Borgese and Norton Ginsburg (eds), *Ocean Yearbook 11* (International Ocean Institute/University of Chicago Press, Chicago, 1994); and Russ Swinnerton and Desmond Ball, *A Regional Regime for Maritime Surveillance, Safety, and Information Exchanges*, Working Paper

specialists meeting in subregional groups on the margins of regional Baltic and Black Sea groups. In the Pacific, the CSCAP Maritime Cooperation Working Group is the appropriate forum to identify how to prepare an initiative in this area for the ASEAN Regional Forum. Such multilateral agreements would include the time-tested provisions of bilateral INCSEA agreements, requiring naval forces on the high seas to communicate and avoid dangerous manoeuvres and harassments. But these agreements could also be tailored to and/or supplemented by separate agreements to address particular subregional non-military maritime concerns, such as surveillance, fisheries, merchant shipping safety (search and rescue) and/or anti-piracy/anti-narcotics cooperation.[13] Provision should be made in such agreements for an annual subregional Review Meeting/Senior Officers Naval Symposium, which would also provide the venue for the bilateral naval contacts and discussions that have proved so valuable and durable in existing (bilateral) INCSEA agreements. Other nations might wish to reflect on the recent successful experience in even the conflict-prone Middle East region before disavowing as too ambitious such proposed multilateral subregional INCSEA/Safety at Sea regimes. In particular, the subregions of the Asia Pacific should regard similar agreements as priority maritime CBMs. It is, however, important to recognise that *INCSEA agreements alone cannot effectively address the problems of inherently covert submerged submarines or Law of the Sea disputes over boundaries of Territorial Seas (and Exclusive Economic Zones).* A flexible variety of bilateral and multilateral actions is needed to minimise these latter more difficult causes of incidents at sea. Such actions might include continuing bilateral and/or multilateral negotiations on agreed

---

No.278 (Strategic and Defence Studies Centre, Australian National University, Canberra, 1993).

13   As indicated by the furore surrounding the Canadian seizure of a Spanish fishing trawler in early March 1995, disputes over fishing rights, even beyond the EEZ boundaries, are becoming increasingly serious as global stocks of ocean fish

interpretations (under the Law of the Sea) of Territorial Sea and EEZ boundaries; the exercise of prudent caution in all forward naval operations near disputed boundaries; and agreed emergency communications procedures, such as those in the 1989 US-Soviet Dangerous Military Activities Agreement, for ships or aircraft entering or crossing those disputed boundaries, and perhaps even provisions for submarine underwater communications in extreme situations of perceived close danger. A proper complementary mix of these suggested actions can help further reduce global incidents at sea in the post-Cold War maritime environment.

* *Exclusion/Separation Measures.* Despite long-standing Soviet and Russian proposals to 'keep out' other navies operating in the strategically significant Sea of Japan/Sea of Okhotsk area and certain strategic straits, such 'keep-out' sea zones are seen by the United States and other maritime nations as undercutting traditional freedom of the seas and mobility of naval forces, and are a source of contention rather than confidence building.

* *Constraints on Personnel, Equipment, Activities.* These constraints have tended to prohibit military operations that have not been properly forecast or notified, or that take place within certain exclusion or separation zones. In their European, Middle East, and South Asian form, such measures have almost exclusively focused on ground forces. Such measures come closest of all CBMs to technical arms control or limitation, and thus pose significant challenges of negotiation and verification. Such constraint measures - with the broader exception of nuclear-free zones - are not a well-suited or promising focus for maritime CBMs in the post-Cold War world.

---

continue to diminish. One recent report documented 30 international fishing incidents in 1994 alone. See *Washington Post*, 16 March 1995, p.A33.

Conclusion

In the post-Cold War maritime security environment, many navies, particularly in the Asia Pacific region, are extending their regional reach and capability.   To reduce uncertainty and risk regarding naval forces and plans, maritime CBMs, particularly a variety of information and transparency measures, are a high priority, even more so in these regions where such CBMs are still largely undeveloped. To address potentially dangerous encounters of naval forces, and to address new regional and/or subregional maritime challenges through the establishment of routine procedures and meetings, selected bilateral INCSEA agreements and subregional multilateral INCSEA/Safety at Sea agreements should also be a priority. The CSCAP Maritime Cooperation Working Group is the appropriate forum to identify how to prepare an initiative in this area to recommend to the ASEAN Regional Forum.

CHAPTER 5

MARINE SCIENTIFIC RESEARCH

I AN EXAMPLE OF COOPERATIVE MARINE SCIENCE RESEARCH IN THE ASIA PACIFIC

George Creswell

Introduction

In this short paper I will describe the ASEAN-Australia Regional Ocean Dynamics Expeditions that took place from 1993 to 1995.[1] I will conclude by looking at the expeditions in a way that draws inspiration from the excellent paper presented by Mark Valencia at the inaugural meeting of this Working Group last year.[2] As an aside, in Appendix A, I have a partial list of regional and bilateral programmes assembled from information provided by colleagues in ASEAN.

Before I begin, however, I would like to quote from Valencia concerning the role of epistemic communities in marine science (that is, communities interested in knowledge). Valencia has argued that:

> these communities have enormous value for international and regional organisation because their loyalties are more to the production and application of their knowledge than to any particular government. Through networks and 'invisible colleges' these communities seek to promote cooperation across national boundaries'.[3]

---

[1] The participating organisations are referred to below in the text and they are sincerely thanked. I thank the officers and crews of *Baruna Jaya I, Pesek, Penyu* and *Atyimba* for their excellent efforts. I thank all the expedition members for their work at sea and ashore - and their friendship.

[2] Mark Valencia, 'Cooperation in Marine Scientific Research as a Confidence Building Measure' in Sam Bateman and Stephen Bates (eds), *Calming the Waters: Initiatives for Asia Pacific Maritime Cooperation* (Strategic and Defence Studies Centre, Australian National University, Canberra, 1996).

[3] ibid., p.138.

According to Valencia, '... cooperation in this seemingly innocuous field [of marine science] can build ... the confidence necessary for initiatives in other spheres'.[4] Cooperative studies, he argues, 'reduce the asymmetry of information' across the region.[5]

The ASEAN-Australia Expeditions 1993-95

These expeditions grew from the ASEAN-Australia Marine Science Project to establish a tide gauge network throughout the ASEAN region starting in 1984. The Project Management Committee represented all ASEAN nations and Australia and it met regularly. The project was guided by the distinguished expert in tides and oceanography, Professor Geoff Lennon of the National Tidal Facility in Adelaide, South Australia.[6]

In the course of a few years the project realised its aim of establishing the tide gauge network, and time enabled trust to be built up and friendships to be forged. In the late 1980s the Project Management Committee agreed to include shipboard and moored instrument studies of the currents and water properties in the seas and straits of the region. The data from these would be complementary to data from the tide gauge network. I joined the project in 1990 to assist in both planning the study and running the expeditions. I shared the position of Chief Scientist with Dr Abdul Gani Ilahude of the Indonesian Institute of Sciences (LIPI).

The objectives for the expeditions can be expressed simply:

- To share oceanographic skills across the ASEAN-Australia region.

- To achieve this through research voyages to strengthen our understanding of the ASEAN seas and the exchange of water between the Pacific and Indian oceans.

The participating organisations were:

---

4   ibid., p.139.
5   ibid., p.140.
6   G.W. Lennon, 'ROD and the Significance of the ASEAN Seas', Proceedings of the Symposium on *The Seas of South East Asia - the Key to Regional Climate Patterns*, Lombok, Indonesia, June 1995.

Brunei
Ministry of Communication Brunei

Indonesia
BPPTeknologi Indonesia
Indonesian Institute of Sciences (LIPI)
Indonesian Hydrographic Service (Dishidros)
Institute Pertanian Bogor

Malaysia
Royal Malaysian Navy
University Terengganu, Malaysia

Philippines
National Mapping and Resource Information Authority (NAMRIA)

Singapore
Port of Singapore Authority

Thailand
Royal Thai Navy

Australia
AusAID (Project funding)
AMSAT Ltd (Project management)
Australian Oceanographic Data Centre
Bureau of Meteorology
CSIRO Marine Laboratories
National Tidal Facility

The study area is shown in Figure 5(I).1. The bulk of the work was carried out with the Indonesian vessel *Baruna Jaya I* on voyages of three and a half weeks' duration in June/July in both 1993 and 1994. Scientists and engineers from five of the ASEAN nations and Australia participated in the voyages. At sea the work was shared, lectures were given, and data were analysed, written up and presented at daily meetings by multinational teams of expedition members.

Figure 5(I).1: The Southeast Asian Study Area

The stations of the wide-ranging expeditions of *Baruna Jaya I* are numbered, with those for 1993 going to station 29 and those of 1994 being from 30 onward. Many stations were repeated and expendable bathythermographs were dropped while underway. Three deep-water moorings collected data in Makassar Strait for over one year; similar single moorings operated in the Maluku and Halmahera seas. Bottom-mounted moorings were installed in Malacca and Singapore straits for a total of five several-month deployments. The Malaysian and Philippine ships *Penyu* and *Aryimba* were used for lines of closely spaced stations in Malacca Strait and around Mindanao in November 1994 and June 1995 respectively.

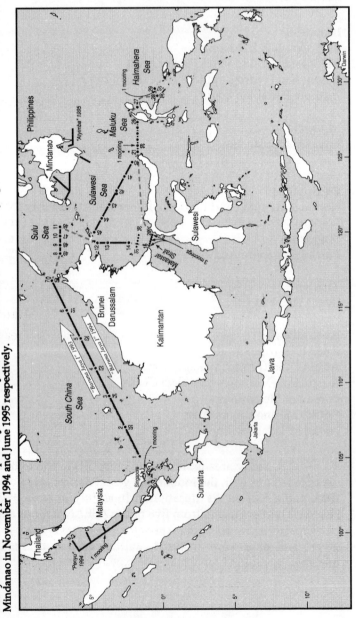

In addition to the work with *Baruna Jaya I*, the Port of Singapore Authority's vessel *Pesek* and the Royal Malaysian Navy's vessel *Penyu* were used to install bottom-mounted acoustic current meters in the straits of Singapore and Malacca for many months.

The knowledge acquired by the expedition members in turn led to further work being planned and carried out within the framework of the overall project. One part of this was a voyage with the Royal Malaysian Navy's *Penyu* to measure water properties along the axis of Malacca Strait in November 1994. A second part was a voyage by the Republic of the Philippines vessel *Atyimba* to measure water properties around southern and eastern Mindanao in June 1995.

In early 1995 a dozen of the ASEAN expedition members came to CSIRO and the National Tidal Facility in Australia to work on the data. They presented their reports in June 1995 at a symposium at Lombok that marked the end of the project. A selection of their reports is listed below:

'Physical property variations between the Sulu Sea, South China Sea and Balabac Strait', N. Saadon (Malaysia);

'Current conditions in Makassar Strait, Maluku Sea and Halmahera Sea', Hadikusumah, S. Saimima, and T. Soedarmadji (Indonesia);

'Physical properties of the Sulu Sea', E. Caradang and H. Catapang (the Philippines);

'Characterisation of sea water properties in Malacca Strait', P. Oei (Singapore);

'Time series analysis of currents in Singapore Strait', T.M. Wong (Singapore);

'Analysis of the XBT data collected on the Regional Dynamics Expeditions 1993/94', N. Saadon (Malaysia) and Hadikusumah (Indonesia);

'Observations of the Indonesian throughflow through the major straits', P. Swangsang and V. Kaenchan (Thailand);

'Aanderaa current meter data processing procedure and synopsis of early results', Mohd Khalis bin Haji Jaafar (Malaysia).

The technical aspects of the expeditions are discussed in a little more detail in the following three sections.

Deep-Water Moorings

The arrangement of the instruments on the three year-long moorings in Makassar Strait appears in the schematic Figure 5(I).2. The symbols, starting from the tops of the moorings, represent floats at roughly 200 m depth containing upward-looking Acoustic Doppler Current Profilers (ADCPs) that measure currents every eight metres up to near the surface; conventional 'paddle wheel' current meters (recording every hour) and glass floats along the mooring; acoustic command releases; and concrete anchors. Similar moorings were installed in the eastern Maluku Sea and in the Halmahera Sea, where the depths were 2500 m and 950 m respectively.

Eighteen of the twenty conventional current meters on the five moorings returned a little over one year's data; one returned nine months' data; and one failed due to leakage. All ADCPs failed due to a shortcoming in manufacture.[7] To soften this failure the manufacturers were encouraged to provide three ADCPs for deployment with refurbished moorings for a second year in Makassar Strait - 1994-95. This they did. However, when *Baruna Jaya I* sailed in July 1994 we found that our request to the Indonesian security forces for approval to install the moorings had been submitted too late.

A flavour for the tidal components detected by the conventional meters can be acquired from Figure 5(I).3, which shows predicted and observed currents for March 1994 at roughly the same depth (~700 m) in the three seas. The semi-diurnal tides are strong at Maluku and Halmahera, with amplitudes at the latter reaching 0.4 ms^{-1}.

In Figure 5(I).4 the tides have been filtered out and stick vectors are plotted twice daily for the upper pairs of current meters in Makassar Strait. A predominant southward flow is evident, certainly in the records from the uppermost meters on each mooring. At shorter than seasonal time scales there appears to be little vertical or horizontal coherence, but of course rigorous analyses are needed.

---

[7]   A. Poole, 'Electronics and instrumentation CME', Proceedings of the Symposium on *The Seas of South East Asia - the Key to Regional Climate Patterns*, Lombok, Indonesia, June 1995.

Figure 5(I).2: The mooring arrangement in Makassar Strait that was part of the ASEAN-Australia Expeditions 1993-95.

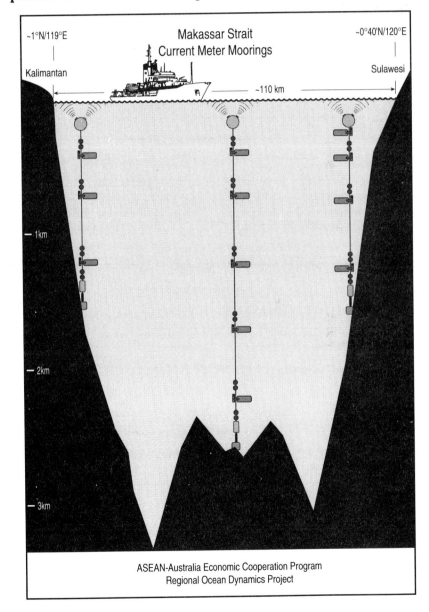

Figure 5(I).3: The observed, predicted and residual currents at ~700 m depth in Makassar Strait and the Maluku and Halmahera seas in March 1994.

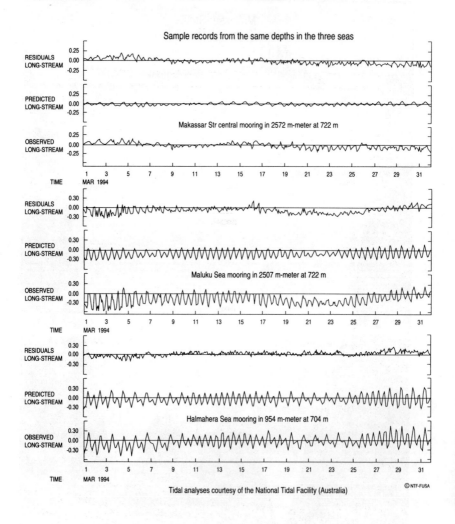

Figure 5(I).4: 12-hourly stick vectors for the upper pairs of current meters on the three moorings in Makassar Strait. The tides have been filtered from the data.

Makassar Strait

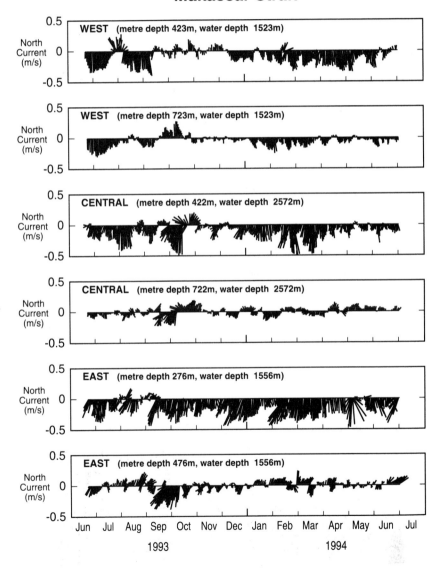

Figure 5(I).5: The arrangement for the 3-tonne anchor used to house the Acoustic Doppler Current Profiler and acoustic release in the straits of Singapore and Malacca as part of the ASEAN-Australia Expeditions 1993-95.

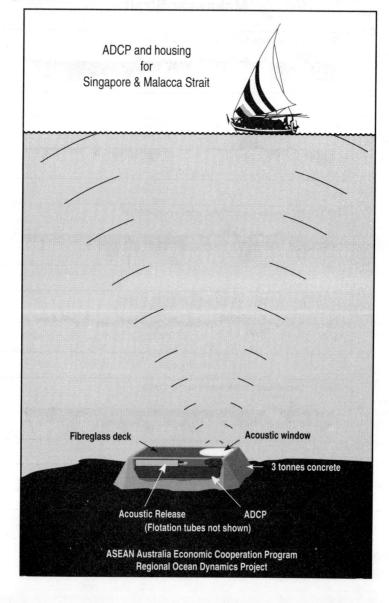

Shallow-Water Moorings

The arrangement used to house the ADCP and acoustic release in a 3-tonne trawl-proof anchor at depths of ~60 m in the straits of Singapore and Malacca is shown in Figure 5(I).5. These ADCPs suffered the same affliction as their sisters on the deep moorings, despite shipping them back to the manufacturers in the United States and, in one case, having the manufacturers' engineer set one of them up in Singapore. Only the fifth of the five deployments in the Singapore Straits operated perfectly. Another one in the Malacca Straits appeared to operate properly for part of its several months' deployment.

The Singapore Straits are aligned roughly North-East - South-West. The record is shown in Figure 5(I).6.[8] The tidal currents reached over 1 ms^{-1} during the springs. The bottom temperature record shows a sudden increase in October, in step with the reversal of the monsoons and the entry of South China Sea water into the strait. The 1 m vertical resolution of the ADCP allowed us to see that during the neap tides, presumably when stratification is established, the deeper waters were carried off to the south-west (Figure 5(I).7). In other words, there was a fortnightly injection of South China Sea water into the bottom of Malacca Strait. After the monsoon reversal this flow extended from top to bottom.

Water Properties

The June 1995 transect of salinity and temperature across the Mindanao Current with *Atyimba* (Figure 5(I).8) serves as an example of water property measurements. Note the strong salinity maximum at 100-200 m depth and the minimum at 300-500 m. Such structure is well known from earlier work[9] and could be seen in our observations farther downstream in the Makassar Strait. Another feature that we noted was apparent overturning at stations 40-43, perhaps due to bottom topography. Incidentally, during the daylight hours a simple

---

8   T.M. Wong, 'Currents in the Singapore Main Straits', Port of Singapore Authority Internal Report, 1995.

9   R. Lukas, E. Firing, P. Hacker, P.L. Richardson, C.A. Collins, R. Fine and R. Gammon, 'Observations of the Mindanao Current during the Western Equatorial Pacific Ocean Circulation Study', *Journal of Geophysical Research*, Vol.96, 1991, pp.7089-7104.

drifter was released before and recovered after each station and fixed with Global Positioning System (GPS). The resulting current speeds are shown at the top of the figure.

Concluding Comments

Valencia spoke of communities of marine scientists whose overriding aim was the acquisition and application of knowledge.[10] Some countries - probably even my own in some circumstances(!) - may have trouble with the idea of the free communication of information and ideas across international boundaries. However, and while it might be trite and obvious to say so, water properties (perhaps the trigger for climate change and variability), fish larvae, and pollution are given free communication across international boundaries by ocean currents. Cooperative multinational teams are needed to address the sorts of problems surrounding these. The trusts and real friendships necessary for such projects are established through a progressive escalation of cooperation. These, as it were, 'came out of the wash' in the ASEAN-Australia Expeditions through all parties being fully briefed and therefore pulling in the same direction. The legacy of the expeditions is substantial. Young scientists from different ASEAN nations now have the shared history with which to discuss very freely the projects and problems that their nations share. Universities in ASEAN have access to modern data sets from their seas that can be used for research and teaching. My colleagues around ASEAN receive from me copies of any recent papers on scientific work in their region - they are also assured of my responses to their queries for a period that will extend many years beyond the life of the project.

I conclude by listing some of the elements that I think are necessary for successful cooperative marine science work in the Asia Pacific region. These are: a suitable problem, goodwill, local manpower and knowledge, a source of trained people to plan and guide the work, and money.

---

10   Valencia, 'Cooperation in Marine Scientific Research as a Confidence Building Measure'.

Figure 5(I).6: The along-channel flow and the bottom temperature in Singapore Straits in 1994.

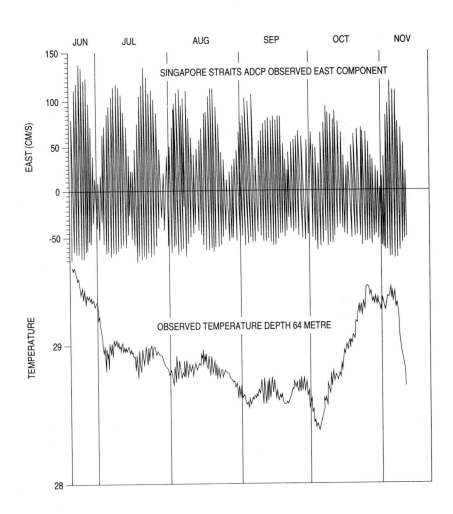

Source: Wong, 'Currents in the Singapore Main Straits'.

Figure 5(I).7: 12-hourly current vectors for all depths measured by the ADCP in Singapore Straits.
Note that vectors having a southwesterly component are thick, while those with a northeasterly component are thin. The depths of the vectors range from 12 m (52 m above the bottom) to 62 m (2 m above the bottom).

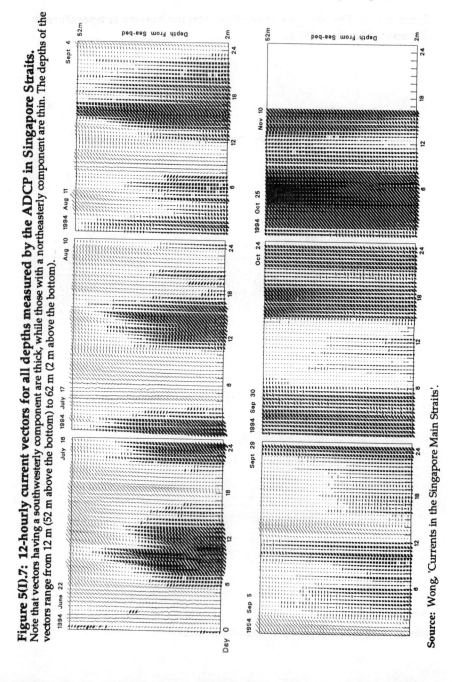

Source: Wong, 'Currents in the Singapore Main Straits'.

Figure 5(I).8: Salinity and temperature transects across the Mindanao Current with RPS *Atyimba* in June 1995.
Note the drifter speeds along the top of the diagram.

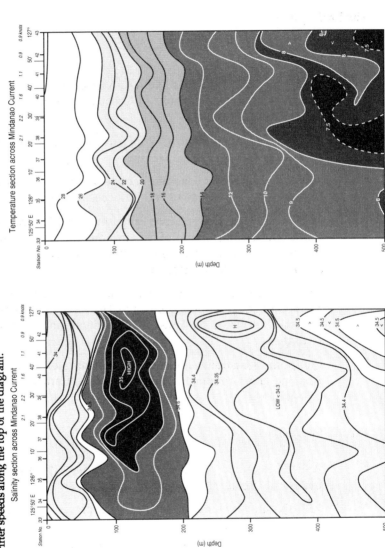

Appendix A: A Partial List of Regional and Bilateral Programmes

The Philippines

Ongoing Programmes

* Philippines-United States NOAA: Vulnerability Assessment and Evaluation of Adaptions of Coastal Resources due to Sea Level Rise.

* Philippines-United States PTWC: Satellite Telemetry Upgrade to the Legaspi Tide Gauge Station.

* ASEAN-Australia Economic Cooperation Programme III: Coastal Zone Environment and Resource Management Project.

* ASEAN-Canada Cooperative Programme on Marine Science Phase II: Establishment of Environmental Criteria for the Development and Management of Living Marine Resources and Human Health Protection.

* ASEAN-European Community: Interdisciplinary Scientific Methodologies for the Sustainable Use and Management of Coastal Resources Systems - Conceptual and Exploratory Activities.

* Philippines-Australia: Integrated Seafarming of Giant Clams, Abalone and Grouper in North Bais Bays, Campoyo, Negros Oriental.

Future Programmes

* ASEAN-Republic of Korea: Cooperative Programme on Industrial Use of Marine Biological Resources.

* ASEAN-Japan: Management of Multispecies Resources and Multigear Fisheries.

* Philippines-Australia: Development of Improved Mud Crab Culture Systems in the Philippines.

Indonesia

- CIDAR: Red tides.

- Indonesia-United States: ARLINDO studies of the Pacific to Indian Ocean Throughflow.

- Indonesia-France: JADE (Java Australia Dynamics Experiment).

- ASEAN-Australia: Coral reef studies.

- Indonesia-United States (Scripps Institution): Throughflow studies with submerged pressure gauges.

Singapore-Malaysia

- Studies prompted by concern for the low-oxygen waters of the east Johore Straits.

Malaysia

- Malaysia-Japan: Current measurements in Terengganu.

II MARINE SCIENTIFIC RESEARCH IN THE PHILIPPINES: STATUS, PROBLEMS AND PROSPECTS

Miguel D. Fortes

This paper briefly describes the status, problems and prospects of marine scientific research in the Philippines and situates these aspects within the broader perspective of initiatives in Southeast Asia. It aims to provide guidance about the steps that need to be taken to promote and support the objectives of sustainable development. This is in response to the rapid and largely unquantified loss and degradation of coastal habitats and the urgent need for their management in coastal Southeast Asia. The information provided here would likewise be useful in national and regional efforts towards a comprehensive appreciation of maritime benefits, risks and responsibilities.

Philippine Territorial Waters and the Coastal Zone

The Philippines is located in a zone with a population growth rate averaging between 2.0 and 2.99 per cent and where the population doubles every 24 to 34 years. By 2000, Manila alone will be the eighteenth most populated city in the world with about 11.1 million people. It is no wonder that at present, people are turning to the sea and the coastal waters for their basic needs.

The Philippine marine territorial waters cover about 2.2 million km^2. This is the Exclusive Economic Zone (EEZ) comprising 1,934,000 km^2 (88 per cent) of oceanic waters and 267,000 km^2 (12 per cent) of coastal waters. There are some 185,000 km^2 of shelf area with a depth over 200 metres. The enormous expanse and promise of the Philippine EEZ pose a great challenge to the expanding role of marine scientific research in the coming years.

The most prominent geographic fact of the Philippines is that it consists of 7,107 islands with a total coastline of more than 17,000 km. Political boundaries reflect this prominence as 80 per cent of the country's provinces and two-thirds of all its municipalities share the coast. About 55 per cent of the population resides in some 10,000 coastal *barangays* (the smallest political unit), plus larger urban centres. Seventeen of the twenty-five cities having populations in excess of 100,000 people are on the coast. Associated land use activities that are concentrated on the coast are transportation infrastructure, industrial and commercial development, lowland agriculture, aquaculture, tourism and recreation, land reclamation, and waste disposal.

In addition to the 267,000 km^2 of coastal waters, the Philippine coastal zone also covers a total area of about 11,000 km^2 of land. Within this area resides about 59 per cent of the country's total population, which is indicative of the close link that most Filipinos have had to the sea during their formative years. About 70 per cent of the 1,525 municipalities in the country, including ten of the largest cities, are located in the coastal zone. In this shallow portion of the sea, the beaches, gulf and coves provide significant livelihood opportunities and recreational values. The large diversity of floral and faunal species that these coastal areas contain constitute valuable resources.

The special significance of the Philippine coastal zone lies in the fact that it is the focus of intense urban and industrial pressure. Its natural resources are critical to the livelihood base of the people and many historical and cultural resources are to be found here. The marine realm may be of equal, if not greater, importance to people, but for a developing country like the Philippines, where resources to explore the oceanic parts are wanting, this portion of the sea is virtually unknown.

With over 18, 000 km of coastline, the Philippine coastal zone continues to be a rich source of fish and other aquatic products, a primary mode of transportation, a major area of human settlement, a breeding ground and habitat for wildlife, and a predominant feature of the country's natural beauty. Much of the growth in this area comes from the use of renewable resources such as crops, seaweeds, water, crustaceans and fish. Philippine fisheries production comes primarily from the coastal areas. The annual fish yield (excluding invertebrates) of Philippine reefs ranges from 5 to 24 metric tons per km^2. The bulk of the fish catch is taken in the near shore areas of the coastal zone, where mangroves. seagrass beds and coral reefs abound. This feature alone is sufficient to justify a strong research effort into the country's coastal zone. The marked dependence of coastal municipalities upon their marine resources makes the improvement in the quality of the marine environment a policy objective that is common to all these communities.

Coastal Ecosystems and Resources

Coral reefs, seagrass beds and mangroves are among the world's most important - and most endangered - ecosystems. They are the three major life support and protective ecosystems that abound along the Philippine coastal zone. Hence, they perform a wide range of biological and physical functions which are the basis of their environmental and economic roles. They nurture the sea and protect the land. They provide vital breeding grounds and habitats for fish, shelter for coasts from the effects of storms, and they inhibit erosion. Nearly two thirds of all fish caught throughout the world are hatched in mangroves and tidal areas. Roughly 80 per cent of all commercial species of fish and shell fish in the Philippines depend on coral reefs, seagrass beds and mangroves at critical stages in their life histories.

Coral Reefs

Among the oldest and richest living communities of plants and animals on earth, coral reefs are geomorphologic structures of biological origin which may be found growing as a fringe to a land mass (fringing reefs), in proximity to coastlines but at some distance out to sea (barrier reefs), or as an isolated structure surrounded by deep water in the form of a ring of coral with a central shallow lagoon (atoll). They constitute a very important component of the Philippine coastal zone. They are highly productive complex communities sustained primarily by coral-algal symbiosis. Historically considered to be one of greatest natural treasures of the country, they are home to about 488 species of corals, 971 species of benthic algae and 2,000 species of fish. They have a high economic value. They are not only the source of many varieties of food, they provide shoreline protection from waves and storms and are a source of sand for the replenishment of beaches. They have aesthetic and recreational value and are an important tourism attraction. They are also a site for the extraction of minerals such as sand, coral rubble aggregate and quarry stone. As a habitat for rare species and with their high biodiversity, they are a valuable educational and scientific resource and a source of new medicines. A single reef may contain 3,000 species of corals, fish and shellfish. These can yield up valuable medicines. Didemnin, which comes from sea squirts, is active against a broad range of viruses from the common cold to herpes and meningitis. Potential anti-cancer drugs are also being found. The Philippines with 27,000 km^2 of coral reef area has the largest area of coral reefs in the world.

Nearly one-third of all fish species live on coral reefs, while others are dependent on reefs and seagrass beds at various stages in their life cycles. Although estimates as to the amount of fish that can be harvested from reefs vary, it should be possible to take some 15 metric tons per km^2 without destroying stocks. Almost 55 per cent of the fish consumed by Filipinos depend on coral reefs. It is estimated that coral reefs contribute 10 to 15 per cent of the total marine fisheries production.

Gomez *et al.*, from the 1991 data, give the status of Philippine coral reefs.[1] Table 5(II).1 summarises this is in terms of live coral cover with the following ranges: excellent = 75-100 per cent; good = 50-74.9 per cent; fair = 25-49.9 per cent; and poor = 0-24.9 per cent. The number of sites in the country where studies were conducted and their percentages (in parentheses) are also given.

1   E.D. Gomez, P.M. Aliño, W.R.Y. Licuanan and H.T. Yap, 'Status Report on Coral Reefs of the Philippines 1994' in C. Wilkinson, S. Sudara and L.M. Chou (eds), *Proceedings Third ASEAN-Australia Symposium on Living Coastal Resources*, Vol.1: *Status Reviews* (AIMS, Townsville, 1994), pp.57-76.

Table 5(II).1: Status of Philippines Coral Reefs

		Living Coral Cover			
	Sites	Excellent	Good	Fair	Poor
Luzon	336	12(3.6)	86(25.6)	146(43.4)	92(27.4)
Visayas	363	24(6.6)	95(26.2)	131(36.1)	113(31.1)
Mindanao	43	3(7.0)	6(14.0)	13(30.2)	21(48.8)
Total	742	39(5.3)	187(25.2)	290(39.0)	226(30.5)

Seagrass Beds

Seagrass beds are a discrete community dominated by flowering plants with roots and rhizomes (underground stems), thriving in slightly reducing sediments and normally exhibiting maximum biomass under conditions of complete submergence. In contrast to both marsh grasses and algae, seagrasses support large numbers of epiphytic organisms, the biomass of which may be almost as great as that of the seagrasses themselves.

For decades, the research of local marine scientists focused almost solely on the corals, seaweeds, animals or fish that either live in coastal habitats or are associated with them.[2] On the other hand, the traditional orientation of the country's marine science has been to view the ocean as a deep-water mass, neglecting the shallow coastal fringes where seagrass abounds. Investigators with an interest in seagrass research are few and priorities for research and developmental activities are usually directed towards other resources with immediate economic impacts. Ironically, in the Philippines, where the second-highest seagrass diversity in the world

---

2 M.D. Fortes, 'Seagrasses: A Resource Unknown in the ASEAN Region', ICLARM Education Series No.5 (International Centre for Living Aquatic Resources Management, Manila, 1989).

is found, it is only in the last 15 years that the seagrass ecosystem has been a focus of scientific inquiry and only in the last five years that it has been an an object of natural resource management.[3]

Many plants and animals live in Philippine seagrass beds. This is due to the rich nutrient pool and diversity of physical structures protecting young marine life from predators. Fish and shrimp are probably the most important components of the beds, although coastal villages derive their sustenance from other components of the grass beds. The major invertebrates found in the beds are shrimps, sea cucumbers, sea urchins, crabs, scallops, mussels and snails, while the major vertebrate species include fishes, reptiles and mammals. Some endangered species of sea turtles reported in Philippine seagrass beds include the green sea turtle, the Olive Ridley, the loggerhead and the flatback. Snakes are also a common inhabitant. The sea cow ('dugong'), a mammal which is endangered all along its range of distribution in the world, is almost completely seagrass-dependent.[4]

The economic usefulness of a seagrass bed resides primarily in the fisheries it supports. In the Philippines, coral reefs with their associated seagrasses potentially could supply more than 20 per cent of the fish catch.[5] A total of 1,384 individuals and 55 species from 25 fish families was identified from five seagrass sites in the country. All the members of these families have economic value, mostly as food and aquarium specimens. Estacion and Alcala reported adults of about 52 fish species from 31 families from seagrass beds in central Philippines.[6]

Few reports acknowledge the crucial role of fishes which migrate from seagrass beds to other ecosystems. In Southeast Asia, most coral reefs are in developing countries where they are

---

3   M.D. Fortes, 'Seagrasses of East Asia: Environmental and Management Perspectives', RCU/EAS Technical Report Series No.6, United Nations Environment Programme, 1995.
4   ibid.
5   J.W. McManus, 'Coral Reefs of the ASEAN Region: Status and Management', *Ambio*, Vol.17, No.3, 1988, pp.189-93.
6   J. Estacion and A.C. Alcala, 'Associated Fisheries and Aquatic Resources of Seagrasses' in *Proceedings of the First National Conference on Seagrass Management, Research and Development* (National Environmental Protection Council, Diliman, Quezon City, 1986), pp. 79-97.

associated with seagrasses. These two ecosystems potentially could supply more than one-fifth of the fish catch in these countries.[7] Five times as many fish live above seagrass beds as above sea floors made up of mud, shells and sand.[8]

Seagrass beds have the potential to filter sewage, thus reducing the threat from pollution which would otherwise affect coral reefs and mangroves. They are also biotic heavy metal reservoirs or sinks in the marine environment. The habitat is also known to stabilise the coast due to its ability to trap sediments. The seagrass bed, as an ecotone between coral reefs and mangrove forests in tropical coasts, is an area of tension between these two habitats. It mediates the structural and dynamic components of the neighbouring ecosystems via control of material, water and energy flows between them. More importantly, the seagrass system, as an ecotone, supports a rich diversity of species from adjacent systems and provides primary refugia for both economically and ecologically important organisms. As such, seagrass habitats are sensitive to fluctuations because species coming from their neighbouring systems encounter 'marginal conditions' and are at the extremes of their tolerance levels to environmental alterations. This sensitivity makes seagrasses useful indicators of changes not easily observable in either coral reef or mangrove forest.

Worldwide, there has been a rapid increase in seagrass decline.[9] As natural resources, seagrass beds are subject to varied and destructive disturbances mediated by both natural and man-induced influences. At the Seagrass Workshop held in Bangkok in December 1993, seagrass scientists of the ASEAN-Australia Living Coastal Resources (LCR) project indicated that seagrass habitats in East Asia are rapidly being destroyed. In Indonesia about 30 to 40 per cent of the seagrass beds have been lost in the last 50 years, with as much as 60 per cent being destroyed around Java, while in Singapore the patchy seagrass habitats have suffered severe damage, largely through burial under landfill operations. In Thailand, losses of the

---

7   McManus, 'Coral Reefs of the ASEAN Region'.
8   G. Lean, D. Hinrichsen and A. Markham (eds), *World Wildlife Fund Atlas of the Environment* (Prentice Hall, New York, 1990).
9   G.W. Thayer, S.M. Adams and M.W. La Croix, 'Structural and Functional Aspects of a Recently Established *Zostera Marina* Community' in L.E. Cronin (ed.), *Estuarine Research* (Academic Press, New York, 1975), Vol.I, pp.228-96.

beds amount to about 20 to 30 per cent. Very little information on seagrass loss is available from Malaysia. In the Philippines, seagrass loss amounts to about 30 to 50 per cent. With the exception of seven sites, the total cover of seagrasses in the country is currently unknown.

Mangrove Forests

Mangroves in the Philippines are the communities of trees that are restricted to tidal flats in coastal waters, extending inland along rivers where the water is tidal, saline or brackish. For purposes of conservation and area protection, certain features of the mangrove ecosystem are directly relevant. These features include both structural and functional attributes: species composition, spatial distribution (zonation), physiological ecology, responses to impacts, and function (including resource, protection and information). Local true mangrove trees number 25 to 30 species with an equal number of associated species. Ecologically, mangrove coverage is most extensive on low-relief coasts where tidal penetration prevents competition from non-salt-tolerant species. It is more lush in areas influenced by fluvial inputs, due to the large pool of nutrients and freshwater inputs which dilute seawater to levels (less than five to ten parts per thousand) that promote best development. Mangroves are often found in sheltered environments. This is because, being shallow-rooted, both trees and seedlings are subject to uprooting in landforms which can be eroded and scoured by waves and currents. They also favour areas with high terrestrial sediment inputs which are important sources of inorganic nutrients.

In 1918, the country's mangrove forests were estimated to be 5,000 km^2. By 1970, this had gone down to 2,880 km^2 and to only 2,420 km^2 a decade later. Recent estimates indicate that the resource comprises only 1,397.25 km^2, although the Philippine Forestry Statistics for 1993 gives the most recent estimate of total mangrove cover at 1,234 km^2.

Table 5(II).2: Coastal Marine Ecosystems of the Philippines

Ecosystem	Definition	Description	Distribution	Use	Threats
Coral reef	system on calcareous foundation of plants and animals which have developed their own biogenic substrate	Shallow, less than 50 m, clear waters; circumtropical; high-low energy system	fringing throughout the country; oceanic and flatform reefs present	ornaments; fisheries; tourism; construction materials; fish pens; seaweed culture; industrial uses	mining; cyanide, blast, muroami fishing; crown-of-thorns; land-based pollution; siltation; storms; El Nino; tourism; expanding coastal population
Seagrass bed	dominated by flowering plants living totally submerged	usually shallow to subtidal waters; 20-30 m beds found in clear waters	reefal and non-reefal (in coves and sheltered bays)	spawning nursery grounds; food production; fertilizer; roofing materials; substrate stabiliser; fisheries	siltation; trawling; wastes and effluents; seaweed farming; dredge and fill; reclamation; shell collection; anchor damage; sand mining
Mangrove forest	intertidal plants living in sheltered low-energy areas	often associated with estuarine systems; intertidal	island and riverine types	firewood; spawning, nursery grounds; fishing; lumber; aquaculture; land stabiliser	fish pond conversion; reclamation; human population expansion; over-exploitation; pollution; mining; poultry; pests/diseases; solid wastes; salt production

In the Philippines, 68 families of fish inhabit mangrove areas. These areas are also a source of firewood, charcoal, tannin and dyebarks and serve as land builders and buffers against typhoons and wave action.

Table 5(II).2 represents a summary of the important features which characterise the ecosystems of the coastal marine environment in the Philippines, including their uses and the threats to these uses.

Associated Marine Fishery Resources

A connecting link between the coastal ecosystems and one that is of utmost importance to archipelagic countries like the Philippines is the fisheries the ecosystems support. In 1993, the Philippines ranked twelfth among the fish producers in the world.[10] It was the second-largest producer of tuna and tuna-like fishes in the Indian Ocean and Southeast Asian region in 1991. In 1994, the fishing industry accounted for 3.9 per cent and 4.3 per cent of the country's GDP at current and constant prices, respectively. It also accounted for 17.7 per cent (PHP65.9 billion) of the Gross Value Added (GVA) of PHP372.1 billion in the Agriculture, Fishery and Forestry Sector at current prices (the largest share next to agricultural crops). The annual growth rates achieved by the Philippine fishing industry from 1985 to 1994 were 3 per cent in quantity and 11.3 per cent in value. The industry provided a livelihood for about 1 million or about 5 per cent of the country's labour force as well as their dependents, with municipal fisheries contributing 68 per cent (675,677) and commercial fisheries 6 per cent (56,715).

Fish production in 1994 was 2.686 million metric tonnes valued at PHP81.299 billion. Production was contributed mainly by municipal fisheries (38 per cent) followed by commercial (33 per cent) and aquaculture (29 per cent). The Philippines exported a total of PHP15 billion in 1994, up by 6.8 per cent over 1993. The leading fishery exports, shrimps/prawn and tuna, accounted for PHP10.8 billion or 72 per cent of the total exported.

More and more resources in the form of boats, gear and labour are being expended to catch the existing limited stocks; there

---

[10]   Infofish Fact Sheet, August 1995.

are simply too much investment in boats and gear, too many fishers, and too few fish to be harvested. In addition, coastal fisheries in many parts of the country are on the verge of collapse due to overfishing and poor management. In the Philippines the situation is especially acute as more and more fish stocks are increasingly overfished and their habitats destroyed. Coastal fisheries continue to serve as the 'sink' for surplus labour displaced from land-based activities.

Meanwhile, for two decades, considerable changes have taken place: technological advances, increased public awareness of environmental and natural resource uses, and increased support from donors and policy makers for environmental and natural resource management. The fishery sector could have responded to these changes with more effective management. Unfortunately, it has remained inept. Management interventions are typically myopic and short-term measures to relieve symptoms rather than to treat causes. Furthermore, the sector operates in isolation as a small, inconsequential offshoot of the agriculture sector. The low profile of fisheries is reflected by its relatively small budgetary allocation in most developing countries. Considering its role, both actual and potential, in the improvement of the coastal and marine environment, the Bureau of Fisheries and Aquatic Resources (BFAR) could be more effective if it was incorporated in the environment sector.

Marine Scientific Research in the Philippines

Status and Problems

From an environmental perspective, the country's bleak situation is one in which the natural environment has almost completely broken down.[11] This is generally true for the coastal and marine environment. While the government has not been remiss in offering solutions to improve the situation, these solutions give short-term benefits to select groups and degrade the environment at society's cost (for example, artificial reefs or ARs). For decades, these

---

[11] Foundation for Rural Economic Enterprise and Development, Inc. (FREED), *DENR Internal Assessment: Gearing the DENR* (Organization for Sustainable Development, Philippines, 1994).

have been talked about in countless forums, recommended to some extent, initiated, but not sustained. The present situation can be likened to that of a deeply rooted malignant tumour that is eating away the lifeblood of the natural environment and its people. Unless there is a substantial change in the national legislative agenda, the lack of national commitment to supporting and encouraging the development of coastal and marine science in the country will remain a major deterrent to economic and environmental sustainability.

Key Issues and Concerns

The key coastal and marine issues can be placed under three broad categories: biophysical issues; sociocultural issues; and institutional/policy issues. This categorisation, however, is artificial as these issues are interconnected and interdependent. If they are separated in this report, it is only for the sake of convenience in presentation and to facilitate understanding.

(i) Biophysical Issues

The priority biophysical issues confronting the coastal zone in the Philippines are:

- degradation of coastal ecosystems and habitats;
- declining water quality and pollution;
- declining coastal fisheries;
- endangered marine species and coastal wildlife; and
- coastal hazards including ocean storms and flooding.

Human activities such as industrialisation, development of recreational areas along the coasts, agricultural land uses and 'dredge and fill' operations are increasing in many parts of the country. These activities have led to a well-documented decline of coral reefs and seagrass beds in both temperate and tropical areas.

On the other hand, natural perturbations such as cyclones, typhoons, tidal waves, volcanic activity and the rapid encroachment of sand waves constitute physical issues which can also be responsible for the decline. However, they do not seem to be as widespread as man-induced changes. Pests, diseases and population and community interactions similarly act as stressors which have affected coastal ecosystems.

As a result of pollution from waste water discharge and what appears to be a disease, seagrass and reef populations along the coasts of the Philippines are declining. This decline is a product of the intense development of coastal areas, which has reduced water quality and hence the growth of marine biota; any pollution resulting in reduced water clarity limits their production and survival in coastal areas. In the Philippines, only about 25 per cent of industrial firms nation-wide comply with water pollution control laws, and at least 31 municipalities and ten cities discharge their sewage, industrial effluent and domestic wastes into strategic river systems and coastal areas. With an increase in pollution, there has been a concomitant decrease in seagrass and coral biomass and a reduction in species diversity.

The two main factors contributing to water clarity reduction are suspended sediments and nutrient loading. Resulting primarily from upland runoff, boat traffic, wind mixing, and gleaning, suspended sediments shade the plants directly. Sand, silt and clay derived from deforestation (and swidden agriculture) wash into streams which carry the suspended materials into seagrass and coral areas. Industrial, residential and commercial development, which cause rapid rates of clearing and soil stripping in watersheds, also contribute suspended sediments in the coastal waters.

The major long-term threat to seagrass and coral populations around the world comes from coastal eutrophication. Nutrient loading or eutrophication, which is particularly a problem in embayments with reduced tidal flushing, is caused by waste waters which reach the coasts from industrial, commercial and domestic facilities; inadequate septic systems; boat discharges of human and fish wastes and storm-drain run-off carrying organic waste and fertilisers. Its direct impact is the enhancement of growth in many plant forms leading to a reduction of light. Ultimately the cause of nutrient loading along coasts is people, and increases in population density aggravate the problem.

In many parts of coastal Philippines, blast fishing is a popular, albeit extremely destructive, fishing technique. In Cape Bolinao alone, six blasts per hour have been recorded. The blasts create blowouts or coral- or grass-free depressions within the reefs. In blowout areas, any one point will be recurrently eroded and re-established at intervals of the order of 5 to 15 years (in seagrass). Such processes limit successional development (as is evidenced by the absence of a well-developed epifauna and flora that is characteristic of an advanced stage of seral development), disrupt sedimentary structures and may result in deposits much coarser than those characteristic of the sandy seagrass carpet. In coastal population or market centres, boat traffic causes scouring of the beds. This is brought about by the boats themselves or by the anchors and poles used to manoeuvre the boats at low tide. The traffic also increases suspended sediments, contributing significantly to the increase of water turbidity and a decline in its quality.

(ii) *Sociocultural Issues*

The priority sociocultural issues in coastal zone management in the Philippines are:

- poverty and conflict over the use of, and loss of access to, natural resources;
- rapid population growth;
- limited involvement of resource users;
- low credibility of the government (loss of people's trust); and
- absence of a shared vision.

Other equally important issues include:

- lack of sensitivity to gender concerns;
- public health; and
- certain misconceptions which have guided mankind's interaction with the environment.

The causes of the first major issues are well identified and their solutions are relatively well laid out, hence they need not be elaborated in this report. On the other hand, the misconceptions which have guided people's actions towards their environment need to be mentioned. People have an unclear perception of what the environment is in relation to themselves, the view being often anthropocentric, not sociocentric or naturalistic. In addition, development is predicated largely upon environmental exploitation, not its protection, as the latter is not yet a perceived social need but an expensive and time-consuming activity. Environmental preservation and the pursuit of economic goals are considered to be in conflict with one another because they are based on two incompatible basic principles: the ecological principle of 'stability', as a precondition of the sustainability of ecological systems; and the economic principle of 'growth', as the inherent logic of economic systems. The important point about these different viewpoints is that they will remain divergent so long as groups have different interests and different sources of information and knowledge.

Taken for granted partly because of the limited involvement of the people in planning and management, a 'shared' vision for the environment is nowhere in sight. For the last two decades, the Philippines Department of the Environment and Natural Resources (DENR) has made vision statements which have changed rapidly with changes in the administration. More importantly, these visions have been formulated largely without incorporating what the people want their environment to be. Hence, the results are almost parochial statements that alienate the people, making them feel that they do not 'belong'. With this scenario, how can one expect them to actively participate in government projects?

(iii) *Institutional/Policy Issues*

The priority institutional/policy issues are:

- low level of institutional capability for coastal area management (especially at the local level, where the capacity to implement sound policies is very limited);

- government's inadequacy in addressing the problem of dealing with commercial operators and implementing existing rules and guidelines;

- lack of mechanisms to limit the free-access nature of some resources; and

- lack of national policy on strategic development of the coastal zone (especially a strategy that addresses the causes of habitat degradation).

The other institutional issues include:

- top-down modes of governance;

- overlapping jurisdictions/interagency conflict;

- lack of cross-sectoral and integrated approaches at the conceptual and policy levels and especially at the implementation level;

- discontinuities in policy and policy implementation because of political instability and the loss of qualified staff to the private sector or to other countries;

- inadequate public support and priority given to the environment as a unifying resource and to environmental management initiatives;

- inadequate implementation and enforcement of existing regulations (poor pollution control, sanitation and waste treatment facilities);

- use of unsuitable technologies and approaches; and

- lack of an alternative paradigm of economic development that is also ecologically sustainable and politically acceptable.

Political interference and mismanagement is a 'normal' ingredient in any developmental effort in less developed countries. This results from misguided priorities arising from a meagre information base, the lack of expertise, political favouritism and an inefficient bureaucracy in the face of a dire lack of financial resources. The much needed but least felt 'political will' to support the new movement of coastal environmental protection is locked in the traditional bureaucracy and political élite in the region. Unfortunately, mitigative efforts being undertaken by the government and private sectors are insufficient, ineffective and largely socially unacceptable.

Case Study: Seagrass Research in Southeast Asia

In Southeast Asia, seagrass beds are the least studied among the ecosystems of the coastal environment. As noted above, there are two main reasons why seagrasses receive little attention. First, most people consider that they are not as important as coral reefs or mangroves or the corals, seaweeds, or fish associated with them. Second, the traditional orientation of the region's marine science has been to view the ocean as a deep-water mass. In fact, it was only in the mid-1960s that the shallow benthic coastal fringe was recognised by oceanographers as a discrete ecosystem, forming a part of the larger ocean systems.[12] On a per country basis, the following factors could also be considered:

* the presence/absence of sizeable seagrass habitats associated with the length and nature of the coastline;

* the available expertise; and

* the current state of knowledge on the ecosystem.

Expertise in seagrass research and knowledge of the ecosystem in Southeast Asia are extremely limited. This is reflected by the number of publications, which totalled only 177 for the period 1983-94.[13] Eighty per cent of the total number were published only after 1986, when governments recognised the fundamental importance of seagrasses to coastal ecology and economy in the region.

Current research activities in seagrass ecosystems in Southeast Asia fall into five categories: seagrass structure, dynamics,

---

12   R.C. Phillips, 'Seagrasses and Coastal Marine Environment', *Oceanus*, Vol.21, No.3, 1978, pp.30-40.

13   M.D. Fortes, 'Seagrass Resources of ASEAN' in C R Wilkinson (ed.), *Living Coastal Resources: Status and Management* (Australian Institute of Marine Science, North Queensland, 1994), pp 106-9.

fisheries, environmental factors, and applied aspects.[14] Among the member countries, these activities are largely concentrated on the structural aspects (species composition and distribution) of the seagrass plants and their associated fisheries (finfishes and invertebrates), indicating, among other things, the relative novelty of the subject. With the exception of Indonesia and the Philippines, the Southeast Asian countries have shown much less research interest in the dynamic aspects of seagrass ecology. This is one reason why the functions of seagrasses still have only limited application in addressing environmental issues in the region. Compared with other countries in the region, in the last five years the Philippines has made some substantial advances in understanding the basic trophic processes and the broad-scale distribution of its seagrass resources. Using the data available, it has initiated a programme of research to investigate both the role of seagrasses in protected areas and their usefulness in the rehabilitation of degraded coasts and in monitoring the impacts of the environmental stress imposed by industry.

Competitive Capacity

From the broader perspective, competitive capacity is a function of a country's macro-economic situation, its industrial structure, its socio-institutional structure and its techno-scientific infrastructure. This paper focuses on the last component. In general, the technological and scientific infrastructure of the Philippines is characterised by scientific isolation, a low quality and low volume of research and development (R&D) institutes, low public spending on R&D, lack of private spending on R&D, and a weak relationship between the scientific community and the 'market'. The subject of enormous political pressures and decisions and stiff international competition, our competitive ability for funds and opportunities is diminished primarily because of the above factors. Although the Philippines has the second-largest population of the eight countries in Southeast Asia, in terms of science and technology performance it has the smallest number of productive researchers.[15] With a much

---

14   Fortes, 'Seagrasses of East Asia'.
15   F. Lacanilao, 'Research and Development Problems of Philippines Fisheries', Lecture presented at the Scientific Symposium 'Sustainable Development of

smaller population, Taiwan had a research output that was 24 times that of the Philippines in 1994. This partly explains why Taiwan is now ahead even in milkfish breeding research and development.

Trends and Prospects in Marine Scientific Research

Future Directions

The future direction of marine scientific research in Southeast Asia is dictated by certain factors which chart the course of marine science world-wide. Essentially, these factors include:[16]

* the developing new occupational areas that require exclusive or partial expertise in seagrass science;

* key knowledge and skills which will be required at that time and methodological changes in their teaching;

* the rapid growth in information and specialisation; and

* constraints and what is needed to overcome them.

A shortage of government funds and a tendency on the part of the private sector to fund only marketable research will largely determine the research climate in Southeast Asia, with the result that only those areas with brighter occupational prospects will be developed. Hence, expertise in marine science will be developed to address the needs of the following developing occupational areas:

* integrated coastal zone management and marine parks development;

* the management of marine information;

* 'mariculture' or sea ranching;

* marine environmental toxicology, pollution monitoring and control;

Fisheries Resources', National Research Council of the Philippines, University of the Philippines, 22 November 1995.

16   United Nations Educational, Scientific and Cultural Organisation (UNESCO), 'Year 2000 Challenges for Marine Science Training and Education Worldwide', UNESCO Reports in Marine Science No. 52, Paris, 1989.

- coastal and marine tourism;

- the development of new products from the sea;

- coastal remote sensing interpretation and application;

- marine species taxonomy; and

- environmental management and protection.

The specific fields of research interest which will attract attention and resources will include: coastal processes, coastal water quality, land-sea and ocean-atmosphere interactions in the coastal zone, global climate change and sea level rise, resource valuation, and management. In the conduct of research, the constraints will come largely from the use of computers, models and modelling; the applicability of mathematics and statistics; the lack of communication, information transfer and electronic networking; and the failure to translate results into a form which is acceptable to people in general.

To complement existing specialisations in biology, engineering, navigation and economics, new subjects will be developed to integrate the knowledge of marine and human ecology involved in coastal activities. These subjects, which are characterised by their multidisciplinary approach and their solid grounding in biology, chemistry, physics, geology and mathematics, include: computer literacy, information management and transfer, interpretation and application of remotely sensed data, taxonomy invoking interdisciplinary skills, mariculture, ecological processes, restoration ecology, ocean-atmosphere interactions, hindcasting of climate, sea levels, the sub-lethal effects of pollutants, traditional knowledge of coastal communities, and marine resource and environment economics. If greater support were made available, computer-assisted research in seagrass science would increase in scope and sophistication.

Because of its ability to increase massively the capacity for storing data, CD-ROM and associated technology could be useful in dealing with the rapid growth of information. Also useful here would be electronic networking, the visualisation of data using graph processors and the establishment of regional databases. Seagrass information could be readily available from information networks, especially those of the United States, European Union and Australia.

The Controlling Factors

Coastal Zone Issues

The factors which have brought about a decline in fisheries production in the recent years include environmental degradation, an increase in the demand for fish, intense competition for land and water resources for fish production, inadequate institutional and organisational arrangements, and the poor performance of our researchers and scientists. Environmental degradation was a direct result of rapid population growth and accelerated industrial and other economic developments after the Second World War. While economic growth has improved income and increased employment opportunities, it has also resulted in adverse environmental changes that are threatening human health and the functional integrity of the ecosystems.

The increasing demand for fish was brought about by three factors: population growth, increase in disposable income and increase in the relative preference for fish over other foods.[17] The present supply of fish permits an average per capita consumption of 12 kg per year. But projected population increases will make it impossible to maintain current patterns and levels of fish consumption without substantial production increases. World population is projected to increase from the present 4 billion to 6 billion by the year 2000 and Asia will have at least 3.2 billion people living in our already congested environment.[18] The Food and Agriculture Organisation (FAO) estimates that another 30 million tons at current prices will be needed to maintain the present level and pattern of fish consumption.[19] Without increases in supply,

---

[17] T.-E. Chua, 'Asian Fisheries towards the Year 2000: A Challenge to Fisheries Scientists' in *Proceedings of the Third Asian Fisheries Forum, Singapore* (The Asian Fisheries Society, Manila, 1994), pp.1-14.

[18] World Bank projection, 1990.

[19] Food and Agriculture Organisation of the United Nations (FAO), Living Marine Resources Research Paper 5, commissioned by the United Nations Conference on Environment and Development (UNCED), Rome, 1991.

consumers will have to bid against each other for the limited supply, causing prices to rise. As a result, there will be a shift in the consumption of fish, skewing the allocation away from those less willing and able to pay more.

Real income in the developing world is increasing. This will continue to put an upward pressure on the demand for high-quality fish for the domestic market. This upward pressure is being further strengthened by an increasing desire by people in affluent nations to consume healthy food, as fish is widely recognised and promoted as a healthy source of animal protein.

The coastal zones of most developing nations are densely populated. In Southeast Asia more than 200 million people (about 60 per cent of the population) live close to the shore.[20] The United Nations Conference on Environment and Development (UNCED) projects that, by the year 2000, between 60 and 70 per cent of people in coastal nations will reside within 60 km of the shoreline and over two-thirds of these will be in developing countries. In short, the coastal zone will be densely populated and urban centres will proliferate along the coastlines, leading to an increase in environmentally degrading activities. There will thus be intense competition for land and water resources for fish production.

Because property rights are unclear or unenforceable, there is a lack of an effective mechanism for allocating scarce resources among competing users. An example of this is the decade-long struggle between inshore fishers using traditional fishing gear and commercial trawlers operating in the same fishing grounds for the same target commodity (shrimp). The resolution of this problem requires a better understanding of its root causes and their effects, as well as a clearer perspective of the community, its socio-economic and cultural characteristics and the application of economic

20 T.-E. Chua, 'Managing Coastal Resources for Sustainable Development: The ASEAN Initiative' in T.-E. Chua and L.F. Scura (eds), *Managing ASEAN Coastal Resources for Sustainable Development: Roles of Policy Makers, Scientists, Donors, Media and Communities* (ICLARM Conference Proceedings, 1991), pp.21-35.

incentives or disincentives. Many of these actions go beyond the realm of the fishery sector.[21]

As for the poor performance of our researchers and scientists, it is alarming to note that the Philippines ranks last among eight Asian countries assessed for science and technology performance, which is the basis of economic growth.[22] The leading nations in this ranking have also managed their resources better because projects that conflict with social benefits and environmental integrity are often excluded or given up. In Singapore, it has never been a part of economic policy to sacrifice a sector of society or the environment in development strategies. In Thailand, workers have stopped using tyres for the construction of artificial reefs since 1988 but in the Philippines, their unregulated deployment continues without studies.

Due to a lack of political courage on the part of the government, its attempts to conserve the coral reef resources have been too few and have come too late. On the other hand, grassroots demonstration projects have shown that communities themselves can create and implement effective conservation programmes with minimal assistance from the government.[23]

Emerging Development-Environment Paradigms

'A new scientific paradigm triumphs not by convincing the majority of its opponents, but because its opponents eventually die'.

Max Planck, physicist.

In order to be more relevant, more freely acceptable to the people and more effective in performing its mandate and attaining its vision, the country's environmental sector has to actively acquire,

---

21 L.A. Fallon and T.-E. Chua, 'Towards Strengthening Policy and Strategic Orientation for Fisheries Resources Management: The Role of Coastal Area Management', *Tropical Coast Area Management*, Vol.5, No.3, 1990, pp.1-5.

22 Lacanilao, 'Research and Development Problems of Philippines Fisheries'.

23 J.R. Clark, 'Annex C: Management of the Coastal Zone for Sustainable Development' in Dames & Moore International, Louis Berger International, Inc. and Institute for Development Anthropology, *Sustainable Natural Resources Assessment - Philippines* (United States Agency for International Development, Manila, 1989).

disseminate and utilise newer and more pragmatic ideas. These ideas are the driving force behind modernisation (of both staff and facilities), capacity building and the maintenance, even simplification, of procedures. For the most part, they are associated with the new paradigms to which the world environment is opening itself.

The current environmental scenario in the Philippines dictates the need for a reappraisal of existing paradigms and/or a shift to new and more relevant or appropriate ones. In the broader context, the ingredients for such a shift have been made clear:

> ... poverty must be eradicated through community movements and people empowerment; the economy must be resuscitated through the broad-based provision of access to and the mobilisation of resources and investments for higher value, higher multiplier and higher efficiency goods and services; *the environment must be rehabilitated and sustainably managed;* and the government machinery must be reoriented and restructured towards more democratic, more responsive, people-based, and area-oriented approaches of realising sustainable development.

In this paper, the focus will be on the sustainable management of the coastal marine environment. The following are some of those paradigms which have emerged out of the need to refocus environmentally related efforts which obviously did not work or are inappropriate under existing conditions.

- Economic growth as it has been conventionally perceived is no longer tenable as the unquestioned objective of economic development policy. The old concept of growth, ('throughput growth'), with its reliance on an ever-increasing throughput of energy and other natural materials, cannot be sustained, and must yield to an imaginative pursuit of economic ends that are less resource-intensive.[24] This new approach requires a concerted effort to be made to remould consumer preferences and to steer demand in the direction of

---

24 R. Goodland *et al.* (eds), *Environmentally Sustainable Economic Development: Building on Brundtland* (UNESCO, Paris, 1991).

environmentally benign activities, while simultaneously
reducing throughput per unit of final product and services.

- Producing more with less through conservation, higher
efficiency, technological improvements and sound recycling.
Japan excels in this regard, producing 81 per cent more real
output than it did in 1973, using the same amount of energy.

- Economic logic tells us that we should aim to maximise the
productivity of the scarcest (limiting) factor, as well as to
increase its supply.[25] This means that economic policy
should be designed to increase the productivity of natural
capital (natural resources) and its total amount, rather than
to increase the productivity of human-made capital and its
accumulation; there is a need to reorient and adopt policies
for the management of scarce, not abundant, resources, and
to institutionalise ecological knowledge that has direct
relevance to and implications for the management of these
scarce resources.

- Natural capital and human-made capital are complements,
rather than substitutes.[26] The neo-classical assumption of the
near-perfect substitutability of the two is a serious distortion
of reality. The switch from human-made to natural capital as
the limiting factor is a function of the increasing scale of
human presence. Investment must shift from human-made
capital accumulation to the preservation and resoration of
natural capital. Instead of investing mainly in sawmills,
fishing boats and refineries, development banks should now
invest more in reforestation, the restocking of reefs and fish
populations and renewable substitutes for dwindling
reserves of petroleum (the World Bank's new official name is
the International Bank for Reconstruction and Development
(IBRD).

- In any conflict between biophysical realities and political
realities, the latter must eventually give ground.[27] The
environment will inevitably transit to sustainability: the

25 H.E. Daly, 'From Empty-World Economics to Full-World Economics' in ibid.
26 ibid.
27 Goodland *et al.* (eds), *Environmentally Sustainable Economic Development*.

choice is between planning for an orderly transition or allowing physical limits and environmental damage to dictate the timing and course of the transition.

* It is neither ethical nor helpful in terms of the environment to expect the grassroots to reduce or arrest their development. Therefore the richer companies, which after all are responsible for most of today's environmental damage, must take the lead in this respect.

* The newly developing sectors of society need to find a different pathway and to shape models of development that will bypass the ruinous, resource-depleting cycle that the older, more developed sectors went through. The essential fuels of the transition to sustainability - capital and technology - are scarce in these developing sectors, so it is imperative that these sectors optimise the use of such resources in ways which also take advantage of their main resource - people.

* Increasing the ability of scientists to move away from the objectivity and rationality of science into the less rational and more subjective roles of advocacy and policy making. This, however, implies that these scientists have already reached the peak of their careers. Nevertheless, there is a prevailing 'push' for researchers to improve their output, for scientists to perform their role in information dissemination, and for both to train more future scientists who would actively take part in the decision-making process.

* The preservation of the functional integrity of the resource system through integrated and holistic approaches. The natural system maintains itself through a close interaction of various key processes that enable it to reach a stage of ecological equilibrium. To ensure the systematic flow of goods and services from the resource system, human activity should be regulated within the upper biological limits, beyond which adverse ecological changes occur and the resource system fails to maintain its normal functions (its carrying capacity). Unfortunately, scientists have yet to provide such an index. But in the absence of such values,

managers must carefully balance environmental protection with the realities of human needs and expectations. In the meantime, resource managers must use expert judgment and common sense as their guide.

- The 'tragedy of the commons' implies that communities are unable to form functional groups to manage their common resources. But in some isolated cases, these communities do form working cooperatives which are effective in implementing sustainable resource-use practices. Hence, 'tragedy' is transformed into 'benefits'.

- The success of many corporate establishments depends on their ability to make their people feel important by, among other means, involving or consulting them in decision making, communicating to them in acceptable language, and *listening* to them.

- The recognition and acceptance of a new paradigm of economic development where natural resources are used sustainably over a long time frame (intergenerational equity) and where benefits accrue to the mass base of marginal coastal populations.

Research Data Needs for Marine Resource Management

It is important for the sustainable development of marine resources that their uses be developed under a system of integrated planning and management. Attention should be given to future needs, and in particular to encouraging research into their use, protection and conservation. Thus for marine science, the major concerns that need to be addressed and from which the necessary research data could be obtained include the following.

(i) *Coastal Processes*

In coastal development planning, information about coastal processes is important. This is because of their effects on biota, water circulation, sedimentation and erosion. Hence, related research should focus on: land-coastal zone interactions; the mechanisms of coastal processes (for example, sediment transport due to waves, currents, rivers and wind; the effect of man-made structures such as harbours and dams); and the development of techniques for monitoring not only the ongoing process itself but also external forces, such as waves and currents.

There is a need for an education programme in research techniques that is primarily aimed at marine geologists, ocean and coastal engineers, planners and decision makers. Among the subjects to be covered are the monitoring (especially by satellite observations and the interpretation of aerial photographs), modelling and simulation of coastal processes; field measurements; land-sea interactions; and currents.

(ii) *The Effects of Disturbance on Ecosystems*

Coastal area development may disturb the marine ecosystem balance through its effect on the quality of coastal waters. Particularly important here are the modification of water-flow patterns that occurs as the result of reclamation undertaken in the construction of docks, harbours and similar works, and the effects of increased discharges of surface water and domestic and industrial waste waters. Eutrophication and climatic changes also affect the marine ecosystem balance. There is thus a need to promote through research, training and education an understanding of the nature and functioning of the coast, and to establish appropriate environmental measures to deal with these disturbances of the coastal equilibrium. This need can be addressed by effective communication with decision makers, planners and managers as well as by regional cooperation.

(iii) *Water Pollution and Seagrass Habitats*

The pollution of coastal waters from land-based sources, by atmospheric inputs, or by the use of coastal areas for human and industrial activities, is one of the more conspicuous problems arising from the use of the coastal zone. The problem is aggravated by a lack of proper management and knowledge. If there is to be a proper evaluation and assessment of water pollution in coastal marine areas, information, education and training will have to be provided. The basic information that is required for a proper evaluation of the effects of water pollution in coastal areas could come from the following areas: physical oceanography and meteorology, marine ecosystems and their functions, and the study of living resources, particularly those already exploited, of riverine inputs and of the discharge of sewage and industrial effluents.

Education and research are required at all levels - primary, secondary, university and postgraduate - and also for planners, managers and users. Training in analytical techniques is necessary for the assessment of marine pollution, contingency plans, modelling, dispersion/dilution of pollutants in coastal waters, and the use of control devices.

(iv) *Possible Impacts of Climate Change and Sea Level Rise*

Present sea temperatures in Southeast Asian seas are expected to increase by 1 °C, resulting in enhanced evaporation and increased precipitation.[28] With this increase in precipitation, more nutrients will be washed out to sea. Depending on the actual load of nutrients, this can have either positive or negative effects for coastal communities. With erosion enhanced, current patterns in near-shore areas, where seagrasses, coral reefs and mangroves abound, will be altered and the breeding and nursery functions of the ecosystems will be adversely affected.

The effects of a rise in the sea level within the predicted range of 20 cm by 2025 are likely to be insignificant for seagrass systems when compared to the effects of man-induced influences. Nevertheless, such a rise would still have a substantial negative impact on the seagrass community. There would inundation, both the frequency and severity of storms and wave surge would increase as would the rates of shoreline erosion, the dynamic coastal physical properties would be modified, and shoreline protective structures and facilities would be damaged or reduced.[29] There is thus a need to research and to monitor the changes in sea levels, and to develop

---

28 L.M. Chou (ed.), 'Implications of Expected Climate Changes in the East Asian Seas Region: An Overview', RCU/EAS Technical Report Series No.2, United Nations Environment Programme, 1994.

29 M.A. Davidson and T.W. Kana, 'Future Sea Level Rise and its Implications for Charleston, South Carolina' in M.H. Glantz (ed.), *Societal Responses to Regional Climatic Change: Forecasting by Analogy* (Westview Press, Boulder, Colo., 1988).

programmes that assess the possible effects of these changes on seagrass systems at the global, regional and local levels.

(v) *Land-Sea and Ocean-Atmosphere Interactions in the Coastal Zone*

An understanding of land-sea and ocean-atmosphere interactions is vital for planning and management. In the coastal zone, physical and chemical oceanographic parameters are, to a large extent, influenced by the form of the coastline and its topography as well as by meteorological and climatic conditions. The sea also impacts on both the atmosphere and the coast.

University graduates, government planners and managers are in need of education and research programmes that focus on the measurement in the field of those parameters used to describe the interactions between the sea and the atmosphere as well as on modelling and simulation.

(vi) *Management*

Long-term traditional uses are no longer compatible with the sustainable development and management of the coastal zone. Moreover, in most Southeast Asian countries marine practices have not been regulated, and the human population will not quickly accept the new laws of the sea, unless these laws are understood and the reasons for their existence clearly communicated and demonstrated.

For the marine environment as a whole, regulations should be established governing the multiple use of designated coastal areas. These should designate different types of zones for different uses and include zones of complete protection from extractive human activity. The zoning scheme would separate competitive operations and may provide for the periodic closure of zones, for example in seagrass areas where fish-breeding times are known.

Education and research programmes are needed at both the university (including graduate) and government levels, and for policy makers, planners, managers and investors. Research training will be required in monitoring, planning and multiple-use management as well as in the application of methods for sustainable development and environmental impact assessment.

In addition to the research requirements for the management of marine resources listed above, there is a parallel need for data management and information acquisition. There is an increasing amount of data and information on the coastal and marine environment that is available for science and management. A major concern is the need to arrive at an effective mechanism to cope with the present and future problems in managing this data and information.

(vii) *Valuation of Marine Resources*

A primary cause of marine habitat loss is the failure of the present economic policies to give monetary value to its components and the interactions among them. In most Southeast Asian countries, the destruction of coral reefs for the trade of precious biological materials, and the conversion of seagrass beds into seaweed farms or their destruction to build access roads, fish ports, and other industrial facilities, occur for two reasons: to meet the need for increased food production or hard currency, regardless of whether that production is sustainable or not; and because seagrass systems, like the other natural systems, are often undervalued.

There have already been attempts to give monetary value to goods and services from seagrass beds and mangroves. The values were calculated primarily on the basis of the fisheries that seagrass beds support. Thus in Cairns (North Queensland), Watson, Coles and Lee Long estimated that the potential total annual yield from Cairns harbour seagrasses for the three major commercial prawn species was 178 tons per year with a landed value of $A1.2 million per year.[30] In Puget Sound, Washington, a 0.4 hectare eelgrass bed was valued at US$12,325 annually.[31] The valuation took into account the amount of energy derived from the system, and the nutrition it

---

30 R.A. Watson, R.G. Coles and W.J. Lee Long, 'Simulation Estimates of Annual Yield and Landed Value for Commercial Penaeid Prawns from a Tropical Seagrass Habitat, Northern Queensland, Australia', *Australian Journal of Marine and Freshwater Resources*, Vol.44, 1993, pp.211-19.

31 McRoy, pers. comm., 1978.

generated for oyster culture, commercial and sport fisheries, as well as sport charters and waterfowl. In Southeast Asia, the revenues derived from seagrass fisheries alone would be substantial. Even if the calculations used above are only partially correct, if they were applied to Southeast Asian seagrass resources, the economic value of seagrass beds in the region would be considerably higher.[32]

There is a need to undertake the valuation of coastal and marine resources. It should be pointed out, however, that the sole purpose of the valuation process is to provide useful data for making sound management decisions, and that the values arrived at will be underestimates. This is because not all the components, much less the processes that maintain the integrity of coastal systems, can be given monetary values. The active participation of scientists in this process is essential, since they have more knowledge about the true worth of the resources. Otherwise, others less informed will assign much lower values.

The Need for a Regional Approach to Marine Scientific Research

The wide range of research capabilities that exists among the countries in Southeast Asia is a major obstacle to an integrated management of the region's coastal and marine environments. There is a need for regional cooperation in this sector. The following recommendations may be useful in achieving this:

Regional centres should be established with networks for capacity building in order to promote the exchange of successful models and experiences and to act as a knowledge base for policy development.

These centres should aim at building national capacities by assisting sectoral assessments and institutional development, reviewing programmes and managerial capacities within existing educational, training and research establishments, facilitating and jointly undertaking supportive research, and developing and jointly implementing short- and long-term training programmes aimed at target groups at all relevant levels within and, to some extent, also outside governments. These activities should be predominantly on-the-job and

---

[32]   Fortes, 'Seagrasses: A Resource Unknown in the ASEAN Region'.

hands-on, making use of real-life case studies and simulations, developing cross-sectoral thinking and promoting the need for effectiveness. The centres could be attached to existing institutions with excellent track records, ensuring mutual support, but should maintain their autonomous status in order to facilitate their regional activities.

Access should be provided to international centres of knowledge and data networks and regional Southeast Asian equivalents should be developed.

Regional cooperation should be enhanced or further explored to improve access to library materials (journals, books, current contents), electronic information systems (e-mail, databases), and international networks of scientific and professional associations.

Research capacity in the region should be mobilised and better focused.

The research capacity in most member countries is under-funded, under-utilised, and is often poorly focused. The overriding priorities for the future are to ensure that the development of coastal marine resources is sustainable, and that, once developed, such resources are managed within an integrated framework.

Indigenous research capacity should be strengthened with these priorities in mind, so that optimal use can be made of existing facilities. Wherever possible, the work undertaken should be field-oriented and should cover both technical and social aspects.

Particular attention should be paid to the physical and biological processes involved in water and nutrient fluxes and their relation to land use and climate, and to the appropriate technologies for the protection, conservation and sustainable use of marginal areas with vulnerable and fragile ecosystems.

A regional consensus should be forged on the strategic approaches needed to ensure the long-term sustainability of coastal marine environment sector programmes and projects.

Countries have to recognise and address the pressing need to improve the performance of key agencies and institutions and their regional extensions, where the demand for a better environment is greatest. Initially, and for purposes of pragmatic systematisation, the region needs to look at capacity building in the coastal marine environment sector at three levels: at the local level, where field operations are carried out; at the central government level, where policies are made; and at the international level of external support agencies. In addition, the region should adopt strategies to strengthen capacity both in the short term (that is, coastal villagers operating a fish cooperative) and in the long term (that is, strengthening educational institutions to build a nation's capacity in the environment sector). It should also look at the 'enabling factor' in the capacity-building process, the role of community-based organisations, of the private sector and of NGOs. Further, the region needs to ensure that it continues to adapt these strategies to changing economic and social conditions.

Conclusion

The main obstacles to the formulation and implementation of programmes for marine research in Southeast Asia are still the shortage of funds for research, low salaries for staff, the lack of access to needed technologies, weak technical support infrastructures, poor public appreciation of coastal resources and environment, and the relatively small number of researchers trained in promoting an integrated management approach. Unless there is a substantial change in the legislative agenda within the majority of developing countries in Southeast Asia, the lack of commitment by governments to support and encourage the development of seagrass science will remain a major deterrent.

In order to overcome these obstacles, there is a need:

- to develop expertise in marine scientific research, at least in key institutions in the region;

- to give more intellectual stimulation and a sense of mission to the region's marine scientists;

- to foster more public understanding of the relevance of seagrasses and other lesser known resources to the welfare of coastal populations;

- to conduct more public-relations activities to stimulate governmental willingness; and

- to provide the necessary facilities for the training and retraining of educators.

In the longer term, the sound management of seagrass and other coastal ecosystems will depend on an educated community in which members understand the importance of a mix of conservation, development and community participation. The scientific community needs to develop and nurture an ethic that views the seas as a resource in need of our stewardship and not simply a commodity. The extent to which local community participation in marine environmental protection and resource management can be fostered will be a significant factor in determining the quality of the marine environment and the availability of its resources in the future.

CHAPTER 6

MARINE ENVIRONMENTAL SECURITY

Grant Hewison and Mohd Nizam Basiron

At the initial meeting of the CSCAP Maritime Working Group it was agreed that firm practical proposals for cooperation and confidence building between Asia Pacific nations be developed for this meeting. After discussion, those that met with the approval of the Maritime Working Group would then be passed on for consideration by the CSCAP Steering Committee.

The representatives of New Zealand and Malaysia agreed at the initial meeting to develop proposals in the area of the marine environment. This report is the product of joint work undertaken by those representatives.

It should be acknowledged at the outset that within the Asia Pacific region the 'marine environment' is a field that is already subject to enormous study. There are, in addition, many existing examples of cooperation and confidence building.

Rather than attempting to cover all possible avenues in this field, the proposals suggested here for cooperation and confidence building in Asia and the Pacific are those of particular interest to the representatives of New Zealand and Malaysia. They include suggestions for CSCAP to consider environmental security issues in Asia and the Pacific, environmentally responsible defence, the establishment of an effective regional oil spill response and control network and a response to land-based causes of marine pollution.

Proposal One: Environmental Security Issues in Asia and the Pacific

Although this proposal may fall outside of the strict terms of reference of the Maritime Working Group of CSCAP, there appear to be significant opportunities for CSCAP, apart from the Maritime Working Group, to undertake further concerted work on the potential for environmental security issues to be used to build confidence and security within the Asia Pacific region.

The concept of 'environmental security' has already been the subject of considerable study and evaluation.[1] It is not a new issue for those concerned with 'security' in the broad sense. Indeed it is widely acknowledged as a key element in the study of comprehensive security.[2]

More recently, there has been recognition of the role of environmental security both as a source of conflict and as a means for building confidence and security. Moreover, there has been increasing interest in environmental security within an Asia Pacific context.[3]

Nevertheless, the predominant dialogue on emerging security issues in Asia and the Pacific has to date given little regard to environmental security. The environment remains largely at the edge of domestic and international politics and in Asia and the Pacific immediate conventional security worries tend to dominate. Yet, as R.T. Maddock notes in a seminal article on environmental security in East Asia, 'in no other area of the world are the imperatives of economic growth and environmental protection on a more direct collision path'.[4]

---

[1] See H. Sprout and M. Sprout, *The Ecological Perspective on Human Affairs: With Special Reference to International Politics* (Greenwood Press, Westport, Conn., 1965); Richard Ullman, 'Redefining Security', *International Security*, Vol.8, No.1, 1983; Lester Brown, 'An Untraditional View of National Security' in J. Reichart and S. Sturm (eds), *American Defence Policy* (John Hopkins University, Baltimore, 5th edn 1982); Arthur Westing, 'The Environmental Component of Comprehensive Security', *Bulletin of Peace Proposals*, Vol.20, No.2, June 1989; Jessica Mathews, 'Redefining Security', *Foreign Affairs*, Vol.68, No.2, 1989; Norman Myers, 'Environment and Security', *Foreign Policy*, No.74, 1989; Alexandre Timoshenko, 'Ecological Security: Global Change Paradigm', *Colorado Journal of International Environmental Law and Policy*, Vol.1, No.1, 1990; Gunther Handl, 'Environmental Security and Global Change: The Challenge to International Law', *Yearbook of International Environmental Law*, Vol.1, 1990; Sergei Vinogradov, 'International Environmental Security: The Concept and its Implementation', in A. Carty and G. Danilenko (eds), *Perestroika and International Law: Current Anglo-Soviet Approaches to International Law*, (Edinburgh University Press, Edinburgh, 1990); Peter Gleick, 'Environment and Security: Clear Connections', *Bulletin of the Atomic Scientists*, Vol.47, No.3, April 1991; Michel Frederick, 'La securité environmentale [:] éléments de définition', *Etudes Internationales*, Vol.24, No.4, December 1993; Peter Gleick, 'Water and Conflict: Fresh Water Resources and International Security', *International Security*, Vol.18, No.1, Summer 1993; and Daniel Deudney, 'Muddled Thinking', *Bulletin of the Atomic Scientists*, Vol.47, No.3, April 1991.

[2] See, for example, the articles noted in footnote 1. See also Terence O'Brien, 'Track Two: Creating a Meltingpot', *New Zealand International Review*, Vol.20, No.4, July/August, 1995, pp.10-12.

[3] See, for example, R.T. Maddock, 'Environmental Security in East Asia', *Contemporary Southeast Asia*, Vol.17, No.1, June 1995, pp.20-37; Mary B. Powers, 'DOD's Gary Vest Speaks out on Its New Global Cleanup Links', *Engineering News-Record (ENR)*, 6 March 1995, pp.58-9.

[4] Maddock, 'Environmental Security in East Asia'.

In East Asia, the combined problems of a large and expanding population with phenomenal rates of economic growth mean that environmental limits will be reached very soon.[5]

While it seems that no complete study has been undertaken to identify all potential environmental security issues within the Asia Pacific region, R.T. Maddock suggests that the following environmental issues also have the potential to become trans-border security issues.

- Vietnam is concerned that Thailand draws excessive amounts of water from the Mekong River in the dry season, thus increasing the intrusion of salt water from the sea into the Mekong delta region of southern Vietnam, its main rice-growing area.

- Russia dumps low-level nuclear waste into the Sea of Japan, which is a cause of concern to Japan and South Korea.

- Japanese scientists have been disconcerted to discover that up to 65 per cent of Japan's measured disposition of sulphur dioxide emanates from sources outside the country - 50 per cent from China and 15 per cent from South Korea.[6]

As part from these specific examples, considerable potential exists for conflict over trans-border air pollution, marine pollution, migratory animals and birds, and sustainable forest development.[7]

Recommendations

It is recommended that the Maritime Working Group advance the idea that further concerted study of environmental security issues be undertaken within the Asia Pacific region. This suggestion might be usefully taken up first within CSCAP itself and then possibly at the Asia Pacific Roundtable. As noted from the examples above, there seems to be potential, particularly with regard to trans-border problems, for further identification of potential environmental security concerns and further dialogue on the issue generally. While environmental agencies within the region may already be engaged in work on solving these specific issues, it seems very useful that the

---

[5]   ibid.
[6]   ibid.
[7]   ibid.

military/defence establishment be made aware of the potential for environmental problems to escalate into conventional security concerns. There seems to be potential for regional research leading to a workshop on the issue of environmental security.

Proposal Two: Environmentally Responsible Defence

Although the concept of 'environmentally responsible defence' may be viewed as an element of environment security, it seems more appropriate, particularly in the context of these proposals, to discuss the concept separately.

In recent years and particularly since the late 1980s, the military establishments in many countries have recognised a need to improve their environmental performance.[8] The military have in the past caused, and to a great extent continue today to cause, considerable environmental degradation.[9] Although the primary mission of the military remains that of defending the nation, rather than environmental protection, concern for the environment is increasingly becoming part of the military mission. In many countries, for example, military programmes have been created that aim to reduce the amount of pollution generated, achieve full compliance with environmental laws and regulations, preserve natural resources, protect endangered species and clean up past toxic contamination.[10]

The United States Department of Defense (DOD), for example, has established a number of programmes concerned with

---

[8] See for example, Powers, 'DOD's Gary Vest Speaks out on Its New Global Cleanup Links'; Barry P. Steinberg, 'The Hidden Costs of Closing Military Bases', *Public Management*, Vol.73, No.5, May 1991, p.3; Martin Calhoun, 'The Big Green Military Machine', *Business and Society Review*, No.92, Winter 1995, pp.21-4; Ann Hills, 'Conservation: Britain's Defence Ministry Fights back', *Geographical Magazine*, Vol.63, No.5, May 1991, pp.16-20.

[9] See, for example, Reto Pieth, 'Toxic Military', *The Nation*, 8 June 1992, p.773. Reto Peith notes that 'the world's armed forces are the single biggest polluters on the planet. According to [a] report ... prepared researchers of the Science for Peace Institute at the University of Toronto, "10 to 30 per cent of all global environmental degradation can be attributed to military activities." The military establishments also use up tremendous amounts of environmental and human resources and deplete massive amounts of energy'.

[10] Of interest in the maritime sector will be the United States Navy's effort to reduce the contribudon of its warships and submarines to pollution of the oceans by compacting, sorting, offloading and burning shipboard wastes and reducing the volume of materials it takes on board. See Calhoun, 'The Big Green Military Machine'.

environmentally responsible defence.[11] Within NATO, the DOD has been involved in education, information sharing about the environment, and now (with the former Soviet and Warsaw Pact countries) enhancing clean-up capacities. This has involved the creation of networks among defence and environmental experts to facilitate the sharing of knowledge, approaches and technology. It has also involved those from the private sector who might be engaged in the work of actual clean-up.[12]

Along with senior environmental defence officials from Canada and Australia, the DOD has, as part of a comprehensive environmental security trilateral relationship, been examining the potential for environmentally responsible defence in Asia and the Pacific. A Pacific Rim-Southeast Asian defence environmental security conference is, for example, planned for September this year in Hawaii. The DOD has also been discussing with the US State Department, the National Oceanic and Atmospheric Administration and the US Environmental Protection Agency about how environmentally responsible defence programmes might fit into existing multilateral environmental programmes.[13]

A number of other conferences on this issue have also already taken place within the Asia Pacific region. For example, the Australian Defence Studies Centre in the Australian Defence Force Academy hosted a conference titled 'Environmentally Responsible Defence: A Fenner Conference on the Environment' in November 1995. This conference considered a range of issues, including Australia's environmental politics; the contribution from Australia's research organisations' conservation management; remediation; legislative frameworks and international responsibilities; legal perspectives; international trends in environmental law; the concept of environmental security; information management; the role of the private sector; the role of non-governmental organisations; and the environmental assessment of projects.

The Royal Australian Navy also held a conference in 1995 concerning environmentally responsible defence, titled 'The Significance of Environmental Management within the RAN: Its Impact Now and in the Future'. The conference covered a wide range

11 See Powers, 'DOD's Gary Vest Speaks out on Its New Global Cleanup Links'.
12 See ibid.
13 ibid., pp.58-9.

of issues, including discussion of environmental operating procedures in the RAN, commonwealth and state environmental issues, environmental law and its implications for the RAN, practical aspects concerning the control of pollution and waste in the RAN, conservation of wildlife, and the environmental management of RAN facilities.

In addition to this conference, the RAN has also recently established a Directorate of Environmental Management which has undertaken a range of activities, including:

- the publication and distribution of the RAN Environmental Policy Manual (ABR 6111 Volume 1) and Environmental Law Compliance Manual (Volume 2);

- initiating a navy-wide environmental awareness programme, which includes a regular feature in the naval newsletter titled 'Managing our Environment';

- providing an environmental Point of Contact service;

- preparing the RAN Waste Minimisation Strategy;

- reviewing RAN projects to ensure environmental compliance;

- representing the RAN on various committees addressing environmental issues.

Recommendations

It is recommended that the Maritime Working Group advance the following ideas:

- That CSCAP be represented at the Pacific Rim-Southeast Asian defence environmental security conference planned for September 1996 in Hawaii to determine if there is a role CSCAP could play with regard to this aspect of environmentally responsible defence.

- That either the Maritime Working Group or CSCAP itself investigate the possibility of hosting an initial conference or workshop on environmentally responsible defence for naval forces that operate in the Asia Pacific region (there is also considerable potential to involve all military forces apart from naval forces). It may be likely that the Australian or United States naval forces are already considering this possibility. Past conferences, particularly that undertaken by the Royal Australian Navy, might be used as models. It should be noted that the Royal Australian Navy has already established links concerning environmentally responsible defence with the Royal New Zealand Navy, the United States Navy and the maritime element of the Canadian Defence Force. In addition, the Royal Australian Navy has sent documents and other information to naval forces in Japan and India, although at this stage there does not appear to be significant interest in this issue.

• Apart from, or in addition to, a conference or workshop, the Maritime Working Group might also recommend that naval forces within the Asia Pacific region undertake, as part of their association with other naval forces, aspects that include environmentally responsible defence. This might potentially include a wide range of activities, such as the exchange of personnel, training, the sharing of equipment, evaluation of environmental performance, assistance in the preparation of manuals or codes of conduct, and/or assistance in the establishment or functioning of environmental directorates. As noted above, this appears to be already occurring between naval forces in Australia, New Zealand, Canada and the United States.

Proposal Three: Establishment of an Effective Regional Oil Spill Response and Control Network

Southeast Asia is inextricably linked to the petroleum industry from the standpoint of a producer as well as a user, and by virtue of its geography as a region which envelops major petroleum transportation routes from the Middle East to markets in Japan, Korea, China and Taiwan (see Figure 6:1).[14] Oil production began in the region in 1885, and by 1985 daily production in the region had reached about 2 million barrels of oil.[15] Accidental spills from the transportation and production of petroleum are a real threat to the region's marine

---

[14] See Chia Lin Sien, 'Alternative Routes to the Straits of Malacca for Oil Tankers: A Financial, Technical and Economic Analysis', paper presented at the Kuala Lumpur Workshop on the Straits of Malacca, Kuala Lumpur, 24-25 January 1995.

[15] See M.J. Valencia, *South-East Asian Seas: Oil under Troubled Waters: Hydrocarbon Potential, Jurisdictional Issues, and International Relations* (Oxford University Press, Singapore, 1985).

environment and potentially disastrous for a region which is highly dependent on the sea as a source of protein and for other environmental services.

The high level of petroleum production, and an increasingly large movement of oil through the region,[16] has prompted the establishment of a number of regional and subregional initiatives to enhance the ability of ASEAN member countries to respond to an oil spill outside of national capability. One such initiative is the ASEAN Oil Spill Response and Preparedness (ASEAN-OSRAP) project. The project is designed to enhance the ability of ASEAN member countries to respond to oil spills beyond national response and control capacity and encompasses several subregional oil spill contingency plans such as the Straits of Malacca and Singapore Standard Operating Procedure; the Sulawesi Sea Oil Spill Network and the Malaysia-Brunei Standard Operating Procedure for Joint Spill Combat In the South China Sea Including Brunei Bay.[17]

The existence of ASEAN-OSRAP, however, does not necessarily guarantee effective response in the event of oil spills. ASEAN-OSRAP is yet to be tested under real conditions and no study has been conducted to determine the effectiveness of ASEANOSRAP under such conditions. Indeed in his overview of ASEAN-OSRAP Raja Malik Kamarulzaman suggested a number of priority areas for the ASEAN Council on Petroleum (ASCOPE, the coordinating body for ASEAN-OSRAP) to address, such as 'availability of skilled personnel; training and exercises to improve deployment capability; and communication and coordination'.[18]

Oil spill preparedness and response costs money, and countries in the region, particularly in the Straits of Malacca, have always sought a mechanism which provides for a more equitable sharing of the environmental protection costs. To date only Japan (through the Petroleum Association of Japan) has contributed significantly to the effort by helping to fund the establishment of equipment stockpiles in Singapore and Port Kelang. Equipment stockpiles have also been established in Muara in Brunei Darussalam;

---

16 In 1992, 185.3 million tonnes of oil traversed the region on its way from the Middle East to Japan. See *British Petroleum Statistical Review of World Energy*, June 1993.

17 See Raja Malik Saripulazan Raja Kamarulzaman, 'ASEAN-OSRAP: Strengthening Regional Capabilities', paper presented at *1995 International Oil Spill Conference*, Long Beach, California, 27 February-2 March 1995.

18 See ibid.

Figure 6.1: Major and Alternative Routes for Supertankers from the Middle East to Markets in East Asia

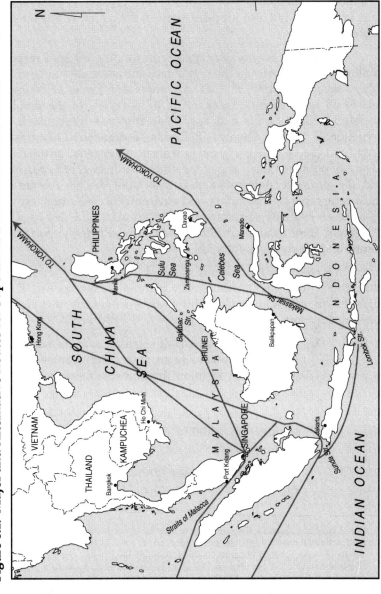

Source: Chia Lin Suien, 'Alternative Routes to the Straits of Malacca for Oil Tankers'.

Balikpapan in Indonesia; Port Kelang, Pulau Pinang, Johor Baru and Laboan in Malaysia; Manila, Cebu and Davao in the Philippines; as well as in the south of Thailand and in Singapore.[19] There is a need to find a more sustainable way of financing such projects, not only for the Straits of Malacca but also for other parts of the region where oil spills can occur.

Apart from issues associated with funding oil spill response activities, most countries in the region lack sufficient data to be able to analyse several parameters that are important for establishing an effective oil spill response mechanism. In its review of the problems associated with oil spills and applicable response mechanisms, the International Tanker Owners Pollution Federation Ltd. (ITOPF) pointed out the need to carry out 'a realistic assessment of the nature and size of possible threat, and of the other resources at risk, bearing in mind the probable movement of any oil spill'.[20] This requirement entails comprehensive economic and environment resource surveys as well as the availability of quality meteorological data. A case to note is the *Nagasaki Spirit* incident in 1992, which pointed to the importance of accurate and timely meteorological data.[21]

In reviewing the various national, regional and subregional arrangements for oil spill contingency planning and response, ITOPF suggested an easy-to-use ten-point framework which includes the following questions:

1   Has there been a realistic assessment of the nature and size of the possible threat, and of the resources most at risk, bearing in mind the probable movement of any oil spill?

2   Have priorities for protection been agreed, taking into account the viability of the various protection and clean-up options?

3   Has the strategy for protecting and cleaning the various areas been agreed and clearly explained?

---

19   See Akio Ono, 'Japan's Contribution to the Safety of Navigation and Pollution Mitigation Efforts in the Straits of Malacca', paper presented at the *Workshop on the Straits of Malacca*, Kuala Lumpur, 24-25 January 1995.

20   See International Tanker Owners Pollution Federation Ltd., *Response to Marine Oil Spills* (ITOPF Ltd., London, 1986).

21   Geoffrey Davison, Project Director, World Wide Fund for Nature Malaysia, pers. comms.

4   Has the necessary organisation been outlined and have the responsibilities of all those involved been clearly stated - will all who have a task to perform be aware of what is expected of them?

5   Are the levels of equipment, materials and manpower sufficient to deal with the anticipated size of spill? If not, have back-up resources been identified and, where necessary, have mechanisms for obtaining their release and entry to the country been established?

6   Have temporary storage sites and final disposal routes for collected oil and debris been identified?

7   Are the alerting and initial evaluation procedures fully explained as well as arrangements for continual review of the progress and effectiveness of the clean-up operation?

8   Have the arrangements for ensuring effective communication between shore, sea and air been described?

9   Have all aspects of the plan been tested and nothing significant found lacking?

10   Is the plan compatible with plans for adjacent areas and other activities?[22]

Recommendations

A review of the present arrangements for combating oil spills in the Southeast Asian region could provide the Maritime Working Group with a practical and useful project which could later be expanded to cover the whole of the Asia Pacific region. The existence of a number of bilateral and multilateral arrangements for combating oil spills is a good starting point for research into establishing a region-wide oil spill contingency plan. At the same time, the existence of regional institutional frameworks such as ASCOPE and ASEAN-OSRAP provides the Working Group with convenient sources of information and referral points for its research efforts.

---

[22] See International Tanker Owners Pollution Federation Ltd., *Response to Marine Oil Spills*.

The present regional arrangements can be examined within the wide framework suggested by ITOPF (see above) or, alternatively, more specific focus could be given for enhancing various aspects of oil spill response capabilities and navigational safety in the region; for example, by establishing a more sustainable funding mechanism for oil spill control and by improving operational effectiveness through joint training and exercises. The Maritime Working Group could undertake a project to identify mechanisms for an 'equitable burden-sharing' system for oil spill response and planning and navigational safety system between littoral states bordering the Straits of Malacca, and oil-importing states in East Asia, particularly those which are not contributing to the upkeep of the Straits of Malacca, such as Taiwan, China and Korea, as well as other Pacific nations which benefit from the movement of oil through the region.

Apart from the two ideas mentioned above, attention could also be focused on reviewing the present information database with a view to contributing towards the establishment of a regional data centre for oil spill contingency planning and response. Individual countries in the region are known to have prepared 'sensitivity maps' detailing areas vulnerable to oil spills. Data on coastal and marine resources can also be obtained from existing regional cooperation programmes such as the ASEAN-Australia Living Coastal Resources Project and the ASEAN-Canada Cooperative Programme on Marine Sciences.

Proposal Four: Regional Mechanisms for Protecting the Marine Environment from Land-Based Activities

The Global Programme of Action for the Protection of the Marine Environment from Land-Based Activities (the Washington Programme) noted in its perambulatory chapter that '(t)he major threats to the health and productivity and biodiversity of the marine environment result from human activities on land, in coastal areas and further inland'.[23] The threats mentioned are pollution from land-based sources (which constitutes nearly 80 per cent of all marine pollution) and physical alteration of coastal environments.[24] Based on this premise, the Washington Programme outlines strategies for national,

---

[23] See United Nations Environment Programme (UNEP), *Global Programme of Action for the Protection of the Marine Environment from Land-Based Activities* (UNEP, Nairobi, 1995).
[24] See ibid.

regional and international efforts for the protection of the marine environment from land-based threats, and the purpose of this proposal is to explore the opportunities for regional cooperation in minimising, preventing and eliminating land-based threats to the marine environment.

The task of protecting the marine environment from land-based activities in any region or area is a difficult one as it needs the cooperation of all countries sharing coastlines, semi-enclosed seas or straits in reducing or eliminating the impact of such activities on the marine environment. Non-performance on the part of one country could easily lead to the failure of regional, bilateral or multilateral programmes,[25] but regional success is possible, as illustrated by the achievements of the Mediterranean Action Plan.[26]

As far as the countries in the East Asian seas region are concerned, the task at hand is a difficult one. Of the thirteen regional seas programmes administered by the United Nations Environment Programme (UNEP), the East Asian seas region is described as being the most 'diverse'.[27] The diversity extends beyond just geographical or physical characteristics. Countries in the region also have a multitude of national laws for protecting the marine environment and possess varying institutional capabilities and capacity for protecting the marine environment from land-based activities.

Figure 6:2 shows the geographical distribution of the eight seas in the East Asian region. The wide geographical spread of the seas can hamper the effectiveness of a programme designed to achieve region-wide objectives of protecting the marine environment from land-based activities. Figure 6:2 also illustrates the potential for cooperation on a bilateral or maybe even multilateral basis for the protection of a particular sea in the region.

---

25 See Qing Nan Meng, *Land-based Marine Pollution: International Law Development* (Graham and Trotman, London, 1987).

26 See A. Vallega, 'ICCOPS International Workshop on Regional Seas Towards Sustainable Development - Challenges for Research and Policy' in Aldaberto Vallega *et al.* (eds), *Special Issue of ICCOPS Newsletter*, 1995.

27 See United Nations Environment Programme (UNEP), *Programme of Action to Control Land-Based Sources of Pollution in the East Asian Seas Region - Regional Report* (UNEP, Bangkok, 1994). The East Asian seas region covers an area which includes the seven ASEAN countries, as well as Cambodia, Myanmar and the People's Republic of China, with the South China Sea forming the largest body of water. In addition, the region also includes other seas, namely the Gulf of Thailand, Straits of Malacca, Java Sea, Banda Sea, Sulu Sea, Andaman Sea, parts of the Indian Ocean and the western Pacific Ocean.

Figure 6.2: East Asian Seas Region

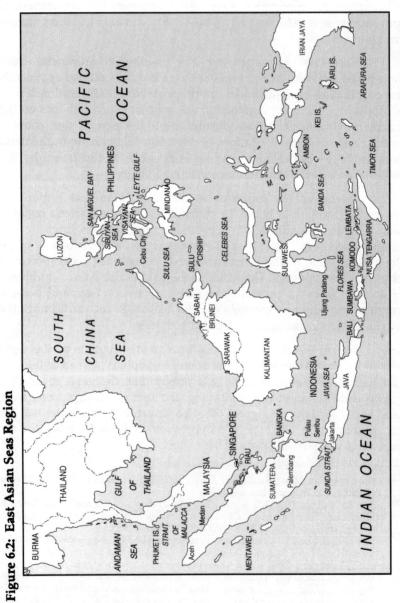

Source: United Nations Environment Programme, *Programme of Action to Control Land-Based Sources of Pollution Into East Asian Seas Region.*

The areas or seas where it would be possible for 'site-specific' protection efforts to be organised are:

- the Andaman Sea - bilateral effort between Thailand and Myanmar;

- the Straits of Malacca - multilateral effort between Indonesia, Malaysia, Singapore and possibly Thailand;

- the Straits of Singapore - bilateral effort between Malaysia and Singapore;

- the Gulf of Thailand - multilateral effort between Thailand, Cambodia and Vietnam; and to a lesser extent

- the Sulu Sea, where bilateral efforts could be established between Malaysia and the Philippines.

One of the best ways to ensure the success of the proposed programme structure is to incorporate it within a regional regime for the protection of the marine environment in the East Asian Seas. The regional convention, if accepted by countries in the region, should include protocols added for the site-specific efforts mentioned above and for the protection of the marine environment from land-based activities.[28] Examples of such regimes include the Mediterranean Action Plan,[29] the Paris Convention,[30] and the Lima Convention.[31]

However Meng noted that protection of the marine environment from land-based activities can be made difficult by issues of national sovereignty and the right to economic development, and it may be the case that countries in the region may not necessarily want to commit themselves to a legally binding instrument on land-based pollution.[32]

Some measure of regional protection can also be achieved if countries in the region ratify relevant international instruments for

---

[28] See Qing Nan Meng, *Land-based Marine Pollution.*

[29] See Adalberto Vallega, *Sea Management: A Theoretical Approach* (Elsevier Applied Science, London and New York, 1992).

[30] See United Nations Environment Programme (UNEP), *The Convention for the Prevention of Marine Pollution from Land-Based Sources* (UNEP, Nairobi, 1974). The Paris Convention, as it is known, was concluded on 4 June 1974 and involves States bordering the North Sea and Northern Atlantic and was the first international convention which focuses on land-based pollution.

[31] See Lima Convention for the Protection of the Marine Environment and Coastal Area of the South-East Pacific.

[32] See Qing Nan Meng, *Land-based Marine Pollution.*

protection of the marine environment from land-based activities such as the 1972 London Convention.[33]

Recommendations

The issue at hand presents the CSCAP Working Group with an excellent opportunity to assist in the development of a regional regime for the protection of the marine environment from land-based activities. It is recommended that the CSCAP Maritime Working Group undertake a study to examine the feasibility of developing a regional instrument for the protection of the marine environment in the region from land-based activities. The study could be undertaken in several phases.

The initial phase should focus on examining the willingness of countries in the region to commit themselves to a legal instrument for the protection of the marine environment from land-based and sea-based activities. The question is an important one, given the reluctance of many nations to commit themselves to a legally binding instrument for the protection of the marine environment from land-based activities.[34] In conducting the study, the CSCAP Maritime Working Group could obtain the assistance of the office of the East Asian Seas Programme as well as the ASEAN Senior Officials for the Environment Network (ASOEN).

Conclusions

The marine environment of the Asia Pacific region is a field already subject to wide-ranging study with many examples of cooperation and confidence building. Nonetheless, many opportunities remain unexplored for their potential in enhancing cooperation between the countries of the region and building confidence.

---

[33] See R. Coenen, 'Presentation Notes on the London Convention 1972', presented at the *Seminar on Prevention of Marine Pollution: The Implementation of Marpol 73/78 and the London Convention 1972*, 4 April 1996, Kuala Lumpur.

[34] The Global Programme of Action for the Protection of the Marine Environment from Land-Based Activities concluded in Washington DC is non-binding. However, some have argued that the Washington Programme carries some legal 'weight' given the recognition in the Washington Programme of the legal requirements for the protection of the marine environment from land-based activities contained in the United Nations Convention on the Law of the Sea (UNCLOS).

The four proposals suggested above are only a selection of the wide range of opportunities that exist for cooperation and confidence building in the field of the marine environment. They were selected more because of their interest to the writers than on any other criteria. Consequently, they may not be the 'best' or the 'most suitable' opportunities on offer, but they do, nonetheless, represent useful opportunities that the CSCAP Maritime Group might pursue.

CHAPTER 7

SLOC SECURITY - A JAPANESE PERSPECTIVE

Sumihiko Kawamura

Introduction

At present, economic development in the Asia Pacific region is the most dynamic in the world, and the economic well-being of the region is deeply dependent on seaborne trade. Coastal, intra- and inter-regional trade rely on seaborne transport, which is the most efficient and economical means of transporting large volume/heavy weight cargoes. Increased regional trade will result in increased economic interdependence. It is thus critical that the strategic importance of the major sea routes throughout the region be recognised by all regional states.

Since the end of the Cold War and the 1982 UN Convention on the Law of the Sea (UNCLOS III), which entered into force in November 1994, the importance of the maritime dimension of the Asia Pacific region, particularly Southeast Asia, has changed significantly. The end of the Cold War invited the emergence of some regional powers into the arena of regional security, and UNCLOS III gave regional states greater maritime responsibility. In order to comply with the requirement to conduct extensive patrol and law enforcement activities in the expanded areas of responsibility, regional states are required to enhance the capability of their maritime assets not only for detecting illegal activities in their areas of responsibility, but also for dealing with adversaries when required.

On the other hand, the supply of energy (oil and natural gas) is becoming more critical in the Asia Pacific region, particularly in East Asia, and it is likely to become a major security concern in a few years. Among Asian countries, SLOC (Sea Lines of Communication) security used to be only Japan's concern and was placed at the centre of Tokyo's foreign and economic policies, because Japan was utterly dependent on imported oil. But the issue of an adequate supply of energy is changing the maritime outlook of the Asia Pacific region dramatically. It is certain that the development of offshore energy resources will be of even greater interest as an alternative source of oil and natural gas. Furthermore, the SLOCs from the Persian Gulf will assume a much greater importance to almost all countries in the region because they are likely to need to import oil.

The SLOCs need to be protected, but no one country is self-sufficient in its capability to protect its own SLOCs. The ongoing disputes over natural resources and sovereignty of some islets in the South and East China Seas have the potential to spark open conflict. It is also certain that there are non-military threats such as piracy and marine pollution within the seas of the Asia Pacific region. Piracy is not only a concern for coastal states but for many ships that transit the region.

With regard to how to deal with piracy, experience shows that discussion and cooperation between and among the regional nations can facilitate effective anti-piracy measures, but I would like to emphasise the importance of the naval presence as a method of cracking down on piracy effectively. It should be remembered that Russia deployed naval ships, including a Kara-class missile cruiser, to the East China Sea in June 1993, with orders to attack any threats to shipping, after it had observed repeated live-fire attacks from late 1992 through early 1993 in the shipping lanes off the coast of the Chinese mainland. The number of incidents was dramatically reduced after the Russian naval deployment into the danger zone.

Marine pollution and the safety of maritime traffic will also be increasingly of concern to states having borders on straits and archipelagic countries of the region.

Maritime assets capable of monitoring and protecting the SLOCs are necessary as the volume of regional maritime traffic increases and the risk of non-military threats increases. But in this paper, I would like to concentrate only on military threats.

International Cooperative Scheme for SLOC Security

In order to encourage a widespread desire for at least some cooperation among countries in the region, a cooperative international scheme is desirable.

The development of an international cooperative scheme for SLOC security will aid the goal of deterring local conflicts and preserving regional stability. Moreover, such a scheme should have as its goal the freedom and safety of navigation to ensure smooth economic access to and within the region.

The new scheme should of course be organised on a burden-sharing basis. But the Asia Pacific region is not yet ready for a multilateral security arrangement for the following reasons. First, Asian diversity and absence of a common threat preclude a comprehensive mechanism from obtaining practical results. Second, regional security talks such as the ASEAN Regional Forum (ARF) are helpful, but it would seem they cannot substitute for more important bilateral arrangements. Third, there are problems arising from a lack of systems' inter-operability and of mutually held doctrine.

Consequently, a cooperative SLOC security framework should necessarily feature the following factors:

- retaining the United States as the core or the sole key strategic player in the region;

- a network of bilateral security arrangements between the United States and its regional partners;

- burden sharing by concerned states, particularly to complement US functional deficiencies.

In order to develop the most appropriate burden-sharing formula, I would like to proceed further with my discussion from two different viewpoints: function/capability and geographic area of responsibility.

Burden Sharing by Function/Capability

I would like to describe SLOC security roles in three operational capability categories:

- maintenance of sea control throughout the Pacific Ocean, including routes to the Indian Ocean and the Persian Gulf;

- protection of shipping, surveillance and search and rescue (SAR) in regional areas such as the North Pacific, South Pacific, or ANZAC region; and

- protection of shipping, surveillance and SAR in coastal waters.

Maintenance of Sea Control throughout the Pacific

Only the US Navy is viewed by Asian countries as sufficiently benign for and also as capable of maintaining sea control throughout the Pacific. Potential threats are numerous, but not well defined. However, as long as the United States is engaged, the US Navy can effectively deter or defeat any serious threat.

It is in the best interest of the United States to preserve peace and stability in the Pacific in order to serve US economic interests. US interests in the Asia Pacific region will remain similar to those the United States has pursued in the past, namely supporting global deterrence, preserving political and economic access, maintaining a balance of power to prevent the rise of a regional hegemony, and ensuring freedom of navigation.

A US naval presence has been the backbone of maintaining a strategic balance in the Pacific since the Second World War, and it is true that the continued US presence in the region makes crises less likely. Virtually all Asia Pacific countries, with only a few exceptions, want the United States to maintain a credible presence in order to prevent the creation of a vacuum which would result if it withdrew its naval strength. Any attempt by another state (such as China , India or Japan) to take the place of the American presence is likely to be unwelcome.

Therefore, for the foreseeable future, the US Navy remains the sole entity with the military capability and the sense of national purpose necessary to play a major role in bilateral military cooperation with its counterparts in the region.

Protection of Shipping and Surveillance in Regional Seas

Even though most regional navies are oriented toward coastal defence or other immediate sovereignty protection roles, together with the US Navy (USN), both the Royal Australian Navy (RAN) and the Japan Maritime Self-Defense Force (JMSDF) have sufficient capabilities for long-range surveillance and shipping protection.

In line with its 1981 commitment to protect its sea lanes up to 1,000 miles from Japanese territory, Japan is able to conduct regular maritime surveillance of its neighbouring seas and its sea lanes by utilising maritime patrol aircraft and naval vessels. While the rationale for the US-Japanese security alliance has changed after the end of the Cold War, the bilateral security pact's importance remains high. The alliance provides a reciprocal basis for promoting stability throughout the Northeast Pacific, and Japan has sufficient capability to take responsibility for shipping protection and surveillance under the umbrella of overall sea control provided by the US Navy.

In the South Pacific or ANZAC region, Australia is the most suitable nation, from the viewpoint of capability and national will, to take responsibility for regional shipping protection and surveillance.

Protection of Shipping and Surveillance in Coastal Areas

Shipping protection and surveillance in the coastal regions must be borne by littoral states, in addition to those nations' non-military maritime roles such as the management of maritime laws, the protection of the marine environment and the security of offshore areas under national jurisdiction.

From a geopolitical viewpoint, each country can play an important role in SLOC security because its proximate location enables it to control local sea traffic. The 200-mile Exclusive Economic Zone (EEZ) and the proclamation of archipelagic waters by various regional states have led to a significant expansion in the area of responsibility of regional states.

Surveillance and law enforcement activities in these areas require maritime assets sufficiently capable of dealing with adversaries when required. In a perceived environment of decreasing American military presence within the region, self-reliance is a powerful motive for regional countries, particularly Southeast Asian countries, to modernise their defence forces, especially their navies, which were the least developed of their military forces during the Cold War.

The regional countries can contribute to global SLOC security by providing security in their areas of responsibility and by ensuring US access to and within the region. The responsibility of each regional country can be enhanced by cooperation with the key strategic player (the United States). Such cooperation can be achieved on a role-sharing basis by supplementing deficiencies in the US Navy's capability with the complementary capabilities possessed by the regional states.

As to the capabilities that the regional states can offer, I would like to suggest mine countermeasure capability as one of the most appropriate examples. As we have seen during two recent periods in the Persian Gulf, mines were effective in denying foreign vessels access. The use by potential adversaries of mines can also seriously disrupt trade and naval operations.

At present, with more than 30 countries involved in the development, manufacture and sale of mines, it is of great concern that mine technology poses a low-cost method for rogue nations to thwart safe and free maritime transportation and naval operations in the future. There is an obvious danger that these proliferating arsenals of mines could be used to drastically disrupt passage of ships including tankers - a fact not lost on the regional states, whose supplies of oil and sea transportation would be seriously jeopardised by even minor mine-laying activities.

Consequently, in terms of promoting interdependence between the United States and regional states, the improvement of mine countermeasure capabilities would seem to be a high priority for regional maritime forces for the following three reasons. First, at present, only a few if any minesweepers are generally assigned to the US Seventh Fleet on a regular basis. Second, minesweepers are perhaps the most inherently defensive combatant ship class that exists, and an increase in the number of minesweepers will not foment fears of a military build-up among neighbouring countries. Third, in terms of both cost and time, it is much easier to build up mine countermeasure forces than it is to build up any other maritime capability.

Burden Sharing by Areas of Responsibility

With regard to burden sharing in terms of geographic areas of responsibility, I would like to clarify the most appropriate force assignments for achieving SLOC security.

For the purpose of this discussion I would like to employ the same geographical regions as those used by Australia's Michael O'Connor in his paper for the 1986 SLOC Conference, namely:

- The North Pacific region - that area bounded by the mainland of Asia to the west, the International Date Line to the east, the 20 degrees North latitude to the south, and the 60 degrees North latitude to the north.

- The ASEAN region - that area bounded by the mainland of Asia and the 80 degrees East meridian to the west, thence south to the Tropic of Capricorn, east to the Australian mainland, north and east along the Australian coast to a latitude of 10 degrees South and a longitude of 141 degrees East, thence north by the border of Indonesia and Papua New Guinea to the Equator, thence east to the International Date Line, north to a latitude of 20 degrees North, thence west to the mainland of Asia.

- The ANZAC region - all the sea area south and east of the ASEAN region and bounded on the north by the Equator and east by the International Date Line. (See Figure 7:1.)

The United States-Japan Mutual Security Treaty, designed as a Cold War instrument, seems to have a new life even though the 'enemy' has virtually disappeared. While the security treaty should be continued, other countries in the Asia Pacific region should pay more for part of the US presence. The concept of Japan as 'host nation' to the US forces should be expanded. Since the Asia Pacific countries want the US naval presence, they should develop a 'host region' framework for cooperation to maintain the continued US presence in the region.

Overall sea control throughout the Pacific is the role of the United States. Under the auspices of this, the RAN and the JMSDF can conduct long-range maritime surveillance and protection of shipping in large open ocean areas. Judging by its geographic proximity to the operating area, Australia is the logical candidate for

Figure 7.1: Map showing the North Pacific, ASEAN and ANZAC Regions

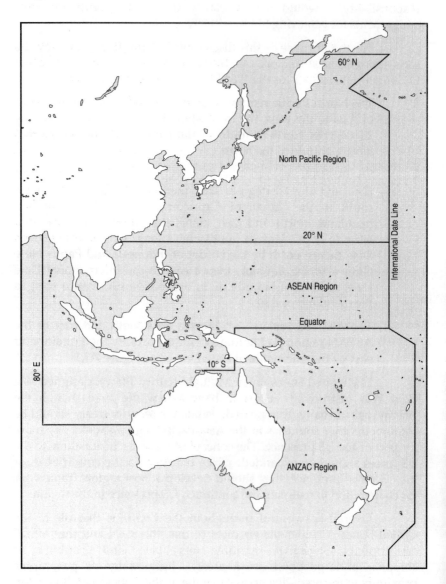

responsibility in the ANZAC region, while Japan should take responsibility in the North Pacific region.

Responsibility for surveillance and protection of shipping within the littoral waters must by borne by the rest of the regional states in the form of bilateral security arrangements on a role-sharing basis.

Conclusion

The security of maritime transport and communication is of vital importance to the prosperity and well-being of the regional countries. It is very desirable that every country bear its share of responsibility by accepting a role in the important task of assuring SLOC security.

In this paper, I have proposed some ideas concerning the common objectives that regional states can share and I have outlined some of the benefits to their national interests that might flow from such international cooperation.

I believe it is very important to both discuss and implement measures that will ensure stability in the region and enable the region to cope with threats such as the interruption of free passage in important international straits, as was exemplified by the trying experiences of the Gulf War.

Even though there are likely to be many difficulties in realising an effective maritime cooperative framework, the potential rewards are significant.

CHAPTER 8

MARITIME INFORMATION AND DATA EXCHANGE

Sam Bateman

Introduction

Arrangements for the exchange of marine or maritime[1] information and data are both:

- a potential maritime confidence- and security-building measure (MCSBM) in their own right, due to the dialogue and cooperation involved in their establishment; and

- a prerequisite or 'building block' for other forms of maritime security cooperation which have been suggested in recent years, including maritime surveillance and sea level/climate monitoring.[2]

The compilation of databases of maritime information, and the exchange of such information between different users and collectors of data, have been facilitated by the tremendous advances in information technology which have occurred in recent years, making the storage, exchange and manipulation of data much easier. Digital maritime databases, for example, may contain an array of hydrographic, oceanographic, geographic, shipping route and traffic, port infrastructure and marine incident (such as groundings, collisions, piratical attacks) data which can be analysed for trends, causal relationships, and so on, with considerable benefits in terms of reduced costs and more effective management of marine industries,

---

1   This paper treats 'marine' and 'maritime' as synonyms (both meaning 'pertaining to the sea') and thus sets aside the tendency in some parts of the world to restrict 'maritime' to shipping and navigational issues. Hence the terms 'marine' or 'maritime' data, as used in this paper, encompass all information related to the sea, seabed, marine resources, and activities at sea.

2   'The ASEAN Regional Forum - A Concept Paper' in Desmond Ball and Pauline Kerr, *Presumptive Engagement: Australia's Asia-Pacific Security Policy in the 1990s* (Allen & Unwin, Sydney, 1996), pp.111-19.

enhanced oceans governance, better marine safety and improved monitoring of the marine environment generally.

The aim in establishing marine/maritime information systems and databases is to present the best data available, in the form of statistics, reports and maps, to the users of such material - that is, the managers, policy advisers, decision makers and strategic planners. In conventional military security terms, the utility of geographic information systems (GISs)[3] for defence planning and operations has long been recognised. The components of a GIS, or indeed any other data system, comprise the data inputs (such as maps, tables, field observations, remote sensor data); the GIS database management facility, providing for the storage, merging, manipulation and analysis of data; and the outputs in the form of maps, reports, statistics, and so on.[4] In the context of the maritime dimension of comprehensive security, recognition of the importance of ideas such as sustainable development and integrated coastal and marine zone management has had a profound impact on the need for marine/maritime information and how we use that information.

The quality of the product from a GIS, or any other data system, depends on the quality of the data inputs, and obviously this will be much better if as many sources as possible are used. These sources include other databases and collectors of relevant data, both nationally and internationally. Thus the full benefits of maintaining databases and information systems will only be realised if there is a preparedness to share information, both between national entities and between countries on a regional basis. Knowledge about the availability of data, or what is referred to as *metadata* ('information about data'), is a useful starting point.

The concept of *regionalisation* is particularly important to ensure that the information system is kept to a manageable size, and to provide some focus to its output. Boundaries of the region covered by

---

3   A geographical information system (GIS) may be defined 'as a system which facilitates the storage and intelligent use of geographic data - that is, data about land and water resources and human activities which use these resources'. See Desmond Ball, 'Introduction' in Desmond Ball and Ross Babbage (eds), *Geographic Information Systems: Defence Applications* (Brassey's Australia, Sydney, 1989), p.1.

4   K.J. Lyons, O.F. Moss and P. Perrett, 'Geographic Information Systems' in Ball and Babbage (eds), *Geographic Information Systems*, p.17.

the information system or database may be defined in terms of the strategic, economic, physical, chemical, biological or geological characteristics of the particular environment, depending on the purpose or function of the information system. It is particularly significant for this paper that these boundaries invariably are not related to national boundaries, and that an information system restricted to national inputs only will provide inferior output.

After first describing some key concepts, this paper discusses the factors which establish the importance of maritime information exchange and databases in the Asia Pacific region. It outlines what is involved with these processes, along with examples of regional databases, before concluding with some thoughts on the possible way ahead. It proposes a widening of the scope of maritime information and data exchange in the region and affirms the need to overcome some of the political sensitivities which inhibit the more comprehensive exchange of maritime and marine data in the region at present.

Concepts

Sustainable Development

The sea and the sustainable development of its resources are important economic interests of most countries in the Asia Pacific region, along with the general dependence of the region on seaborne trade and the keen regional interest in coastal zone management. The broad agenda for the sustainable development of the coastal and oceans environments of the world, including their living resources, is contained in Chapter 17 of *Agenda 21*, agreed at the United Nations Conference on Environment and Development (UNCED) in Rio de Janeiro in 1992.[5] This builds on the regime for managing the oceans

---

5   United Nations Conference on Environment and Development (UNCED), Chapter 17: 'Protection of the Oceans, All Kinds of Seas, Including Enclosed and Semi-enclosed Seas, and Coastal Areas and the Protection, Rational Use and Development of their Living Resources' in *Agenda 21*, UNCED, Rio de Janeiro, 3-14 June 1992.

and seas of the world established by the 1982 UN Convention on the Law of the Sea (UNCLOS).

Chapter 17 of *Agenda 21* provides a long list of what countries ought to do in the following programme areas:

• integrated management and sustainable development of coastal areas, including exclusive economic zones;

• marine environmental protection;

• sustainable use and conservation of marine living resources of the high seas;

• sustainable use and conservation of marine living resources under national jurisdiction;

• addressing critical uncertainties for the management of the marine environment and climate change;

• strengthening international, including regional, cooperation and coordination; and

• sustainable development of small islands.

A particular difficulty of coastal and marine zone management, relevant to this paper, relates to the uncertainty of the data which is available as an input to the process. Section (E) of Chapter 17 of *Agenda 21*, for example, notes the vulnerability of the marine environment to climate and atmospheric changes and that the rational use and development of coastal and marine areas require better information on the present state of these systems and the ability to predict future conditions.[6] Globally, there is a continuous and gradual concentration of human populations towards urban complexes on or close to the coast. The geographic nature of the Asia Pacific region is such that coastal zone development is a priority of most regional countries.

Technical Cooperation and Capacity Building

The actions required by Chapter 17 of *Agenda 21* are complex, innovative and well beyond the capabilities of most countries. Developing countries in particular face considerable difficulties in developing their capacities to fulfil their obligations under Chapter 17

---

6   ibid., para.17.97.

and to follow sustainable development paths. The guidance to assist developing countries in capacity building is provided by Chapter 37 of Agenda 21.[7] This chapter contains the following description of the process of capacity building:

> Specifically, capacity-building encompasses the country's human, scientific, technological, organisational, institutional and resource capabilities. A fundamental goal of capacity-building is to enhance the ability to evaluate and address the crucial questions related to policy choices and modes of implementation among development options, based on an understanding of environmental potentials and limits and of needs as perceived by the people of the country concerned.[8]

Capacity building in developing countries requires cooperation between these countries and relevant United Nations organisations, regional associations and developed countries, as well as among the developing countries themselves. The aim of this process is to enhance the capacities of developing countries in the areas of data and information, scientific and technological means and human resource development. In summary, capacity is usually regarded as including at least three elements: human resources, institutions and enabling environment.

Chapter 37 of *Agenda 21* goes on to note that:

> Technical cooperation, including that related to technology transfer and know-how, encompasses the whole range of activities to develop or strengthen individual and group capacities and capabilities.[9]

Technical cooperation involves moving beyond the exhortative language of documents such as *Agenda 21* to the identification and implementation of practical measures which will assist developing countries with integrated management and sustainable development. The benefits of technical cooperation accrue not only to the developing countries which are the recipients of the assistance, but also to the

---

7   Chapter 37: 'National Mechanisms and International Cooperation for Capacity-Building in Developing Countries' in UNCED, *Agenda 21*.
8   ibid., para. 37.1.
9   ibid., para. 37.2.

entire international community as a result of the overall better management of the world's oceans and seas at all levels - global, regional and national.

The establishment of comprehensive databases and the ongoing collection of data are important elements of the national capacity for the effective development and management of all marine and coastal zones. These processes are facilitated by regional cooperation, but the capabilities of developing countries in this regard are limited, and the programmes that do exist depend heavily on the skills and capabilities of the developed countries (for example, the International Oceanographic Data Exchange or IODE programme).

There are strong incentives for all countries to build their capacity in data and information collection and to participate more actively in relevant programmes. Some regional countries are particularly vulnerable to weather- and climate-induced natural disasters, such as tropical storms, floods and tsunamis, as well as the potential for climates to change and sea levels to rise in the longer term. The capability to deal with these phenomena is markedly enhanced by involvement in the necessary research and data collection. Moreover, the information acquired is important to much economic activity, including the exploitation of resources and tourism developments.

Part III of the 1982 UNCLOS requires states to promote marine scientific research and to cooperate with regard to the conduct of such research. The flow of information and technical cooperation between countries is required by Article 244(2) of UNCLOS, which states:

> ... States, both individually and in co-operation with other States and with competent international organisations, shall actively promote the flow of scientific data and information and the transfer of knowledge resulting from marine scientific research, especially to developing States, as well as the strengthening of the autonomous marine scientific research capabilities of developing States through, *inter alia,*

programmes to provide adequate education and training of their technical and scientific personnel.[10]

Major programmes for the research and monitoring of the world's oceans and seas are carried out under the auspices of the Intergovernmental Oceanographic Commission (IOC) and the World Meteorological Organisation (WMO).

At the regional level, *Agenda 21* encourages cooperation on the exchange of marine data:

> States should use existing subregional and regional mechanisms, where applicable, to develop knowledge of the marine environment, exchange information, organise systematic observations and assessments, and make the most effective use of scientists, facilities and equipment.[11]

Regional organisations offer numerous advantages for the management of marine areas: better scope for cross-fertilisation of ideas with the 'local knowledge' of regional needs and conditions; a stronger bargaining position for dealing with extra-regional ocean users and donors; and the scope for regional trans-sectoral organisations to promote integrated regional ocean management.[12]

Marine Informatics

It has been suggested that the importance of maritime information and databases to the sustainable development of marine and coastal areas could even lead to a new discipline of *marine informatics*, which would involve studying how to supply decision makers with the types of high-quality integrated information they require to make decisions on complex issues of sustainable development.[13] The problems involved include the difficulties that the necessary information may not be available or, if it is available, it may be widely scattered throughout the country or overseas, and even then

---

10 United Nations, *The Law of the Sea: Official Text on the Convention on the Law of the Sea*, UN Doc A/CONF. 62/122, UN Sales No. E.83.v.5. (1983), Art.244 (2).
11 UNCED, *Agenda 21*, para. 17.115.
12 Lee Kimball, 'International Law and Institutions: The Oceans and Beyond', *Ocean Development and International Law*, Vol.20, 1989, note 24, p.158.
13 Roger Bradbury, 'Marine Informatics: A New Discipline Emerges', *Maritime Studies*, No.80, January/February 1995, pp.15-22.

it must be integrated and displayed in such a manner that it can be understood by the decision maker.

The flow of information required for sustainable development of the marine environment can be shown as involving a series of stages such as those in Table 8:1. Relevant tools include databases, directories, geographic information systems and decision support systems. The data will come from many sources, including hydrological and oceanographic surveys, geological surveys, environmental monitoring, statistical surveys and population censuses, and remote sensing. Baselines must be established and long-term historical data obtained by whatever means possible. Overall the types of task involved are quite beyond the means of most developing countries, and yet the availability of such data is essential for the processes of option identification and decision making. Networks are particularly useful for addressing the data and information needs of either specific issues (for example, coastal erosion, mangroves and coral reefs) or particular management strategies (such as geographical information systems, marine parks and environmental impact statements).[14]

Table 8:1: Information Flow for Sustainable Development

Stage	Description
acquiring	gathering the information to required standards
managing	organising and storing the information in a database
accessing	making the information available for others
integrating	bringing different sorts of information together
enhancing	manipulating and analysing the information to create new information
visualising	displaying the integrated information as images
assessing	analysis of the policy implications of the scientific and economic information

Source: Roger Bradbury, 'Marine Informatics: A New Discipline Emerges', *Maritime Studies*, No.80, January/February 1995, p.16.

---

[14] Jens Sorensen, 'The International Proliferation of Integrated Coastal Zone Management Efforts', *Ocean and Coastal Management*, Vol.21, No.1/3, 1993, p.65.

Global Ocean Observing System[15]

The Global Ocean Observing System (GOOS) is now the major global entity for monitoring, modelling and forecasting the state of the world's oceans and seas. GOOS is a global initiative, supported by the Intergovernmental Oceanographic Commission (IOC), the World Meteorological Organisation (WMO), the United Nations Environment Programme (UNEP), and the International Council of Scientific Unions (ICSU). All coastal states are encouraged to participate, with partnerships where possible between developed and developing countries. GOOS represents the culmination of several large coordinated marine scientific research programmes which have been established during the last two decades and have involved expenditures of many tens of millions of dollars by participating countries.[16]

GOOS emphasises the close link between meteorology, as the science dealing with the atmosphere and associated phenomena, and oceanography as the science concerned with the study of the oceans, including the movement of water, temperature, density and salinity variation. The monitoring of ocean conditions is an important activity both in a short-term sense, because of the impact of these conditions on regional weather and climate, and in a long-term sense, because of the need to improve the capability to predict climate and atmospheric changes and the implications for rising sea levels.

Monitoring of the marine environment by the collection of data on the world's oceans has a long history, 'but in recent years it has assumed a more rigorous form, partly in response to an increasing demand for data on which to base regulation and control measures for pollution, and partly thanks to the development of sophisticated

---

15   The information in this section is primarily from the Organisation for Economic Cooperation and Development (OECD), *Oceanography* (Megascience: The OECD Forum, OECD, Paris, 1994).

16   Significant programmes include: the World Climate Research Programme (WCRP) established in 1979 with substantial marine components; the Tropical Ocean Global Atmosphere (TOGA) experiment (1984-94); the World Ocean Circulation Experiment (WOCE)(1990-97); and the Joint Global Ocean Flux Study (JGOFS), sponsored by the ICSU and running from 1991 to 2000.

technology'.[17] The need for pollution monitoring is determined by the increased risks of pollution by contaminants from a wide range of sources: from rivers, from land-based discharges, from shipping, from offshore operations and from the atmosphere.

New satellite technology has become available in recent years which provide oceanographers with real-time pictures that are, in effect, weather charts of ocean currents and eddies. These improve the older techniques in which currents are inferred from satellite-measured sea surface temperatures. By measuring the height of the sea surface, using radar altimeters on board a satellite, together with satellite readings of sea surface temperatures and tracking drift buoys, scientists are able to predict current and ocean movement, including unpredictable eddies.

The applications of GOOS, and the requirements for different data types and forecasts to solve different problems, are being specified by a series of modules as follows.

• *Climate.* Predicting and forecasting climate beyond a period of about ten days requires a capacity to understand and predict ocean processes.

• *Health of the Ocean.* This module is concerned with processes or contaminants which adversely change the state or balance of the ocean. These include changes in temperature or salinity or currents, which alter ecosystems; changes in the supply of nutrients or pollutants; and changes in biological productivity or balance, such as the growth of toxic algal blooms.

• *Coastal and Shelf Seas.* This module provides data to monitor the impact of forces from the open ocean on the coastal zone. The coastal zone is the area of the earth's surface most intensively subjected to exploitation, pressure from industry, and waste products and is the source of the greatest problems regarding the management of resources and conflicts of interest.

---

17   A.D. Macintyre, 'Environmental Monitoring of the Oceans', *Marine Policy*, Vol.19, No.6, 1995, p.497.

- *Ocean Services.* Improved marine forecasts for parameters such as wave conditions, currents, sea ice, wind and sea level, including warnings of severe and extreme weather, and specialised global and regional oceanographic and meteorological services are needed to improve shipping, tourism, marine recreation, the safety of life at sea, and the exploration or exploitation of seabed mineral resources.

- *Marine Living Resources.* In recognition of the significant impact of changes in physical oceanographic phenomena (such as currents, temperature and salinity) on marine life, this module will define the requirements for data and products from GOOS of those industries extracting marine living resources, and of related biological activities and research.

The OECD has estimated that the overall benefit-cost ratio for GOOS is, to a first-order rough estimate, approximately 10:1 to 20:1, with absolute benefits in the order of US$ 8 to 10 billion per year.[18] Particular benefits flow from:[19]

- improved efficiency, reduction of costs, and improved management of the marine environment (for example, the pay-offs to fishing fleets from improved coastal weather predictions);

- enhanced prediction, and mitigation of the effects, of hazards, risks and disasters associated with hurricanes, storm surges, massive coastal erosion, earthquakes, tsunamis, major oil spills, shipwrecks and extreme occurrences of toxic algal blooms;

- enhanced knowledge of the variability of climate, El Nino Southern Oscillation, and decadal variation, which lead to better forecasts for agriculture and better knowledge of global warming and climate change; and

[18] N.C. Flemming, 'Analytical Report' in OECD, *Oceanography*, p.120.
[19] ibid., pp.112-19.

•   insurance against highly improbable and extreme events, such as major erosion of the base of the Antarctic ice shelves, which could be triggered by global climate change.

The IOC Sub-Commission for the Western Pacific (WESTPAC) is taking steps towards the implementation of GOOS in the Asia Pacific region. Many WESTPAC programmes are, directly or indirectly, related to GOOS. A regional component, the North-East Asian Regional-GOOS (NEAR-GOOS), was established in 1994 and one of its aims is to share the data observed in the marginal seas surrounded by Russia, China, Korea and Japan.[19] An objective of WESTPAC is to expand the regional GOOS to the entire WESTPAC region.

The Importance of Maritime Data in the Asia Pacific Region

There are two other factors which should be mentioned as particular features of the Asia Pacific region which highlight the importance of marine information and data exchange in the region. The first is the complex maritime geography of the region, and the second is its particular vulnerability to marine accidents, with many focal areas and choke points where there is a high density of shipping traffic.

Geographical Factors

Along the eastern coastline of Asia, there is a continuous chain of enclosed or semi-enclosed seas between the mainland and the off-lying archipelagoes and islands, stretching from Sakhalin and the Kamchatka Peninsula through the Japanese archipelago and the Philippines to the Indonesian archipelago and northern Australia. The situation is then further complicated by the numbers of groups of island within these seas, such as the Senkaku, Paracel and Spratly islands, which are the subject of sovereignty disputes. The maritime

---

19   Keisuke Taira, 'Message From Chairman', *WESTPAC Information*, No.4, May 1996, p.1 (*WESTPAC Information* is published by the IOC Sub-Commission for the Western Pacific).

geography of this region has great strategic significance and underpins the fundamental importance of regional maritime cooperation.

As a consequence of the extended jurisdiction allowed by UNCLOS (that is, a twelve nautical mile territorial sea, two hundred mile EEZs, and archipelagic waters for Indonesia, the Philippines and other archipelagic states), a large portion of the ocean environment of East Asia consists of territorial seas (and conflicting or overlapping claims to territorial waters), resource-rich EEZs with *their* conflicting claims, and vital straits and choke points for shipping. Achieving straight-line maritime boundaries and clear sovereign jurisdiction over maritime areas in such a region, with its complex maritime geography, is an extraordinarily difficult task and management of these seas is inevitably going to require a high degree of regional cooperation.

The regional seas of East Asia are also relatively complex in oceanographic and hydrographic terms, with plentiful marine life, uneven bottom topography, and sometimes fast currents and tidal streams. Comprehensive knowledge of regional seas is essential for resource development, navigational safety and marine environmental management, as well as for naval operations such as submarine operations, anti-submarine warfare and mine countermeasures. Cooperation in regional marine scientific research, and the exchange of relevant data, are essential because ecosystems and oceanographic features vary so much from one area to another and are not part of the sole jurisdiction of any one country.

Marine Safety

Incidents such as the grounding of the *Exxon Valdez* in Alaska, the foundering of the Greek *Aegean Sea* off the northwest coast of Spain, the breaking up of the Liberian *Braer* off the Shetland Islands, and the burning of the Danish-owned *Maersk Navigator* near the northern entrance to the Malacca Strait, have highlighted the risks to the marine environment posed by the carriage of dangerous or hazardous cargoes at sea. While these particular ships may not have been judged to be unsafe by international standards, the catastrophes that befell them have drawn attention to the problems of unsafe ships at sea and have led to tighter international controls over shipping, as well as providing an incentive for regional cooperation to achieve the objective of 'safer ships and cleaner seas'.

These high-profile marine accidents attract considerable publicity, but they need to be kept in perspective as a source of marine pollution. They account for about 30 to 40 per cent of ship-generated oil pollution of the oceans, with intentional activities (such as bilge-pumping and tank-cleaning) accounting for the remainder.[21] In turn, ship operations are responsible for only about 30 per cent of marine pollution, with the remainder due to land-based sources (both run-off and atmospheric fall-out), natural seepage and offshore production.

The reduction of the risks of marine pollution from shipping and the enhancement of marine safety require systematic consideration of the geography of shipping routes, ship types and cargoes, as well as identification of the more sensitive marine environments, such as mangrove coasts and coral reefs in the tropics.[22] As a consequence of economic development in the Asia Pacific region, shipping traffic has grown significantly in the region, particularly along the route from the Straits of Malacca and Singapore to Northeast Asia. A major feature of this growth has been the increased carriage of hazardous cargoes by sea, especially chemicals.

Examples of Regional Marine Databases

Indonesia

As a large archipelagic nation with many islands and an extensive Exclusive Economic Zone rich in marine resources, both living and non-living, Indonesia is concentrating much of its development effort on its marine and coastal areas. This is being managed through the Marine Resource Evaluation and Planning (MREP) project, which includes development of the Indonesian Marine Resources Information Database (IMRID). The MREP project covers

---

21 Ronald Mitchell, 'Intentional Oil Pollution of the Oceans' in Peter M. Haas, Robert O. Keohane and Marc A. Levy (eds), *Institutions for the Earth: Sources of Effective Environmental Protection* (MIT Press, Cambridge, Mass., 1993), p.289.

22 For a discussion of the requirements of effective environmental management of shipping, see Hance D. Smith, 'The Environmental Management of Shipping', *Marine Policy*, Vol.19, No.6, 1995, pp.503–8.

ten Marine Coastal Management Areas (MCMAs) and three Special Marine Areas (SMAs).

IMRID includes data collected from various agencies and comprises raster data (such as picture, aerial photos and satellite imagery), vector data (for example, bathymetric maps, contour lines) and alphanumeric data (such as data types, plankton data, salinity data, tables). It is grouped into five different classes: marine geology; hydro-oceanography: socioeconomic; flora, fauna and habitat; and marine activities. IMRID data is subject to a data security classifications (that is, top secret, secret, classified and open-file through which the retrieval and access of data is controlled by the Indonesian Armed Forces Headquarters.

Australia

A national inventory of marine data sets is being developed in Australia at present. This inventory is called the Australian Marine Data Inventory (AMIDI) which is part of an overall National Marine Information System (NATMIS) that is being developed as part of the Ocean Rescue 2000 project which is aimed at protecting and managing Australia's marine resources. The term 'marine data' is interpreted widely and loosely, with marine data 'ranging from documents on managerial strategies for pharmacological exploitation of benthic invertebrates on abyssal plains through to trace metal chemistry studies in mangrove swamps'.[23] AMIDI does not contain the specific data sets themselves, rather it holds information about the data: what was collected, where, when, how, by whom and what has been done to it (that is, it is an example of *metadata*).

NATMIS is an umbrella term for several on-line marine and coastal initiatives, disseminating the information via the Internet (the World Wide Web). The aim is to establish a national network of linked sites whereby agencies will maintain and update their own data and information with answers available to key questions such as:

---

[23]   Ocean Rescue 2000, *Australian Marine Data Inventory - An Interim Guide to the Supporting Information - Document 3*, Version 2.0 dated August 1995, p.2.

- What is the current state of Australia's marine and coastal environment?

- Where can information be found on marine and coastal issues?

- What are the main regions and habitats, and where do they occur?

- Where do endangered species occur, and are they conserved?

- How can the effects of pollution be minimised?

- What are the indicator species for marine and coastal degradation?

NATMIS has four main components:

- Coastal and Marine Data Directory
  - Directory of Australian marine data holdings
  - Linkages to the designated custodian agency
  - Network linkages connect directly to data custodians

- Australian Coastal Atlas
  - User-friendly Australian coastal geographic information system/on-line atlas, containing summary-level processed information such as photos, maps, images and summary text (as used by the majority of users, managers, policy makers and community groups)
  - Available through the Internet
  - Input from policy, management and research agencies as to content

- Marine Data Standards Coordination
  - Development and synthesis of appropriate standards for marine data
  - Information to be made available on-line

- CoastNet

  - On-line information to enhance communication between coastal policy makers, coastal managers, researchers and other coastal interest groups. This will include providing access to the Coastal Atlas, the Coastal and Marine Data Directory, CouncilNet, and the ERIN On-line Service.

Strategic Maritime Information System

The Strategic Maritime Information System (SMIS) is being developed by the Information Technology Division of the Australian Defence Science and Technology Organisation (DSTO). It is a database of open-source, maritime information covering Southeast Asian and Australian waters, including map depictions, maritime boundaries, reports of incidents at sea, port details, data on some 32,000 merchant ships over 1,000 GRT which operate in the region, major routes and shipping movements.

The ability to manipulate data related to trade routes and shipping traffic densities is one useful attribute of SMIS. Data sets from Lloyd's are used in SMIS which record all voyages that terminate at any port within the region covered by SMIS over a specified period, by detailing the port, calling vessel and arrival date, plus ports and dates of last departure and next destination. While these data sets do not include details of the actual passage or route used, these can be interpolated using waypoint sequences, abstracted from recommended routeing charts. This information, when matched with the subsets of vessel and port details, can be manipulated to produce data, for example, on traffic densities along the busiest regional routes both in aggregate and for various types of ships - for example, tankers, container vessels, LNG/LPG carriers. Such information is of great utility for tasks related to marine safety and the environmental management of shipping, including monitoring the risks of marine pollution.

Conclusions

Acceptance of the ideas of sustainable development and integrated coastal and marine zone management has a profound impact on the need for marine information and how we use that information. The availability of appropriate data is a prerequisite for the effective development and management of all marine and coastal zones, and countries in the Asia Pacific region have strong incentives to cooperate with regard to the collection and exchange of maritime information.

The maritime geography and oceanography of the Asia Pacific region are such that no one country, using its own resources, will be able to develop an adequate database of maritime information to develop its offshore resources and manage its maritime interests in an effective and sustainable fashion without cooperation with its neighbours. In addition to the direct national advantages of cooperation, all countries who are parties to UNCLOS and *Agenda 21* have an obligation to cooperate on the management of regional seas, including a responsibility to report on the state of their marine environments. In the security context, marine data and information exchange is an important MSCBM.

Despite the importance of pursuing information and data exchange programmes, there are numerous complications and problems to overcome. First, the development of geographic information systems and databases is very dynamic. It is an area of rapid technological development with new technologies providing new means of gathering, storing, manipulating, transmitting and displaying the data, and inevitably different countries will be using different levels of technology. Second, coordination is difficult in view of the number of government departments and research agencies, both national and international, involved. Third, the issue is potentially sensitive both in commercial terms, and with regard to naval operations in view of the relationship with submarine operations, anti-submarine warfare and mine countermeasures. Fourth, the complicated situation with regard to maritime jurisdiction and unresolved maritime boundaries may make countries less willing to cooperate, in case they are perceived to be compromising their own sovereignty. Lastly, there seems to be still a general lack of appreciation of the complexities of the marine environments and of the importance of sound scientific knowledge and comprehensive data to its management. In short, marine scientists may still 'have a message to get across'.

CHAPTER 9

EXCLUSIVE ECONOMIC ZONE AND MARITIME BOUNDARY DELIMITATIONS IN NORTHEAST ASIA

Jin-Hyun Paik

Introduction

For the purpose of the paper, the East Asian region may be divided into two subregions, Northeast Asia and Southeast Asia, based on the geographic and other features related to maritime boundary delimitation. Currently there are three maritime boundary agreements in force in the Northeast Asian area.[1] The geographic circumstances of the area require the conclusion of a few more bilateral and trilateral agreements to complete the maritime boundaries in this area. Yet two territorial disputes over the ownership of tiny offshore islets, one between Korea and Japan over the Dokdo Islands (Takeshima in Japanese) and the other between Japan and China over the Senkaku Islands (Tiao'yutai in Chinese), make the conclusion of boundary agreements extremely difficult, if not impossible.[2]

However, two recent developments have made maritime boundary delimitation in Northeast Asia a real and pressing issue. First, on 16 November 1994, the 1982 Convention on the Law of the Sea (UNCLOS) entered into force, together with the provisional application of the 1994 Agreement (Implementing Agreement), created

---

[1]   The first boundary in the region was delimited between South Korea and Japan in the continental shelf area through the Korea Strait north of Tsushima Island in 1974. In 1986 and 1990, North Korea and the Soviet Union (now Russia) agreed on their territorial sea boundary and continental shelf/EEZ boundary in the northern East Sea or Sea of Japan.

[2]   In the Southeast Asian area, on the other hand, there are currently over 20 maritime boundary agreements in force. However, given the greater number of littoral states and the complicated geographical nature of the region, there still remain a number of important boundaries to be delimited. In fact, the geographical circumstances relating to the delimitation of maritime boundaries in the Southeast Asia subregion are far more complicated than those found in the Northeast Asia subregion. Moreover, this area also has a series of highly complicated territorial disputes involving the ownership of uninhabited islands and coral outcroppings, most of them in the South China Sea. For the details of maritime boundary agreements in force in the East Asian region, see J. Charney and L. Alexander (eds), *International Maritime Boundaries*, Vols. I and II (Martinus Nijhoff, Dordrecht, 1993).

to modify the deep seabed portion of that Convention. As a result, coastal states in Northeast Asia have completed the necessary domestic procedures, or are currently in the middle of doing so, to ratify the Convention. Under the Implementing Agreement, moreover, China, Japan and South Korea, as registered pioneer investors for the development of the deep seabed under Resolution II of UNCLOS III, must become parties to the Convention by 16 November 1996 to keep their privileged pioneer status.[3] The ratification of the Convention gives an impetus to coastal states to review and improve their domestic maritime legislation and practice in accordance with the Convention, and to settle their outstanding or potential maritime disputes.

Second, mainly out of concern for the increasing instances of foreign fishing in their offshore areas, Japan and South Korea have made a long-awaited decision to establish their Exclusive Economic Zones.[4] On 20 February 1996, Japan announced its decision to proclaim its EEZ. A similar announcement by South Korea followed immediately. It is expected that China will do the same. Since the distance from one coast to another in Northeast Asian seas nowhere exceeds 400 miles, it will be difficult to avoid the issue of boundary delimitation once coastal states establish their 200-mile zones. As a result, the question of boundary delimitation (for both EEZs and the continental shelf) has emerged as a real and pressing issue among the coastal states of Northeast Asia.[5]

---

[3] The 1994 UN Convention on the Law of the Sea: Implementing Agreement, Annex, Section 1, para. 12. On 1 March 1996, South Korea became a party to the Convention, and it is expected that Japan and China will do likewise in the near future.

[4] In the Northeast Asian region, the former Soviet Union was the first state to introduce a 200-mile exclusive zone of any kind, when in 1976 it established a 200-mile Exclusive Fishery Zone. This was subsequently replaced by a 200-mile Exclusive Economic Zone in 1984. However, it was not the first regional state to establish an EEZ, North Korea having already done so in 1977. Nonetheless, three major coastal states bordering the Yellow/East China Sea, namely China, South Korea and Japan, have yet to declare EEZs, though Japan reluctantly, and selectively, did establish a 200-mile fishery zone in 1977.

[5] Unlike the continental shelf, where the delimitation of boundaries is largely a hypothetical problem unless seabed resources are proven to exist, the establishment of an EEZ would make a boundary problem real because of the nature of living resources. It would be extremely difficult to manage an EEZ effectively without drawing a boundary through the overlapping EEZs of neighbouring countries.

There are two reasons why the question of boundary delimitation is particularly thorny in the Northeast Asian region. First, there exist some very difficult territorial disputes in the region. Unless these territorial disputes are resolved, which is highly unlikely, it may not be possible to delimit the boundaries. Second, as the continental shelf dispute in the early 1970s showed, coastal states appear to be in serious disagreement as to which laws should apply to boundary delimitation in the region. Moreover, the complicated geography of the region and the uncertain nature of the seabed make delimitation an extremely difficult issue.

The impact of the Convention will, of course, depend on which states in the area become parties to it. At present, virtually all littoral states appear likely to join. Given that the articles which directly address the delimitation of maritime boundaries are general and indeterminate, the entry into force of the Convention itself may have only a limited impact on the issue of boundary delimitation. Nonetheless, it is important to examine the relevant articles of the Convention, as they are the articles that would apply should all littoral states join the Convention. Moreover, should a state or states invoke the compulsory dispute settlement system of the Convention to resolve maritime boundary disputes, once again it would be the relevant articles of the Convention that would ultimately apply.

This paper first examines whether boundary delimitation provisions in the Convention, in particular Article 74/83, would provide a meaningful guideline for resolving potential boundary problems in the Northeast Asian region. The paper then assesses some of the outstanding issues from the standpoint of the applicable laws. Among those issues which require scrutiny are the geographical setting, the relevance of geomorphology or geology, and the status of islands in delimitation. Finally, the paper suggests a possible alternative approach to the question of boundary delimitation.

Applicable Laws

The search for the conventional rules governing the delimitation of extended maritime jurisdiction has turned out to be one of the most difficult tasks of UNCLOS III. Given that the provisions of the Convention are generally supposed not only to establish the new conventional rules, but also to embody, in many parts, the emerging rules of customary international law, and that the provisions on maritime boundaries would directly and critically affect the interests of coastal states more than any other provision, it has been imperative to establish rules which would command the most widespread support.

One of the major controversies of UNCLOS III concerned the delimitation critieria with one group of states - the equity group - favouring 'equitable principles' and the other group - the equidistance group - the 'equidistance principle or method'. The equity group, however, did not completely exclude the use of the equidistance method but was rather of the view that the equidistance method should be employed only when it was in accordance with the equity principle. At the same time, no advocate of the equidistance principle argued that the equidistance method should be applied in all circumstances without modification. Indeed, ever since the Seabed Committee was set up almost all the proposals favouring the equidistance line have been qualified with the insertion of the phrase 'special or relevant circumstances', so as to take into account equity considerations. Thus, the essence of the controversy lay in whether the equidistance method should be given preferential status among the criteria for delimitation. The equity group opposed any preferential status being granted to the equidistance method while the equidistance group supported it.

After some long and difficult negotiations, UNCLOS III eventually adopted Article 74/83, which provides that 'the delimitation of the EEZ/continental shelf ... shall be effected by agreement on the basis of international law ... in order to achieve an equitable solution'. It is generally acknowledged that the provisions that were finally adopted represented a careful compromise and not a consensus of the competing positions. These provisions, however, do not seem to provide a substantial normative standard for actual delimitation. While the provisions set out the goals to be achieved, they are silent as to the methods to be followed in order to achieve them. The task of identifying and elaborating the process to achieve an equitable solution has been left to international tribunals, scholarly works and state practice.

Therefore, despite Article 74/83 of the Convention, it would seem that it is customary international law which should be applied to boundary delimitation in Northeast Asia. As a result largely of past international adjudications, a basic rule of customary law has been established in the area of continental shelf or EEZ delimitation whereby such delimitation is to be effected by agreement in accordance with equitable principles, and taking into account all the relevant circumstances. What then are the most important circumstances in boundary delimitation in Northeast Asia?

Coastal Geography

The coast constitutes a starting point for measuring a state's EEZ or shelf entitlement, and consequently for any delimitation process with neighbouring states. This idea is clearly reflected in the classic principle that the land dominates the sea. Therefore, the starting point for any delimitation operation should be an appreciation of coastal geography.

Given the primary importance of coastal geography, the question arises how it should be interpreted. It has been a basic rule of coastal geography interpretation that nature cannot be refashioned.[6] Thus, the lengths or configurations of the coastlines should be given effect according to their natural character. However, this concept is modified by other equitable considerations such as the avoidance of the cut-off effect or disproportionate effect. Thus, under this rule it is only 'total refashioning' that cannot be justified. The question that has to be answered is whether nature should be respected as such or corrected to some extent in order to reflect other equitable considerations.

In terms of coastal geography, the most distinctive geographical character in Northeast Asia is the existence of two parallel seaward arcs formed by the Chinese mainland and the Ryukyu Islands chain of Japan.[7] The Ryukyu Islands consist of 221 islands with a total coastline of 768 miles, a total area of 1,338 square

---

6   'North Sea Continental Shelf, Judgment', *International Court of Justice Reports 1969*, para. 91, pp.49-50.

7   For a period of over 500 years until their annexation by Japan in 1879, the Ryukyu Islands were an independent kingdom which maintained vassalage successively with the Ming and Ching dynasties. Following Japan's defeat in the Pacific war, the islands were surrendered to the Allies in September 1945 and placed under US military administration in accordance with Article 3 of the 1951 San Francisco Peace Treaty. In 1972 they were returned to Japan in accordance with the Okinawa Reversion Treaty of 1971.

miles and a population of more than one million.[8] They stretch from a point 80 miles south of Kyushu to a point 73 miles north-east of Taiwan or almost 650 miles from the southern tip of Kyushu. The islands are separated by intervening gaps as wide as 120 miles between the Okinawa and Sakishima Guntos.

Given their size and population, there is little contention that these islands are entitled to generate their own EEZs or continental shelves. The question is how these island chains should be treated in delimitation negotiations between China and Japan. As stated above, the rules for the interpretation of coastline geography are based on apparently contradictory criteria. Although one basic criterion is that nature should not be refashioned, it is no less important to avoid the disproportionately distorting effects of certain geographical features. Thus in any interpretation it is a question of striking a balance between these two criteria, and such a balance should be assessed on the basis of the particular geographical characters of a given case.[9]

In order not to refashion nature, it is important to interpret correctly what it is that cannot be refashioned. As the above description indicates, the geography of the region is characterised by two parallel arcs formed by the Chinese mainland and the Ryukyu Islands chain of Japan. Of particular relevance here is the description of the East China Sea as a semi-enclosed or marginal sea. Although they are separated by substantial intervening gaps of water, the Ryukyu Islands nonetheless give the East China Sea the character of a semi-enclosed sea.[10] In other words, the size and direction of these islands as a whole appear to be sufficiently coherent and substantial to create in this area a semi-enclosed sea. This finding seems to make it difficult to interpret the geographical nature of this area simply as one where there are many islands in the middle or on the wrong side of the median line between two opposite facing states.[11] Furthermore, given

8   *Japan Statistical Yearbook 1986* (published in Japanese by Management and Coordination Agency, Statistics Bureau, Tokyo, 1986), pp. 21-7.

9   For instance, the Court in the Channel Arbitration Case found that to ignore the Scillies altogether would have amounted to a refashioning of geography, while to give them full effect would have amounted to ignoring the distorting effect that their location had on the equidistance line.

10   For the same view, see D. Bowett, *The Legal Regime of Islands in International Law* (Oceana Publications, Dobbs Ferry, New York, 1979) p. 283.

11   A possible analogy may be the Aegean Sea continental shelf dispute, where the Greek islands are so numerous and so dominate the whole sea area that the mainland-to-mainland approach with an equitable consideration for the islands in the middle is not appropriate, although in the Agean Sea dispute the case for

that Japan is itself an island state consisting of 3,922 islands including Hokkaido, Honshu, Shikoku, and Kyushu, such an interpretation does not appear to reflect geographical reality.

While the importance of the characterisation of the East China Sea as a semi-enclosed sea or a marginal sea, and of the Ryukyu Islands' role in constituting such a sea, should not be discounted, a quick glance at the map of this area is all that is required to discern a marked difference in the lengths of the coastline of China and Japan. According to one account, the length of the Chinese coastline from the southern headland of Hangchow Bay down to Haitan Island in Fukien Province opposite Taiwan (that is, the coastline which is roughly parallel to the Ryukyu Islands) is approximately 365 miles, whereas the length of the Ryukyus' coastline facing the East China Sea is approximately 205 miles. Nevertheless, this arc of islands, which stretches in almost a single line from the Japanese coast all the way down to the area near Taiwan, is so linearly positioned that the use of the equidistance method with these islands as basepoints would result in the Ryukyus being treated as if they were a long continuous promontory stretching from Kyushu, even though the aggregate of their actual coastal lengths facing the East China Sea is considerably shorter than that of the Chinese coastline.

In a geographical situation of quasi-equality between states, abating the effects of an incidental feature from which an unjustifiable difference of treatment could result is not totally refashioning geography,[12] nor is treating differently a substantial natural inequality in geography. Not to recognise such a fact would be a denial of the obvious. It is quite clear that such a considerable disparity between the lengths of the coastlines should constitute a relevant circumstance

---

rejecting such an approach appears to be stronger. See ibid., pp.249-81. Alternatively, it may be said that the present geographical context has partly the character of the so-called 'distant island' situation, where delimitation involves only the island and not the mainland territory of the state to which the island belongs. The 'distant island' situation should be distinguished from the case where delimitation between the mainland states is affected by the presence of islands that, though they belong to one state, lie near to the other state. See Donald Karl, 'Islands and the Delimitation of the Continental Shelf: A Framework for Analysis', *American Joiurnal of International Law*, Vol.71, 1977, pp.668-9. The most notable example of the distant island situation is a delimitation between France and Canada involving the islands of St. Pierre and Miquelon. For details, see C.R. Symmons, 'The Canadian 200 Mile Fishery Limit and the Delimitation of Maritime Zones around St. Pierre and Miquelon', *Ottawa Law Review*, Vol.12, 1980, pp.145-65.

which is to be reflected in the drawing of an equitable boundary line.[13] Equity cannot remedy natural inequalities, and to attempt to do so would amount to the refashioning of nature. The marked difference in the length of the coastline is nothing other than a case of natural inequality. Given the substantial difference in the length of coastline, the position of these islands stretching all the way down to the coast of Taiwan would have a substantially disproportionate effect on delimitation, were they allowed to generate a continental shelf on equal footing with the Chinese mainland. This consideration seems to make somewhat doubtful the equitableness of a median line using the Ryukyu Islands as basepoints in this region.

The Problem of Islands

The Question of Entitlement

The presence of islands is possibly the main issue likely to cause complications in boundary delimitation. The presence of islands gives rise to two questions: one related to the entitlement of islands to a continental shelf or EEZ and another related to their effect on the delimitation of shelf or EEZ boundaries.

One of the main problems resulting from expanded national jurisdictions concerns the seaward limits of these jurisdictions for islands; that is, whether all islands are capable of generating a continental shelf or EEZ. The importance of this issue becomes clearer when one considers that an uninhabited mid-ocean reef of one square mile commands a 200-mile zone of more than 140,000 square miles. This problem also indirectly relates to the effect of the presence of islands on shelf and EEZ boundaries between neighbouring states. For if certain categories of islands are not allowed to generate their own shelf, then they are from the outset irrelevant to shelf or EEZ boundary delimitations.[14]

---

12 'North Sea Continental Shelf, Judgment', para.91, pp.49-50.
13 'Delimitation of the Maritime Boundary in the Gulf of Maine Area, Judgment', para.91, *International Court of Justice Reports 1984*, para. 218, pp.334-5; 'Continental Shelf (Libyan Arab Jamahiriya/Malta), Judgment', *International Court of Justice Reports 1985*, para. 85.
14 However, this situation should be distinguished from the cases where an island may generate its own maritime zone but may not equitably be granted full effect or any effect at all in drawing a boundary. Such cases are concerned with the effect of islands on delimitation.

Given that granting all islands rights to maritime space would gravely reduce the scope of the international area, the Convention did not grant certain islands continental shelf or EEZ entitlements. Thus Article 121, para. 3 of the Convention provides that *'Rocks which cannot sustain human habitation or economic life of their own shall* have no exclusive economic zone or continental shelf'. However, it is by no means clear what 'rocks which cannot sustain human habitation or economic life of their own' means. An essential difficulty arises from the immense diversity of island situations. Suffice it to say that any assessment of specific cases should take overall account of all relevant circumstances. However, since paragraph 3 was clearly intended to exclude certain types of rocks from shelf and EEZ entitlements, its wording should then be made more exact to keep the exception from becoming meaningless.

The Effects of Islands on Delimitation

Once islands are entitled to their own continental shelves or EEZs, then the question arises as to the amount of the shelf or EEZ that they are entitled to in the delimitation of boundaries between neighbouring states. It would be difficult to devise a general formula applicable to all cases that would indicate the precise effect of the various geographical characteristics of islands on delimitation. Moreover, in assessing the effect of islands on delimitation, one needs to assess not only the geographical circumstances but other relevant circumstances such as demographic, political, economic and legal factors. Such a variety of parameters would appear to make any attempt to categorise the effect of islands even more difficult.

However, it is generally argued that contemporary state practice confers a primary role to an island's relative location and its relative size in determining the weight to be given to the island in delimitation.[15] Based on these factors, islands could be roughly

---

15   Karl, 'Islands and the Delimitation of the Continental Shelf', p.642; 'Continental Shelf (Tunisia/Libyan Arab Jamahiriya) (Diss. Op. Oda)', *International Court of Justice Reports 1982*, p.266. Donald Karl, in his article, suggested a general framework for analysis. In his view, islands would be categorised into three groups according to their location in the first phase. Thus, the islands located near the mainland would be used as basepoints, while islands located midway or near another state would be allowed only territorial sea. This result, however, would be modified in accordance with the size of the islands, particularly the length of their coastlines, in the second phase. Thus, if the size of an island (length of coast) is equivalent to a substantial portion of the mainland (length of mainland coast),

divided into three categories. If the islands were located near the coastline of the mainland, they would be given full effect (that is, the same effect as the mainland) and thus the boundary would be drawn between the islands and the opposite or adjacent coasts. However, if the islands in question were located on the wrong side of the equidistance line, they would be given no effect, and the boundary would be drawn without taking into account their presence. Finally, if the islands were located midway between two mainland coasts, they would be accorded effect depending on relevant factors such as their location, size, political status and population.[16] However, these categories should only be used for reference purposes only. The geographical and other circumstances must be evaluated on a case by case basis in the light of what is regarded as representing equity.

Disputed Islands and Boundary Delimitation

One of the most difficult problems in delimiting maritime boundaries in Northeast Asia concerns the treatment of unresolved territorial disputes over specific islands: namely, the dispute over the Dokdo Islands (or Takeshima) between Korea and Japan; and the dispute over the Senkaku Islands (or Tiao-yu-tais) between Japan and China. These disputes can be considered from two angles: first, as disputes over sovereignty of the islands; and second, as maritime jurisdictional disputes - that is, disputes concerning the effect of the disputed islands on the delimitation of the continental shelf. However, due to the location of these islets, in Northeast Asia the former has been inseparably entangled with the latter. Since a maritime boundary necessarily presupposes the identification of political boundaries,[17] the

---

16 such an island would be given partial effect in accordance with the proportionality test. See Karl, 'Islands and the Delimitation of the Continental Shelf', pp. 642 ff.

For instance, in some cases, full effect has been given to midway islands (for example, the Shetland Islands in the North Sea between the United Kingdom and Norway; Tsushima Island in the Korea Strait between Korea and Japan); in other cases, partial effect has been given to midway islands (for example, two tiny Yugoslav islets, Pelagrus and Kajola, midway in the Adriatic Sea between Italy and Yugoslavia; Pentelleria, Lampedusa and Linosa between Italy and Tunisia); no effect except the territorial sea has been given in some cases (for example, the 1958 Agreement between Bahrain and Saudi Arabia; the 1968 Shelf Agreement between Iran and Saudi Arabia; the 1974 Agreement to delimit the waters between India and Sri Lanka; the 1974 Shelf Agreement between Iran and the United Arab Emirates).

17 'To draw a boundary between the maritime jurisdiction of States, involves first attributing to them ... the title over the territories that generate such jurisdiction'.

dispute over the sovereignty of these islands poses one of the main obstacles to the settlement of any boundary dispute.

On the whole there have been three different views as to how to approach this problem. The first view considers the two issues to be inseparable. Accordingly, it considers the settlement of the territorial issue as a *conditio sine qua non* to the seabed dispute. The second view is that in the light of a new development in the regime of islands, primarily as a result of the deliberations at UNCLOS III, the boundary dispute can be detached from the territorial dispute. Thus, it focuses on the question of whether the territorial dispute is relevant or not under current international law. The third approach seems to be an alternative analysis based on the hypothetical premise that these islets belong either to China or to Japan.

Given the inherent difficulty of resolving the territorial dispute,[18] the first approach is of little assistance in efforts to resolve the boundary dispute. While the second approach appears to be a more practical one, its weakness seems to be that, unless the disputed islands are found to be incapable of generating their own continental shelf, any attempt to estimate their effect on delimitation will prove difficult without having first determined their political status. This is because the effect of these islands on delimitation could vary substantially depending on their relative geographical position in the area, and that position could not be determined without first solving the question of ownership. The third approach may be a more reasonable one, but, like the other two approaches, it misses an important factor. It seems that any discussion of the effect of the disputed islands on delimitation would have to take into account their

---

[18] See 'Beagle Channel Arbitration, Report and Decision of the Court of Arbitration', *International Legal Materials*, Vol.17, 1978, pp.634 ff.
For instance, Article 298 of the Law of the Sea Convention, regarding submission of delimitation disputes to third-party dispute settlement procedures, provides: 'that any dispute that necessarily involves the concurrent consideration of any unsettled dispute concerning sovereignty or other rights over continental or insular land territory shall be excluded from such submission'. This provision expressly reflects the difficulty of solving the sovereignty dispute. Thus it has been argued that it would be beyond the substantive scope of the Convention to determine the status of land territory. See P. Irwin, 'Settlement of Maritime Boundary Disputes: An Analysis of the Law of the Sea Negotiations', *Ocean Development and International Law*, Vol.8, 1980, p.114. Moreover, it is well known that China does not accept any form of compulsory settlement of disputes by a third party.

disputed status as well as other geographical or demographical characteristics.[19]

It is very difficult to determine whether the Senkaku or Dokdo Islands would generate their own EEZs or continental shelves. In the case of the Senkaku Islands,[20] given their relatively large size,[21] the presence of fresh water and valuable medicinal herbs, and the fact that these islets had been inhabited for a substantial period of time in the past,[22] these islands probably cannot be classified under Article 121(3) as a rock which cannot sustain human habitation or economic life of their own.[23] On the other hand, the natural conditions of the Dokdo

---

[19]   See 'Case concerning delimitation of continental shelf between the United Kingdom of Great Britain and Northern Ireland, and the French Republic', *Reports of International Arbitral Awards*, Vol.18, [1978], paras 183-6, pp.88-9.

[20]   The Senkaku Islands consist of five uninhabited islets and three barren rocks scattered between 25°40'N and 26°N, and 123°E and 124°34'E. The total area of the eight islets is approximately 2.5 square miles. The whole group is located approximately 120 nautical miles north-east of Taiwan, about 200 nautical miles west of Okinawa, and about 100 nautical miles north of Ishigaki City, the nearest municipality at the southwest end of the Ryukyu Islands. It has a substantial spring, and is abundant in arbuscula, a precious Chinese medical herb. In the past, these islands would appear to have had little use other than as occasional navigational guides. Although in the first half of this century scores of Japanese people had settled to develop them, the islands have been uninhabited for four decades since the early 1940s. The islets are now under the physical control of Japan.

[21]   For instance, the size of Tiao-yu (1.7 square miles) is much bigger than a 'rock' (less than 0.001 square mile or 2.590 square metres) defined by Hodgson in his celebrated categorisation of islands based on size. In fact, Tiao-yu belongs to the category of isles (1 square mile - 1,000 square miles), which is bigger than that of islets (0.001-1 square mile). See R.D. Hodgson, 'Islands: Normal and Special Circumstances' in John King Gamble, Jr and Guilio Pontecorvo (eds), *Law of the Sea: The Emerging Regime of the Oceans*, Proceedings of the Law of the Sea Institute Eighth Annual Conference (Ballinger Publishing Company, Cambridge, Mass., 1974), pp.43-6. On the other hand, the area of a rock according to the estimation by the International Hydrographic Bureau would be much larger (one square kilometre, that is, 0.3906 square mile) than that suggested by Hodgson, but Tiao-yu is still substantially bigger than a rock under this classification. See R.D. Hodgson and R.W. Smith, 'The Informal Single Negotiating Text (Committee II): A Geographical Perspective', *Ocean Development and International Law*, Vol.3, 1976, p.230.

[22]   That may indicate their capacity to sustain human habitation, which is a factor to be considered under para. 3.

[23]   It is perhaps useful here to compare the Senkaku Islands with the British Rockall Islet in the Rockall dispute. Rockall Islet is about 80 by 100 ft at its base, and has an area of approximately 624 square metres (0.000241 square miles). It lies at a distance of 402 miles from Iceland, 322 miles from the Danish Faeroes, 226 miles from the nearest point of the Republic of Ireland, and about 289 miles from the nearest point of the Scottish mainland. The island is uninhabited and uninhabitable due to the lack of fresh water. Given its inaccessibility, it is

Islands would suggest that these islands might not generate their own EEZs or continental shelves.[24]

However, the finding that the disputed islands may generate their own continental shelf is a far cry from the claim that they should be given full effect in delimitation with neighbouring states. On the contrary, in the light of the reference made above to the islands' geographical context and disputed status, it is difficult to assume that any objective observer could possibly deny that this is a case of circumstances creative of inequity *par excellence* in delimitation. The present case seems to be exactly the case of 'islets, rocks, and minor coastal projections', the disproportionally distorting effect of which should be eliminated in the equal division of the particular area involved.[25] Its sensitive location roughly midway between two states means that any effect given to these islands may substantially affect the whole course of a boundary. In short, given the fact that the islands are located far from the coast of each of the parties, are small in size and have no population apart from a small human presence for security purposes, and given the territorial dispute,[26] there is little

---

unsuitable even as a base for a manned lighthouse, though it does support a light which was placed on the rock in 1972 by the United Kingdom. See E.D. Brown, 'Rockall and the Limits of National Jurisdiction of the UK: Part 2', *Marine Policy*, Vol.2, 1978, p.289.

[24] The Dokdo Islands consist of two tiny islets and scattered shore reefs lying in the East Sea about 30 km east of the Ulung Do and about 50 km north-west of Japanese Dogo. Dokdo is not habitable and is therefore of little economic value on its own, except that it may serve as a basis for claiming maritime jurisdiction in the surrounding sea. The dispute over the Dokdo Islands first surfaced in January 1952 when the Korean government established the so-called Peace Line which included the Dokdo Islands within its limits. Japan immediately protested to Korea on the grounds that it had incorporated this island in 1905. Like any territorial dispute, the Dokdo dispute is not immune from complicated historical and legal controversies. The islands have been occupied by Korea since 1946, and the dispute has remained more or less dormant except for the sporadic Japanese protest over the Korean occupation. However, in early 1996, when both Japan and Korea decided to establish their EEZs and allegedly considered including the disputed islands as their basepoint for EEZs, the dispute instantly flared up.

[25] 'North Sea Continental Shelf, Judgment', *International Court of Justice Reports 1969*, para. 57.

[26] Small disputed islands have been consistently ignored in the delimitation of continental shelves, EEZs or exclusive fishery zones. For instance, the 1968 continental shelf boundary agreement solved the question of sovereignty over two islands located in the middle of the Persian Gulf by recognising the sovereignty of Saudi Arabia over the island of A.'Arabiyah and that of Iran over the island of Farsi. The parties then created a continental shelf boundary which ignored these two islands. See United States Department of State, Bureau of Intelligence and Research, Office of the Geographer, *Limits in the Seas*, No.24. The 1969 continental

doubt that such islets should be accorded only a belt of the territorial sea.[27]

Geomorphological/Geological Considerations

In the past, the geophysical character of the seabed was an important consideration in continental shelf boundary delimitation, since a fundamental rule for the delimitation of the continental shelf was natural prolongation. In the East China Sea, in particular, the

---

shelf boundary agreement between Iran and Qatar also ignored the presence of disputed islands in delimiting a median-line boundary. See United Nations, *United Nations Treaty Series*, No.787 p.172 (or United States Department of State, Bureau of Intelligence and Research, Office of the Geographer, *Limits in the Seas*, No.25). In the 1973 maritime boundary agreement between Uruguay and Argentina, the island of Martin Garcia was ignored and transformed into a wildlife sanctuary. See United States Department of State, Bureau of Intelligence and Research, Office of the Geographer, *Limits in the Seas*, No.64. In the 1973 continental shelf boundary between Canada and Denmark (Greenland), the presence of Hans Island in the Nares Strait was ignored because of the dispute over the sovereignty of the island and because the island would distort an otherwise equitable boundary. See United States Department of State, Bureau of Intelligence and Research, Office of the Geographer, *Limits in the Seas*, No.72. In the 1974 continental shelf boundary between India and Sri Lanka, the disputed island of Kachchativu did not affect the location of the median line. See United States Department of State, Bureau of Intelligence and Research, Office of the Geographer, *Limits in the Seas*, No.66. In a 1976 maritime boundary between Colombia and Panama, the disputed islands of Roncador and Northwest Rocks were disregarded as basepoints in constructing the equidistance line. See United States Department of State, Bureau of Intelligence and Research, Office of the Geographer, *Limits in the Sea*, No.79. The 1978 Torres Strait Treaty solved the sovereignty questions over the islands situated in the northern part of the Torres Strait immediately off the Papua New Guinea coast by creating: (i) a seabed resources delimitation line; (ii) a fisheries resources delimitation line; (iii) a protected zone. The Australian islands located north of the seabed resources line received only a three-nautical-mile territorial sea. No continental shelf or economic zone was allocated to these particular islands. See 'Treaty between Australia and the Independent State of Papua New Guinea Concerning Sovereignty and Maritime Boundaries in the area between the two Countries including the area known as Torres Strait, and Related Matters' in *New Directions in the Law of the Sea*, compiled and edited by Myron Nordquist, S. Houston Lay and Kenneth Simmonds (Oceana Publications, London, 1980), Vol.8, pp. 215 ff. The Chamber in the Gulf of Maine Case ignored Machias Seal Island because of uncertainty as to sovereignty over the island. See 'Delimitation of the Maritime Boundary in the Gulf of Maine Area, Judgment', *International Court of Justice Reports 1984*, para. 211.

27 It should be noted that the concern over the effect of the Senkaku Islands on delimitation essentially emanated from the possibility that the Okinawa Trough could constitute a natural boundary in the East China Sea. In such a case, the question of how these islets should be treated in delimitation was critical to Japan. Given that such a claim is no longer tenable, it may be said that the importance of these islets has been relatively reduced.

applicability of the principle of natural prolongation was a critical factor in boundary delimitation due to the presence of the Okinawa Trough, which it was alleged terminated the natural prolongation of the Japanese territory.

However, the rules for delimitation of the continental shelf have undergone substantial changes since the early 1970s. Those changes have emanated from two important developments in the law of the sea. The first of these has been the emergence, through UNCLOS III, of a new definition of the continental shelf, in particular using distance as a primary criterion. The second development has been the establishment of the 200-mile EEZ regime, which covers both the seabed and the water column within the 200-mile limit. Now that 200 miles constitutes the legal basis for defining the continental shelf in most cases, geological or geomorphological factors are only relevant in delimitation cases involving areas beyond that distance.

In the East China Sea, where the distance between the littoral states does not exceed 400 miles, the geophysical nature of the seabed such as the Okinawa Trough would not affect delimitation under modern international law.

Conclusion

From this brief legal examination of some of the key questions concerning maritime boundary delimitation in Northeast Asia it would appear that, with the establishment of a new definition of the continental shelf and the EEZ regime, the claim that seabed features such as the Okinawa Trough constitute natural boundaries may no longer be tenable. In contrast to the decrease in the importance of geological or geomorphological considerations, the importance of the geographical settings of the case seems to have increased. Thus the marked difference in the lengths of the coastline should be reflected in any delimitation. These broad geographical settings, along with the small size of the islands and their disputed status, seem to make it difficult for these islets to affect the delimitation of boundaries in this region.

Nevertheless, in light of the complexity of the situation in the Northeast Asian region, the littoral states may prefer a more function-oriented approach to the jurisdiction-oriented approach of boundary delimitation. Thus the regional states may wish to resolve the pressing issues of environmental protection and resource development without tackling the underlying sovereignty and boundary issues. For instance, the littoral states may address fishery problems from a regional perspective by promoting a coordinated policy of conservation and effective enforcement procedures. They may also work out cooperative arrangements for the development of seabed mineral resources. Since such arrangements could be established without prejudice to the underlying territorial and maritime boundary issues, they might constitute optimal solutions that would defer the more politically charged issues to the indefinite future. Given the highly sensitive political relations between the littoral states, such an approach may be more constructive.

CHAPTER 10

RESOURCE REGIMES AND MARITIME COOPERATION IN SOUTHEAST ASIA

Ian Townsend-Gault

At first sight, the themes of 'natural resources' and 'regional cooperation' in Southeast Asia appear inimical. Ocean resource conflicts abound in this part of the world, in the form of jurisdictional disputes (and related differences concerning sovereignty over small islands and over features) and arguments on fishing rights and entitlements. These issues tend to dominate regional dialogues at all levels, from the inter-governmental to the academic. The fires are stoked regularly by the media, which dutifully report incident after incident, reminding readers of the numbers of their fishing fellow-countrymen languishing in the gaols of neighbouring states. Bilateral negotiations on offshore boundaries continue against a background of such reportage, and pressure from the international oil industry to settle jurisdictional conflicts so that petroleum operations may commence.

These are high stakes for any region. In Southeast Asia, as with many other areas, they are being played for against a background of other items on agendas in other areas: bilateral, subregional, regional, inter-regional, and international. It is fair to say that issues on the resource/environmental agenda yield precedence to few others in any of these forums. They complicate or assist other areas of concern more than they are complicated or assisted by those other issues. Whether or not this should be the case is, of course, another matter.

It could be argued that this primacy, though understandable, is regrettable at best, and dangerous at worst. Resource and environmental issues make very bad political footballs, domestically or internationally; they are too important to be used in this way. Naturally, this is not an argument that recommends itself to many political leaders, but we have now enough evidence world-wide - and we in Canada have recently contributed our fair share - to make this point with some confidence.

Diamonds may be forever, but not all natural resources have such durability. We know that it is possible to wipe out a fish stock, poison an ecosystem, damage an oilfield beyond recovery, or, *pace* contemporary events in the UK agricultural sector, destroy public confidence in the ability of government to protect the very springs of life.[1] Any or all of this can and will happen if governments mistake their priorities. And it is to governments that such remarks must be addressed. Politically and legally, rights over resources are vested for the most part in states. Almost nothing can be done by industry in the face of implacable opposition by the state. But with these rights come concomitant responsibilities. To put the matter baldly, if there is a disaster, we know, ultimately, who to blame.

This is not to imply that the task of resource and environmental management (domestic or international) facing governments is a simple one. To the contrary, there are sources of assistance in discharging this burden, such as concepts evolved by natural resource regimes. To be truly efficacious, a natural resources regime should be functional, responding not only to policy imperatives (which are, too often, political imperatives) but also in a balanced way to the demands of the resource, in terms of its conservation and optimal management and utilisation. These factors shape and condition the most effective laws and regulations dealing with resource and environmental management. They explain how, why, and when the regimes evolve as they do.

What does this mean for resource and environmental cooperation in Southeast Asia? First, it suggests that a functional response to realities (including jurisdictional impasses) helps to chart a

---

1   The record is an increasingly dismal one. To take the most recent disaster, it now appears that, for reasons of profit enhancement, the government of the United Kingdom permitted farmers to feed contaminated fodder to cattle. The same motive led to denials that there was a problem and scientists demanded that their doubts be shared with the public. Even now, the problem is not proven. But this is a mere detail. Public confidence in government probity has been shattered, as has a once-profitable industry. The point is, this scenario can be repeated anywhere there is a lazy and complicitous government, forgetful of its responsibilities to the public. It is only a matter of time before populations demand greater accountability from those who have brought these events to pass.

more sustainable course than crude jingoistic policies of competitive exploitation, a result that would only benefit people and the resource and their shared environment. Second, it would provide a better road-map towards the sort of confidence and cooperation that will be required to ensure that these resources, and their environment, are available for future generations. This paper explores some approaches to these issues.

Natural Resource Regimes

Regimes in General

The relationship between natural resource activities and legal development is close, if elusive. From time to time, personnel from one of the resource industries inveigh against 'regulation' or some other form of 'government interference'. At the same time, resource industries, especially those requiring massive capital investment, are keen to see the involvement of the legal system in areas such as the granting of rights available to, and the statement of obligations incumbent upon, a grantee of resource rights. (This, in fact, is the nub of the relationship between government and industry in this sector: the contractual expression of mutual rights and obligations. The extent to which this consensual undertaking is wholly authoritative or can set legal precedents is one for debate, and is considered further below.)

The point here is twofold. First, the legal system introduces normative concepts that, ideally, attract interest and investment, while striking a balance between the expectations of the state and resource owner on the one hand, and the industry and profit-making investor on the other. Second, the legal system can (and must) respond to the changing interests of either (or both) state or industry to establish new norms or modify old ones, it being accepted that, so long as it is desired to continue this relationship, both parties are constrained by the extent to which such changes can take place. In other words, the relationship, though stated in normative terms, is essentially consensual. The state makes law in the interests of, and sometimes at the behest of, industry to further this mutually beneficial relationship. This bargain is broken time and time again by one side or the other, and there is nothing very remarkable about that.

This is not to say that government should be a cypher for the wishes of industry, nor should companies be mere agents of the state. When the lines are crossed in this way, the results can be disastrous. Witness the offshore UK safety record in recent years, the present state of the British beef industry or the Canadian east coast fishery. Industry cannot assume governmental responsibilities for the national interest and governments are often not comfortable working at the behest of the profit motive. But when the two parties understand one another and work together, neither forgetting their respective roles, the result is a functional and efficient resource regime, capable of balancing all interests and commanding the confidence of government, industry, and the public at large. Yet how many regimes meet this test?

Natural Resource Regime Offshore

Natural resource regimes were first evolved in the domestic (and usually terrestrial) context, and extended offshore as and when necessary. So far as the petroleum industry is concerned, most of the legal or regulatory techniques or concepts used on the continental shelf were developed - or originated - onshore. The elements of fishery conservation are to be found in the management of the living resources in internal and territorial waters.

So far as the regulation of offshore petroleum activities is concerned, this resulted in the modification and subsequent application of tried and tested concepts to problems that had already been encountered and solved onshore. An excellent example is provided by the phenomenon of oil and gas deposits divided by maritime boundaries. A technique known as 'unitisation' was evolved in the American mid-west in the 1920s, and applied where two different oil companies, working adjacent land areas, subsequently discovered that a common reservoir of hydrocarbons was located subjacent to both in such a way that either (or both) could produce from it. The application of unitisation preserves the correlative rights of interest holders while providing for the safe and orderly exploitation of the field, using appropriate conservation techniques. All of this may be prejudiced if the two companies drill and produce competitively.

The cross-boundary field problem was identified early in the life of the doctrine of the continental shelf as a rule of international law, and contemporary commentators suggested that states should avoid the issue by drawing boundaries around reservoirs. It was assumed that most countries would be unwilling or unable to solve the problem peacefully, and that divided oil or gas fields would simply fuel bilateral tensions.

Drawing boundaries around reservoirs - preserving the 'unity of the deposit' - has been rejected decisively by the international community in favour of provisions, usually contained in boundary treaties, committing the parties to negotiate a mutually agreeable form of joint exploitation. In the North Sea, this took the form of unitisation, as per the American model.

This is not the place for a detailed discussion of the North Sea unitisations,[2] but a summary of the situation will illustrate one example of functional cooperation. In 1965, Norway and the United Kingdom negotiated a continental shelf boundary agreement, applying the median technique. This line was agreed in complete ignorance of the geophysical configuration of the subsoil of the seabed. Article 4 of this agreement commits the two countries to negotiating a form of joint exploitation for any fields found to straddle this boundary line in such a way that they can be worked from either side. It should be noted that the 1965 Boundary Treaty was seen as part of a regulatory response by the two countries to the growing interest in North Sea petroleum exploration. In 1963, Norway had enacted a basic petroleum law, and promulgated detailed regulations in 1965. In 1964, the United Kingdom modified its existing rules for onshore petroleum operations and made provision for extending them to the continental shelf. Thus the boundary agreement was an integral part of what was, in effect, a 'North Sea package' offered to the oil industry. The invitation said, in effect, 'we are stable countries: your rights and obligations are clear if you take petroleum licences, and you can take a licence in areas close to the middle of the northern part of the North Sea knowing that you have complete security, in that no other country

---

[2]   A detailed treatment of the international and domestic legal regimes governing the North Sea cross-boundary fields is to be found in Ian Townsend-Gault, 'Petroleum Development Offshore: Legal and Contractual Issues' in N.D. Beredjick

or its licensees will dispute your rights'. As it turned out, this was an attractive package, bolstered by some promising early finds, and the result was the stable and highly profitable North Sea oil industry, that has transformed Norway from an economic backwater to an industrial force of some consequence.

However, it turned out that the 1965 boundary bisected at least three hydrocarbon fields, including the largest in the North Sea, in such a way that the latter is divided 80:20 in favour of Norway. Needless to say, this line would not have been agreed to so readily had the location of these fields been known, which is one argument in favour of boundary making in ignorance of the location of fields. The first field was discovered in 1972, and the British and Norwegian consortia holding licences on their respective sides of the boundary immediately entered into a series of agreements on cooperation. These were, of course, private arrangements, concluded with the full knowledge of the governments concerned. Under these agreements, the field was mapped with considerable exactitude, and a preliminary estimate made of the percentage of the volume resources in situ on either side of the boundary before the commencement of production. Unitisation requires that profits and costs be shared by the parties according to this formula.

The two governments effectively ratified and extended all this by a treaty agreed in 1976, providing for joint exploitation according to the principles of unitisation. However, it is instructive to note that the companies took the initiative and, almost instinctively, applied unitisation to a situation with which they were familiar in the domestic context, but which had not arisen hitherto in the offshore context anywhere in the world.[3] Indeed, lawyers working for the companies concerned later said that they could not have conceived of any other course, and would have recommended the suspension of operations had the governments not chosen the cooperative route. It might be said that the investors in the project might have made similar demands in such a situation.

and Thomas Walde (eds), *Third World Petroleum Investment Policies for the 1990s* (Graham and Trotman, London, 1989), pp.101-64.

3   Most of the lawyers working in the offices of the British and Norwegian oil companies at this time were either North American, or had had considerable experience there. This helps to explain the 'instinctive' recourse to unitisation.

To my mind, this helps to throw a new light on legal development *vis-à-vis* natural resource activities. We tend to examine situations such as cross-boundary fields from one perspective or another. To the lawyer advising government, the issue is primarily one of international law and the rights of the state. To the lawyer advising the oil company or investor, the issues are very different. No one view is less relevant than the other. If one desires a complete view of the law and policy issues arising here, both must be held in the same focus for a true perspective to emerge. This complicates the picture by increasing the number of 'parties' concerned: states, consortia of companies, companies, merchant banks, investors and workers. But that is how it is. The picture is a complex one, and to deny this, any part of it, is to indulge in delusion. It should be noted, however, that all the players in the picture have a common goal - the effective and efficient exploitation of the resource.

Accordingly, the highly functional and complex nature of natural resource activities must be appreciated and acknowledged. Of course, the complete picture is more complex. Yet in looking at the North Sea field, for instance, a range of other issues (including environmental concerns, impact on the fishing industry and socio-economic impacts on coastal communities) are present. The issues are different, but no less complicated than for any other aspect of marine resource activities.

The Inter-state and Regional Context

One of the consequences of the development of the law of the sea over the past two decades is that countries that, hitherto, were not contiguous are transformed into maritime neighbours through the implementation of 200-nautical-mile economic zones.[4] For some countries, this is an unwelcome development, in that it adds items to the bilateral agendas of states at odds with one another. One response

---

4   The 200-nautical-mile economic zone is more properly known as the Exclusive Economic Zone, or EEZ. The zone extends from the limits of territorial sea to the 200-nautical-mile limit, and within it states exercise sovereign rights for the purposes of the exploration and exploitation of the resources of the sea, seabed, and subsoil, and all other economic activities. The international legal rules applicable therein are codified and developed in Part V of the United Nations Convention on the Law of the Sea of 1982.

to this is to ignore the new items on the agenda, and to continue to engage in ocean development as if the other country did not exist.

This attitude is by no means confined to states that do not enjoy the best relations with their neighbours. Unilateral ocean development was in fact virtually the rule until the extensions of ocean jurisdiction that have taken place over the past fifty years. Indeed, the initial extension of jurisdiction, confined as it was to seabed activities, created few issues requiring cooperation. Cross-boundary petroleum fields represent one exception and pollution issues another. But by and large, petroleum development offshore, until the late 1970s, proceeded as if other users of the sea did not exist. This was partly because the adverse impacts from such activities were localised (that is, almost purely domestic) and were deemed to be of little consequence compared to oil production.

This is not to say that such impacts were of little or no consequence for those on the receiving end. The fishing industry in the North Sea, and in areas such as the Gulf of Mexico, suffered greatly - not from oil pollution damage, but rather from loss of gear and catch after contact with debris, most of which could not be attributed to a specific operator. There was therefore no-one to whom the bill could be presented, or who could be sued. Government response was initially unsympathetic, then conciliatory, with compensation schemes for such damage being established either by government (Norway, the United States federally and some coastal states) or industry (the United Kingdom, Canada). These schemes were restricted to national claimants. Debris damage has a major adverse impact on fishing (oil pollution damage is relatively insignificant), and the presence of installations causes problems by denying access to adjacent waters for fishing, or indeed any other, vessels. But these issues were largely ignored. If there was an ocean policy at work here, it would have been simple: oil development at all costs, every other interest to be subordinate.[5]

Once the EEZ was accepted and implemented, coastal states had a greater stake not only in the ocean space adjacent to the territorial sea, but also in its resources and environmental health. It

5   Of course, most countries did not have an ocean policy, or had one, in effect, by default.

then became important not only to control who fished your EEZ, but how your neighbours fished in their area, especially with respect to stocks that migrated from your waters to theirs or from your EEZ to the high seas. You would also be concerned if your neighbour pursued petroleum operations to the exclusion of environmental considerations, for while you did not care if their oil was wasted, you did not want it in your EEZ, poisoning the fish or habitat that your fishing industry relied upon.

Thus the extension of jurisdiction has created many maritime neighbours, and given them an agenda which includes items where there may be common cause, and items that contain the seeds of bitter conflict. The Law of the Sea Convention of 1982 attempted to forestall these problems by advocating cooperation and/or collaboration appropriate to the circumstances. This is a functional response, but, for many countries, is superimposed on traditions of unilateralism at sea, and, in some cases, enmity, sometimes arising from maritime disputes. That these items are on the bilateral, trilateral, subregional and regional agendas of the coastal states of the world is no longer open to doubt or debate. The only question appears to be: how will they meet the challenge?

One approach is clearly implied by the argument developed in this paper: engage in cooperative policy making to the extent required by functional considerations. This presumes a community of interest and focus similar to that found in the parties identified in the North Sea petroleum operation discussed above. It assumes a situation where every party has priorities shared by the other. There will of course be political and other problems along the way, but at least shared functionally derived goals can help set the course and overcome such obstacles.[6] Such an approach appears simplistic, but this is only because the politically derived divisive issues, which are essentially non-productive, have been allowed to dominate the debate. The functional approach has the merits of principle and utility. It also promises more than the sort of bleak antipathy practised by the South China Sea countries, which is making its own contribution to overfishing and marine environmental degradation there. If

---

[6] At one point in the discussions concerning the Statfjord field, the British government argued for a platform to be placed on the UK side of the boundary, purely for symbolic reasons. After discussion, this demand was dropped.

functionalism is at least part of the way forward, the question is now: to what extent is this happening in Southeast Asia?

The View from Southeast Asian Waters

Even before the EEZ or even the continental shelf were rules of international law, Southeast Asia was a region marked by maritime boundaries of some complexity. Extended maritime jurisdiction has complicated the picture still further, though if we follow the analysis presented above, it is in the seeds of this exacerbated problem - extensions of jurisdiction - that the solution lies. Put simply, the question should be: why is state jurisdiction being extended at all? The answer is: to control, conserve and exploit ocean resources. What is the nature of this jurisdiction? It is a complex mixture of rights and responsibilities. As always, however, the emphasis is firmly on 'rights', with responsibilities coming some way behind.

This is, of course, a world-wide phenomenon. Paradoxically, however, while some states might resist what they might see as enforced cooperation with their ocean neighbours, or resent that fact that their exclusive rights are subject to limitation from outside, there is an increased understanding that, in acting cooperatively, countries gain more than they lose. This underscores the saliency of the functional approach: persisting in a unilateral approach to common problems where the solution absolutely requires cooperation will be dysfunctional. The adverse results of such a policy will be apparent sooner or later.

In Southeast Asia, the jurisdictional impasse in the South China Sea casts an enormous shadow over all ocean debates. Lesser shadows are found in other corners of the region: the Gulf of Thailand; the Strait of Malacca; the issue of archipelagic passage. In those cases where implacable attitudes have been struck, progress is likely to be slow and the adverse consequences identified above are likely to occur.

However, there are many signs of emerging cooperation. One key influence in this process is the gradual acceptance - *qua* treaty or otherwise - of the Law of the Sea Convention and other multilateral legal instruments. Ratification of a treaty is no panacea; if implementation - uniform implementation - proves difficult or impossible, the achievement is chimerical. However I would argue that the moral value of ratification cannot to be overestimated, and the symbolic nature of adherence can provide a powerful foundation for ocean cooperation generally.

Recent examples of resource cooperation would include the joint development agreement concluded in 1995 by Malaysia and Vietnam. This brief treaty provides a framework under which the state-owned oil companies of the two countries will develop jointly a small area of the Gulf of Thailand. It is always difficult to know exactly what motives prompt states to enter into such arrangements, but Malaysia has already shown interest in petroleum opportunities in the Vietnamese offshore area. This agreement solidifies cooperation, and is especially interesting, coming at the time that Vietnam was admitted into ASEAN. A colleague and I have argued that joint development arrangements must be seen in and tested in a functional way.[7] If a joint development arrangement is intended to fulfil a political purpose only, then no-one should be surprised if the arrangement is non-productive from all points of view.

There are many avenues for cooperation in the area of resource development. Apart from topics identified in the Law of the Sea Convention, technical assistance provided by countries with greater experience in such activities to their less experienced neighbours would go a long way to consolidate a truly regional approach, not only to operational standards, but ultimately to policymaking and regulation. In the petroleum sector, cooperation in areas such as pollution response and search and rescue might be enormously important. I am not aware of the response capability of the states of the region in either environmental or safety matters, but would suggest that capacity to deal with a major blow-out in some parts of the region might be low to non-existent. And yet, as with any area of the world with petroleum operations underway, the threat of disaster remains. Is the lack of preparedness another example of policy making by default?

---

[7]   Ian Townsend Gault and William G. Stormont, 'Offshore Petroleum Joint Development Arrangements: Functional Instrument? Compromise? Obligation?' in Gerald H. Blake *et al.*(eds), *The Peaceful Management of Transboundary Resources* (Graham and Trotman/Martinus Nijhoff, London and Boston, 1995), pp.51-76.

Conclusions

In my own work on the Indonesian-led workshops on Managing Potential Conflicts in the South China Sea, I am struck constantly by the extent to which some commentators assume that the problems of the South China Sea are unique. Of course, in this combination, they are, but individual aspects or issues are not. A survey of marine cooperative experience in selected regions presented at the Fifth Workshop made this point very well.[8] In almost all cases, the examples examined, successful or otherwise, were founded on functional considerations.

Functionalism is an acid test. It is not the only test, and to urge that ocean resource considerations be divorced from politics or political realities would be a waste of time. However, the more artificial the arrangement, the less should be expected of it. I return to the point made in my introduction concerning the frailty of the environment, and the finite number of our chances to rectify our mistakes. These are also part of the reality within which ocean cooperation - or the lack of it - should be viewed in the area of natural resources.

---

[8]   Chircop *et al.*, 'Conflict and Co-operation in Regional Seas: A Background Paper', Oceans Institute of Canada, Halifax, July 1994.

CHAPTER 11

COMPREHENSIVE SOLUTIONS TO THE SOUTH CHINA SEA DISPUTES: SOME OPTIONS[1]

Mark J. Valencia and Jon M. Van Dyke

Why is a Solution Necessary Now?

The main driving force for a solution is that the status quo - or what some call the 'do nothing' approach - is unstable and may lead to conflict. In a pessimistic scenario, talks continue in the Indonesian-sponsored workshops, but they remain informal and focused on technical issues. Working groups are formed focusing on innocuous topics like marine scientific research, environmental protection and safety of navigation, purposely avoiding the core issues of conflicting sovereignty and maritime claims. Some claimants, fearing that their flexibility will be restricted, refuse to allow these talks to be formalised or to even to discuss their specific claims and their rationale, let alone joint hydrocarbon exploration. The talks lose focus, positions harden, frustration grows, and the sponsors and some claimants lose interest when they come to believe that China is using the talks only to stall for time to build up its economic and military might, in effect to create a new status quo in which it dominates the region. The islands, rocks and reefs remain occupied in a crazy-quilt pattern by the military forces of five of the claimants (Figure 11.1). Occasional violence erupts when forces or vessels of one party come without warning too close to those of rival claimants.

Some argue that this situation - a 'leaking' status quo - is tolerable at least in the short term and that the claimants may bluff and bluster but will avoid actual conflict as too costly both politically and economically. This school advocates maintaining the 'leaking'

---

[1] This chapter is excerpted from a book-length manuscript submitted to the US Institute of Peace, tentatively entitled *The South China Sea Disputes: Approaches and Interim Solutions*, by Mark J. Valencia, Jon M. Van Dyke and Noel A. Ludwig.

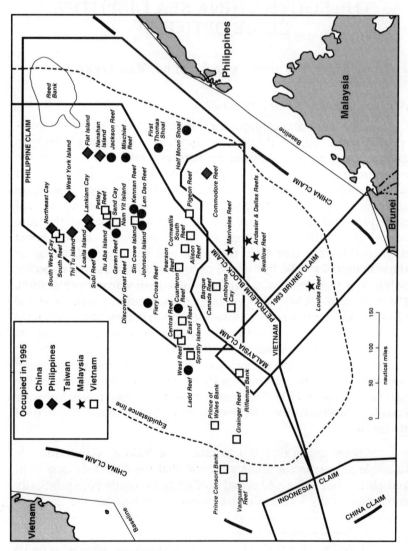

Figure 11.1: Occupation of the islands, rocks and reefs by military forces

status quo until improved political and economic relations ameliorate the tension and reduce the possibility of conflict.

A 'leaking' status quo may be acceptable as long as relations among the claimants remain positive, or at least not hostile. Indeed, during these calms, bilateral arrangements may even be struck and implemented on issues such as mutual fisheries access to areas of overlapping claims, such as that between Malaysia and the Philippines, with little or no reaction from other claimants.[2] But when relations between two or more of the claimants deteriorate, irreconcilable differences will be exposed, tension in the region will rise, forces may be put on full alert, and the frequency of incidents may increase. For example, confrontations occurred in the 1980s when the frequency and intensity of belligerent statements and incidents between China and Vietnam in the Spratlys ebbed and flowed with progress on a Cambodian solution.[3] Nationalism and domestic pressure force government action and reaction, and miscalculation could easily turn this leaking status quo into a flood.

These possibilities underscore the weakness of the 'do-nothing' approach, namely that it is dangerously misleading and inherently unstable.[4] If the status quo were really the operative norm, there would be a freeze on acquisition of military equipment that could produce an advantage in the area, on military manoeuvres, on construction of military installations, ports and airports on the islands, on fishing in sensitive areas, and on seismic surveys and drilling in or near the area. In fact, however, all of these actions are occurring despite the claimants' agreement not to destabilise the situation. Moreover, this 'do-nothing' solution is advantageous to those countries that can use the respite to quietly build up their economic and military power. It also favours China's small-step-by-small-step approach toward a dominant position because each step is so small and the costs of calling its bluff are so large. Thus this 'do-nothing' approach could eventually lead to de facto Chinese control of much of the South China Sea. Indeed, some

---

2   'Spratly Joint Venture', *Indochina Digest*, 24 December 1993, p.4.
3   Mark J. Valencia, *South-East Asian Seas: Oil Under Troubled Waters* (Oxford University Press, Oxford, 1985), p.113.
4   Justus van der Kroef, 'The South China Sea Problem: Some Future Scenarios', *The American Asian Review*, Vol.12, No.4, Winter 1994.

observers believe that the Chinese occupation of Mischief Reef was part of this inexorable advance and was designed to test both ASEAN and US reaction.[5]

At a minimum, the fundamental issues remain unresolved and the area remains a scab over a festering sore, ready to be picked for political leverage. The present unresolved situation also offers an opportunity for outside powers to intervene; for example, to protect the security of sea lanes or their nationals and companies involved in offshore oil exploration. Although China rails against 'internationalising' the issue, it was the first in recent times to let a concession in the Spratly area to an 'outsider' - Crestone Energy Corporation of the United States - thereby precipitating a diplomatic row with Vietnam. Indeed the Mischief Reef incident is only the most recent indication of how quickly the 'status quo' can be transformed into a dangerous situation. The United States, Japan, Australia, New Zealand and even the European Community expressed concern and US policy seemed to shift from 'passive' to 'active neutrality'. Moreover, US and Japanese companies are right in the middle of a possible clash between China and Vietnam over conflicting claims to the Vanguard Bank area.

The pattern presented by these incidents indicates that the current status quo, or 'do nothing' approach, could deteriorate through an unexpected political or military event into open conflict. Worsening of relations between, for instance, Vietnam and China, or, more likely now, Taiwan and China, could foreshadow more fighting in the Spratlys.[6] This possibility was brought to the fore in the wake of Taiwan President Lee Teng-hui's visit to the United States in 1995 when, for the first time, a Chinese boat stopped, boarded and inspected two Taiwan fishing boats in the Spratlys. Unilateral actions by any one of the claimants - the capture of an occupied island from another's forces, unilateral drilling in the area, the capture or killing of fishermen, or large, aggressive naval manoeuvres - could trigger a spiral of increasingly frequent and violent incidents. The naval and air force arms build-up in the region, originally designed to enhance

---

5   Adam Schwarz, 'Where oil and water mix', *Far Eastern Economic Review*, 16 March 1995, pp.54-8.
6   Julian Baum and Matt Forney, 'Strait of uncertainty', *Far Eastern Economic Review*, 8 February 1996, pp.20-1.

capability to protect resources in Exclusive Economic Zones, could become a real arms race, involving the acquisition of submarines, aircraft carriers, and bombers and fighters capable of reaching the islands.[7] Because intensifying and spreading violence could endanger freedom of navigation along the strategic sea lanes in the South China Sea, the interests of Japan and the United States could be affected. Indeed, the control of this area by a potential adversary or its allies has implications for the national security interests of Japan, the United States, and even Russia. On the other hand, a common stance by Vietnam and ASEAN, tacitly supported by the United States, could confirm China's worst fears of being surrounded by hostile nations, thus spurring it to violent action.[8] These possibilities, together with this worst-case scenario of open conflict, could even have implications for longer term geostrategic alliances in the region.

There is thus a growing sense of urgency to resolve these issues. The window of opportunity for half-measures, let alone a multilateral interim solution, may be closing as nationalism increasingly influences positions on the disputes. The increasing frequency and intensity of incidents as well as the uncertainty about China's foreign policy in the post-Deng era further heighten concern. The time to make peace is now, when there still is peace.

A Glimmer of Hope?

A glimmer of hope for a way out of this conundrum was provided in July 1995 at a meeting with ASEAN officials at the ASEAN Annual Meeting in Brunei, when Chinese Foreign Minister Quian Qichen said that China would be willing to use international law and the 1982 Convention on the Law of the Sea as a basis for negotiating the issues and that it would discuss the issues with all seven members of ASEAN. China thus appears to have implicitly abandoned its historic line claim, and may even be considering

---

7   'Manila sees China as threat despite assurances', *Reuters*, 27 October 1995; Joseph R. Morgan, *Porpoises Among the Whales: Small Navies in Asia and the Pacific*, East-West Center Special Report No.2, March 1994; 'Russians deny jet sales fuel Asian arms race', *Honolulu Advertiser*, p.C-4.

8   Frank Ching, 'Vietnam: a challenge to ASEAN', *Far Eastern Economic Review*, 3 November 1994, p.38.

formally revising its claim to be restricted to all territories ceded by Japan in 1945.[9] Taiwan is also reportedly considering changing its claim to be only to those islands occupied by it and China. Such claims would not encompass major sea lanes or have the potential to affect freedom of navigation. Quian also said that China had always attached great importance to the safety and freedom of navigation in the region and that it did not believe there would be any problems in this regard.[10] Indeed, in August 1995, China and the Philippines announced a code of conduct rejecting the use of force to settle their dispute.[11] This agreement could become the basis of a region-wide code of conduct. In November, the Philippines and Vietnam negotiated a similar creed.[12]

A change in China's position might also make an allocation or a multilateral solution more feasible, particularly if China relinquishes or suspends its claim to portions of the continental shelves of ASEAN members. In this context, it may be significant that Taiwan, in sharp contrast to China, has proposed *multilateral* joint development.[13] Even some Beijing officials seem to be saying that a gradual evolution from bilateral to multilateral projects in the area may be possible, under the convenient fiction of a 'bilateral' ASEAN-China 50/50 arrangement.[14]

These rays of hope are dimmed, however, by Quian's statement that China had indisputable sovereignty over the Spratly Islands and their adjacent waters, and that China's national laws asserting its sovereignty over the islands would play a role in resolving the issue. More ominous was the report that China plans to

---

9   Rigoberto Tiglao, 'Remote control', *Far Eastern Economic Review*, 1 June 1995, pp. 20-1.

10   Michael Ricchardson, 'China takes softer stand in dispute on Spratly isles', *International Herald Tribune*, 31 July 1995, p.1.

11   'China agrees to discuss Spratlys "code of conduct"', *Reuters*, 10 May 1995; 'PRC limits claim', FBIS-EAS-95-094, 16 May 1995, p.47.

12   'Philippines, Vietnam agree on Spratlys pact', *Honolulu Advertiser*, 9 November 1995, p.A17.

13   'Li Teng-hui proposes South China Sea development', FBIS-CHI-95-072, 14 April 1995, p.69.

14   'Spratlys: China wants in on development', *Straits Times*, 1 June 1995, p. 1; 'Ramos' preference for diplomacy, dialogue noted', FBIS-EAS-95-068, 10 April 1995, p.70; 'Qian views Spratlys with Vietnamese counterpart', FBIS-CHI-95-096, 18 May 1995, p.8.

hold naval exercises in the Spratly area.[15] Moreover, these changes in position may stimulate a race by China and Taiwan between themselves, or between them and Vietnam, to occupy as many islands as possible, particularly those at the far edges of the group, as a basis for their claims.

Nevertheless, China's words have for the moment somewhat allayed ASEAN's fears and relieved tension in the region. But it is not clear whether China's seeming change of heart is the product of a desire not to antagonise ASEAN at a time when China's relations with the United States are strained,[16] or of a genuine interest in regional cooperation inspired by the priority of economic reform, or only a consequence of present limited military capability. Heretofore, China has never shown the slightest interest in compromising its sovereignty claim to the South China Sea, and particularly to the islands therein, despite the hegemonic implications of this position.[17] Moreover, at the ASEAN Regional Forum (ARF), Chinese spokesman Shen Guofeng reasserted China's 'indisputable sovereignty over the islands and their adjacent waters and said that the most effective way to handle this dispute is through bilateral negotiations'.[18] The issue is whether the economic necessity of regional cooperation will serve as a sufficient constraint on its long-term nationalist purpose. The evidence is not encouraging in this respect, particularly since it is driven by a strong sense of regaining lost Chinese stature and territory, and it continues to improve its military capabilities to do so, unconstrained by the former Cold War balance of power. Thus the situation in the South China Sea could get worse before it gets better. The proof will be in the pudding. To truly instil confidence, China must follow up its soothing words with positive actions.

---

15   Murray Hiebert, 'Comforting noises', *Far Eastern Economic Review*, 10 August 1995, pp.14-16; 'Paper: Beijing planning naval games in Spratlys', *Honolulu Advertiser*, 25 July 1995, p.A-6; 'China stands firm on Spratlys, Harry Wu', *Reuters*, 30 July 1995; 'China is firm on Taiwan, Spratlys ahead of ASEAN meeting in Brunei', *Japan Times*, 22 July 1995, p.4.

16   'China seen defusing tension in South China Sea', *Reuters*, 2 August 1995.

17   Michael Leifer, 'The Maritime Regime and Regional Security in East Asia', *The Pacific Review*, Vol.4, No.2, pp.126-36.

18   'ASEAN and the ASEAN Regional Forum', *Pacific Research*, August 1995, p.22.

What To Do?

Many approaches and half-measures have been proposed that would help build confidence to move beyond the unstable status quo to an interim solution that is both equitable and stable: for example, preventive diplomacy such as by an eminent persons group; a code of conduct; institutionalisation of the multilateral dialogue; a maritime safety and surveillance regime; and various other CBMs. Also suggested were conciliation, mediation or arbitration through the good offices of a third party or judiciary body such as the International Court of Justice (ICJ) or the Law of the Sea Tribunal. But these approaches seem highly unlikely in this case. China, for one, has made it crystal clear that it will not accept the involvement of outside entities, and most Asian nations are deeply suspicious of Western methods.[19] Moreover, although internationalisation can have benefits, it can also restrict the flexibility of regional actors. Direct negotiations are the current preferred method, whether bilateral, serial or multilateral. Because modest measures will neither stabilise the situation nor address the questions of resource access and allocation, an initiative which directly addresses the allocation issues seems necessary. Options range from a series of bilateral arrangements; the allocation of the features and/or the maritime space; a high seas or regional commons; to single-purpose, or comprehensive, multilateral management regimes.

Any solution has to address or take into account the following regional political realities:

- the conflicting sovereignty claims to features and the need to demilitarise them;

- the conflicting claims to maritime space;

- the conflicting definitions of the area that might be subject to a resource management agreement;

19 However, Malaysia and Singapore have agreed to take their dispute over Pulau Batu Pateh/Horsburgh Light to the ICJ, and Malaysia has proposed to China that the ICJ be asked to resolve the Spratly issue. 'Regional Briefing', *Far Eastern Economic Review*, 22 September 1994, p.13; Nayan Chanda, 'Long shadow', *Far Eastern Economic Review*, 28 December 1995 and 4 January 1996, pp.17-18.

- the claimants' primary interest in the petroleum potential of the area;

- the need to establish a stable administrative decision-making structure that is perceived as fair and equitable;

- China's insistence on separate negotiations with each party;

- a necessity to allocate some power and benefits to the smaller powers;

- the need to acknowledge and accommodate the interests of non-claimant South China Sea countries;

- the need to acknowledge and accommodate the interests of extra-regional maritime powers.

China is unlikely to enter into a cooperative arrangement in which others benefit equally. For its cooperation, China will expect to receive rewards. Thus if Beijing is to participate in a joint development effort, the other claimants will have to make it sufficiently attractive to China. Moreover, China prefers a loose form of joint development.[20] To extract a long-term commitment from China will require the provision of considerable benefits and significant exit costs, to make it more difficult for China to defect. Achievement of this goal might involve tying a Spratlys solution to other issues on which ASEAN has more leverage such as economic investment and trade, thus making China keenly aware of the opportunity costs it will incur by defection.

Bilateral Negotiation of Provisional Arrangements

China has consistently insisted that all the issues are bilateral and that they should be resolved through bilateral negotiations.[21] If the claims of China and Taiwan are taken as one and the same, this position is partially accurate. That is, large sections of the South China Sea to the west and north of the Spratlys are claimed respectively only by China/Taiwan and Vietnam, and China/Taiwan and the Philippines (Figure 11.2). Thus these areas could indeed be

---

20 FBIS, Daily Report: East Asia, 2 July 1992, p.1.
21 David Lague, 'ASEAN: China flexes its muscles', *Sydney Morning Herald*, 2 July 1994.

Figure 11.2: Categorisation of claims by number of claimants

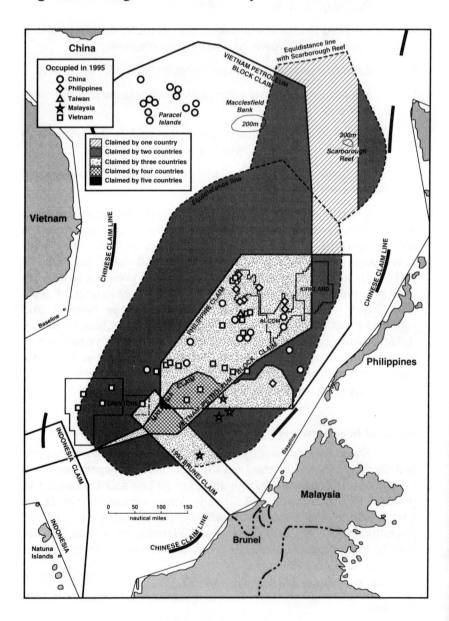

hived off for separate bilateral negotiations. It is conceivable that a combination approach could be used in which these two areas are negotiated separately from the multiple-claim area. Some observers believe it is easier for two parties to agree to cooperate than for larger groups and that a web of bilateral agreements can form the basis for a multilateral process and solution.[22]

But there are problems with the bilateral approach. Bilateral negotiations are clearly to the advantage of a major power, in contrast to multilateral negotiations, which offer an opportunity for the smaller powers to band together to extract greater concessions from a major power. Furthermore, the outcome of each set of bilateral negotiations would set precedents and restrict flexibility in ensuing negotiations. The tactical issue for the other claimants is that, if they choose to negotiate with China bilaterally, they will have to recognise China's claim implicitly or explicitly and thus allow China leverage over the other claimants. Bilateral negotiations for the entire area would also be costly, inefficient, and impractical. Moreover, where more than two parties claim the same area, bilateral negotiations would not resolve all the conflicting claims, and a joint development agreement between two claimants of an area also claimed by a third party could be a violation of the rights of the third party.

Allocation

One solution suggested by some observers is simply to divide up the maritime space and the islands among the claimants. Such an allocation could include only the features, only maritime space, or both the features and maritime space.

Allocation of Only the Features

There are several options for allocation of only the features. In one scenario, a limited sovereignty over the features might eventually pass to the present occupants (see Figure 11.1) but the features would be entitled only to a 500 m safety zone, could not be used for military purposes, and access for scientific research or other

---

22   Lee Lai To, *CALS Newsletter*, Vol.1, No.2, September 1994.

peaceful purposes would be allowed for other claimants. Another possibility would be an agreement that all the features are 'common property - *res communis*', together with an agreement on a set of guidelines for their use for peaceful purposes. Much less likely would be a Svalbard-like solution in which one claimant, presumably China or Vietnam, gains a very limited sovereignty over all the features with all others having access for peaceful purposes, including resource exploitation.[23]

None of these scenarios is, however, likely to be acceptable to all the claimants. The present pattern of occupation is considered unfair by China; China, Taiwan and Vietnam claim sovereignty over all the features; and few, if any, claimants are likely to be willing to limit their rights to use the features. In fact, the allocation of the features might accentuate strategic concerns and exacerbate the disputes if the recognised owners reserve the right to claim EEZs and continental shelves extending from the islands. Moreover, establishment of maritime boundaries would be dysfunctional for the management of living resources.

Another possibility is to allocate the features between the claimants through a judicious combination of proximity, occupation and *Realpolitik*. Although China would get no Spratly features if equidistance lines were chosen from the coasts of countries bordering on the South China Sea, if a system of 'rough equity' were used, China could be granted close to half the features, including the three largest islets: Itu Aba, Thitu and Loaita (Figure 11.3). This approach would give China all but two of the features it now occupies. The other claimants would get the features closest to their own coastlines. In this scenario, the potential owner is usually the present dominant occupant in the area.

---

23 See Mark J. Valencia, 'Cooperation in Marine Scientific Research as a Confidence Building Measure' in Sam Bateman and Stephen Bates (eds), *Calming the Waters: Initiatives for Asia Pacific Maritime Cooperation* (Strategic and Defence Studies Centre, Australian National University, Canberra, 1996), pp.166-8. See also Oran R. Young and Gail Osherenko, 'International Regime Formation: Findings, Research Priorities and Applications' in Oran R. Young and Gail Osherenko (eds), *Polar Politics: Creating International Environmental Regimes* (Cornell University Press, Ithaca and London, 1993), pp.223-62.

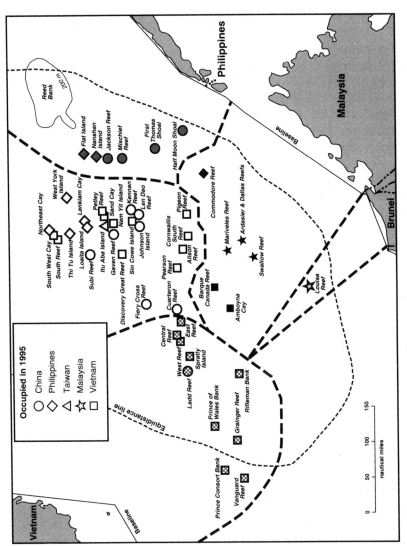

Figure 11.3: Allocation of South China Sea by a system of 'rough equity'

Allocation of the Features and Maritime Space

Scenario 1. Allocation of the entire South China Sea and its features by equidistance lines from claimed or approximated coastal baselines, ignoring the Spratly and Paracel islands (Figure 11.4).

Under this scenario, China/Taiwan, Vietnam, and the Philippines would gain roughly equal areas. Although Pratas Island, most of the Macclesfield Bank, and all but two Paracel islands would go to China, it would not get any of the Spratly geologic block. The Philippines and Vietnam would split fairly evenly the area that would be considered high seas in Scenarios 3 and 4. The Philippines would receive the northeastern portion of the Spratlys geologic block including Reed Bank, one of the most promising areas for hydrocarbons. Of the islands the Philippines occupies, all but Commodore Reef would fall in the Philippine sector. Vietnam would receive the Vanguard Bank and Crestone Concession area, while Indonesia would get the Natuna gas fields it disputes with Vietnam. Malaysia would receive two sizeable sectors off Sarawak and Sabah separated by Brunei's narrow corridor.

Vietnam already occupies all the features in its hypothethetical sector except Ladd Reef. Six Vietnam-occupied islets would, however, be allocated to the Philippines sector, and five to the Malaysian sector. All islands occupied or claimed by Malaysia except Louisa Reef would be situated in the Malaysian sector.

Scenario 2. Allocation of the entire South China Sea and its features by equidistance lines from claimed or approximated coastal baselines, ignoring the Spratlys but giving the Paracel features full effect as Chinese territory (Figure 11.5).

The main difference between Scenarios 2 and 1 is that in Scenario 2 China gains part of the central South China Sea at the expense of Vietnam and the Philippines. It would also get Macclesfield Bank. But China's sector would barely reach the Spratly geologic block and it would thus get no share of the Spratly area most likely to contain petroleum, let alone the continental shelves of other South China Sea claimants. However, it would give China a solid legitimate presence in the central South China Sea.

Figure 11.4: Allocation of South China Sea by equidistance lines from claimed or approximated coastal baselines, ignoring the Spratlys and Paracels

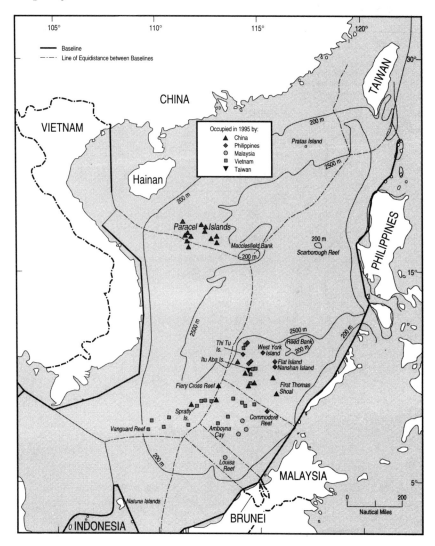

Figure 11.5: Allocation of South China Sea by equidistance lines from claimed or approximated coastal baselines, ignoring the Spratlys and Paracels but giving the Paracels full effect as Chinese territory

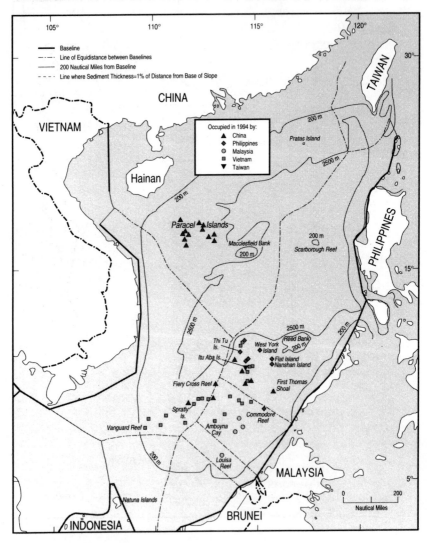

Scenario 3. Allocation of the Spratly features and maritime space based on 'rough equity' and *Realpolitik* concerns (Figure 11.6).

This approach is designed to give each claimant a substantial sector, based on the extent of their claims, their present occupations, their relative positions of power, and a sense of 'rough equity'. Dividing lines are drawn according to three factors: island occupation, natural spatial divisions between island clusters, and continental shelf claim limits. The boundary between the zones of China and the Philippines generally follows the natural gap between the eastern islands (Flat and Nanshan) and the rest, a boundary which is reinforced by both the bathymetry and the geology of the area. The precise line between Vietnam's zone and that of China is based on Vietnam's present occupation of East Reef and China's present occupation of nearby Cuarteron Reef. Malaysia's zone is bounded mainly by the limits of its claimed continental shelf, while Brunei's zone begins at its coastal borders and ends at the seaward limit of its maximum EEZ based on equidistance.

China would receive the majority of the land features, but the seabed in its maritime space has no hydrocarbon and shows only limited prospects for such. All other claimants receive areas of known hydrocarbon potential: the Philippines receives Reed Bank and Malaysia the Luconia Gas Fields and areas further north, both of which are either presently in production or slated for such. Vietnam receives all of the Wan'an Bei area, plus the Blue Dragon field and prospective areas further north, which it also is striving to develop. The island and seabed awards thus tend to balance out to achieve a rough sense of equity.

Scenario 4. Allocation of the South China Sea and features on the basis of equidistance lines out to the limit of the countries' 200 nm EEZs and their geographical continental shelves, ignoring both the Spratly and Paracel features (Figure 11.7).

If allocation followed the rules in the Law of the Sea Convention, but ignored the tiny islands altogether, an area of high seas beyond both 200 nm and the legal limits of the continental shelf would remain in the central South China Sea. The ocean area beyond 200 nm would be classified as 'high seas'. The overlapping claim areas within 200 nm of baselines or within the legal continental shelf

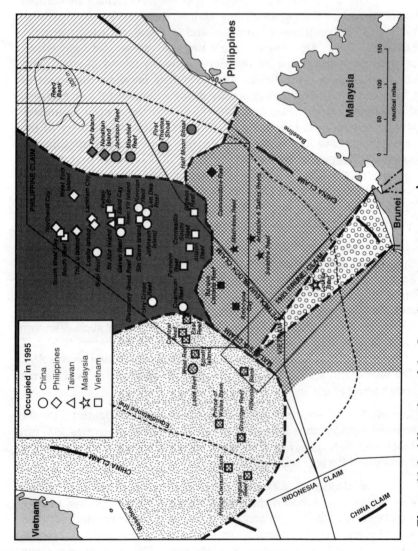

Figure 11.6: Allocation of the Spratlys by 'rough equity' and *Realpolitik* concerns

Figure 11.7: Allocation of the South China Sea by equidistance lines out to 200 nautical miles, ignoring both the Spratlys and Paracels

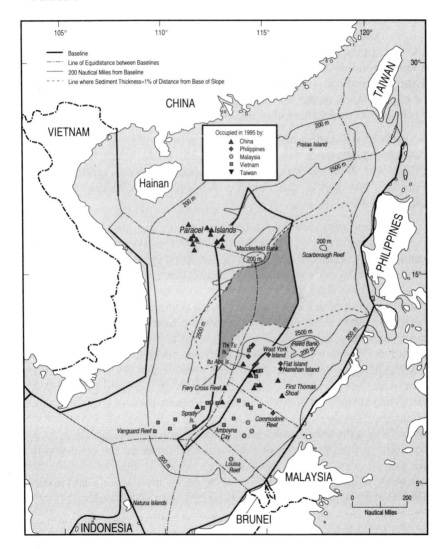

could be allocated on the basis of equidistance. The features inside the high seas area would have only 500 m safety zones, would be controlled by the regional regime, and might be used as multilateral bases for exploration and exploitation of resources.

Because of the morphology of the ocean floor, Vietnam and the Philippines would lose significant portions of their continental shelves relative to Scenario 1 and China would lose one or two Paracel islands plus Macclesfield Bank to the high seas regime. Seven or eight islands of the Spratlys occupied by China, Vietnam and the Philippines would also fall in the high seas area beyond 200 nm.

Scenario 5. Allocation of the South China Sea and its features on the basis of equidistance lines out to the limit of the countries' 200 nm EEZs and their geographical continental shelves, ignoring the Spratlys, but giving the Paracels full effect as Chinese territory (Figure 11.8).

This approach might be justified on the grounds that the Paracels are somewhat larger than the Spratlys, have water and have been inhabited historically, are now occupied by some 4,000 Chinese citizens (mostly on Yongxing or Woody Island), and are considerably closer to China than the Spratlys.[24] In addition, China has protested overflights over the Paracel area.[25] If this scenario were followed, the high seas area in the north that would be beyond both the 200 nm limit and the legal limit of the continental shelf would be considerably reduced compared to Scenario 4. China would gain Macclesfield Bank plus a significant area of sea floor that would otherwise be beyond national jurisdiction in Scenario 3. Perhaps more importantly, it would legitimise China's presence in the heart of Southeast Asia in the context of a multilateral regime. However it would still gain only a small fringe of the Spratly geologic block, and no share of the producing or high-potential areas on the continental shelves of Vietnam and Malaysia, to which it desires access. A variation of this scenario would be to leave the Paracels and their attendant maritime area to be resolved by China and Vietnam.

---

24   Jon M. Van Dyke and Dale L. Bennett, 'Islands and the Delimitation of Ocean Space in the South China Sea' in Elisabeth Borgese and Norton Ginsburg (eds), *Ocean Yearbook* 10 (University of Chicago Press, Chicago, 1993), p.62.
25   ibid., p.57.

Figure 11.8: Allocation of the South China Sea by equidistance lines out to 200 nautical miles (Paracels have full effect)

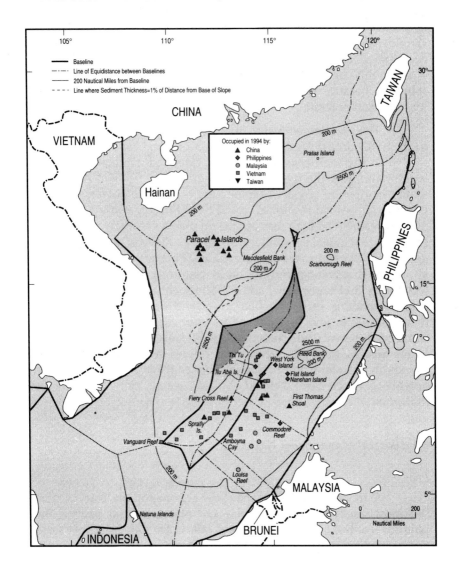

While interesting as geographical exercises, all of these allocation scenarios have serious shortcomings. Aside from the sovereignty issues, first and foremost is the lack of agreement on the definition of the area in dispute and therefore what and how it should be allocated. Second is a likely lack of agreement on what constitutes equity and an equitable allocation - that is, who gets what. In this context, China is unlikely to be mollified by any of these solutions because it remains excluded from any areas with good hydrocarbon potential.

The problem with any 'high seas' approach is that, according to the 1982 United Nations Convention on the Law of the Sea, the seabed in the high seas area beyond extended continental shelves would fall under the regime of the International Sea-Bed Authority, would be open to resource exploitation by outside powers, and the profits from seabed resources would have to be shared with the rest of the world.[26] The high seas approach, unless somehow modified to incorporate regional sensibilities, is thus not likely to be acceptable to any of the claimants, particularly China. Furthermore, a free access approach is advantageous to those countries with more capital, technology and know-how, and may only enhance competition and conflict resulting in the familiar tragedy of the commons - for the living resources and for peace. This approach, although removing some of the area from contention, would also leave unresolved a larger area of multiple overlapping claims. It also excludes some islands in the south with relatively better fishing grounds and oil potential, which are claimed by Malaysia, Vietnam and the Philippines.

Multilateral Management Regimes

Principles

A model multilateral maritime regime for the South China Sea must satisfy agreed principles and objectives and address the political realities of the region. Listed below are principles that seem applicable to any regime for this region:

---

26 *United Nations Convention on the Law of the Sea*, 10 December 1982, UN Doc.A/Conf.62/121.

1   The territorial sovereignty and sovereign integrity of every claimant should be equally recognised in the regime. Thus, although the conflicting claims to maritime space in the Spratly area should be set aside, the ultimate resolution of these claims should be unaffected by the establishment of the regime. Further, the principle of non-interference in each other's internal affairs should be reaffirmed.

2   Regional disputes should be resolved through regional mechanisms. Regional issues should not be internationalised.

3   Regional disputes should be resolved through peaceful means. The resources of the South China Sea should continue forever to be used exclusively for peaceful purposes and should not become the scene or object of regional or international military conflict. Provocative military activities such as the establishment of military bases and fortifications should be prohibited from this region.

4   The resources of the South China Sea should be exploited pursuant to the principles of equity and fairness toward all countries and all peoples of the region.

5   Cooperative regional exploration, development and management of the living and non-living resources of the South China Sea is the most equitable solution to the controversies concerning this area and will promote rational resource use and peace in this region.

6   Each country has the responsibility to ensure that activities within its jurisdiction or control do not cause damage to the claimed territory, resources or environment of any other country.

7   Rare and fragile ecosystems, as well as the biodiversity of the living resources of this region, should, as far as is practical, be protected and managed to ensure their preservation for future generations.

8   The Spratly area should be included in the Southeast Asia Nuclear Weapon-Free Zone.[27]

Objectives

The objectives of any multilateral regime for the South China Sea should include the following:

1   to enhance peace and security in the South China Sea;

2   to create a stable, predictable maritime regime for the South China Sea based on mutual restraint, transparency, trust and confidence;

3   to demilitarise the Spratly features through an agreed, mutual, step-by-step process;

4   to manage the resources in a cooperative, equitable, efficient, rational and sustainable manner;

5   to ensure safe navigation and prevent piracy, drug smuggling, poaching, purposeful pollution and other illegal activities;

6   to accommodate the interests of other South China Sea states, including the land-locked and geographically disadvantaged states;

7   to accommodate the interests of extra-regional maritime powers for peace, stability, freedom of navigation and security of sea lanes;

8   to accommodate the existing interests of companies in the area;

9   to provide a mechanism for consultations on maritime matters and for resolving disputes among the South China Sea countries;

10   to maximise accumulation and availability of information on the area;

---

27   Nayan Chanda, 'Long Shadow', *Far Eastern Economic Review*, 28 December 1995 and 4 January 1996, pp. 17-18.

11 to promote scientific research and the exchange of scientific data regarding the resources of the South China Sea;

12 to promote the transfer and exchange of technology among interested countries; and

13 to transcend the sovereignty claims in order to avoid politicising the issues.

Definition of the Area to be Managed

The basic problem for a multilateral management regime is to obtain agreement on the definition of the area to be covered. Among the possibilities are: (a) the area enclosed by a line equidistant between undisputed territory of the littoral countries and the Spratly features (Figure 11.9); (b) the area beyond national jurisdiction if either the Paracel or Spratly islets are ignored and the 200 nm exclusive economic zones and continental shelves are drawn in accordance with the procedures allowed in the Law of the Sea Convention (Figures 11.7 and 11.8); (c) the area claimed by three or more claimants (the multiple claim area) (Figure 11.2); and (d) a line connecting the outermost main islands (or all drying reefs) (Figure 11.10).

(a) If China/Taiwan's claim is only to the Spratly features and the maritime zones they are entitled to generate, then the area of focus could be that area within the line equidistant between the Spratly features and undisputed national territory (Figure 11.9).[28] In other words, China's maximum claim, based on giving full effect to all the islets, would be to the equidistant line between these islets and the coast of the claimant states. Although it is highly doubtful that any of the features should have full effect, pretending that they have this capacity is a convenient legal fiction for defining an area for managed sharing which would include many of the promising areas for hydrocarbons. Under this approach, however, all claimants except China/Taiwan would be denied portions of their possible EEZs and continental shelves.

---

[28] This line is from Victor Prescott, 'Sharpening the geographical and legal focus on the potential regional conflict in the Spratly Islands', paper presented at the ISEAS Workshop on *The Spratly Islands: A Potential Regional Conflict*, Singapore, 8-9 December 1993.

Figure 11.9: Area within the line equidistant from the Spratly features and undisputed national territory

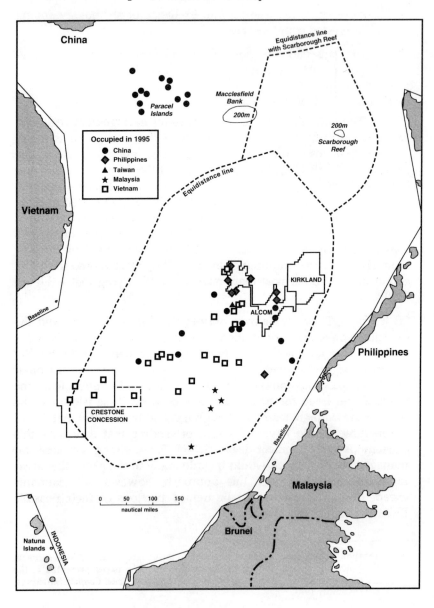

Figure 11.10: Area enclosed by a line connecting the outermost islands or, in the case of the Spratlys, the outermost main reefs

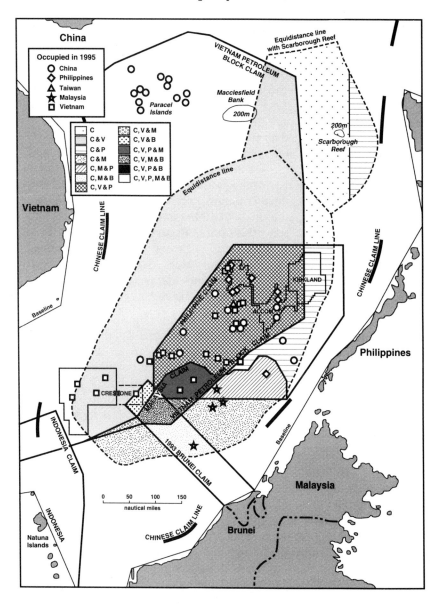

(b) The area beyond 200 nm from acceptable baselines and/or beyond the legal limit of the continental shelf (i) ignoring the Paracel and Spratly islands (Figure 11.7); or (ii) giving the Paracels full effect (Figure 11.8). The area beyond 200 nm or the limit of the continental shelf is really a combination allocation-regional commons solution. It seems most equitable in the sense that all get a portion of the area they claim and a share in the rest. However, it is unlikely to be acceptable to China, because the commons area with or without the Paracels having full effect is unlikely to contain any significant resources. This unacceptability is likely to be accentuated if islands in each sector are allocated to the claimants and if the Paracels and its attendant maritime area remain disputed between China and Vietnam. If Vietnam could see fit to trade off its claim to the Paracels and their surrounding maritime space for a full uncontested EEZ and a hefty share in the regional commons, perhaps this definition of the 'area' would be acceptable to both China and Vietnam. Brunei and the Philippines may support this option, in part because it gives them access to or a share in areas they do not even claim. Taiwan would probably not agree with it, but does support multilateral development in principle. Vietnam and Malaysia have difficulties with it but may be willing to accept it in the end.

(c) In the Multiple Claim Area (MCA) option (Figure 11.2), the area of focus would include only the area claimed by three or more entities, counting the claims of China and Taiwan as one. This approach would considerably narrow the area in question and leave disputes in areas outside the MCA to be resolved by the claimants themselves. China would perhaps prefer this definition because it allows it to dominate bilateral or trilateral negotiations outside the smaller MCA.

(d) A minimalist approach would focus on the area enclosed by connecting the outermost main islands or, alternatively, the outermost drying reefs in the Spratly group (Figure 11.10). This idea is analogous to the definition of archipelagic baselines in the Law of the Sea Convention, although only an archipelagic state claimant, namely the Philippines, could incorporate the area in this manner. The problem with this definition is that, at its smallest, it excludes much of the Reed Bank in the northeastern portion of the area with good gas potential, thus ignoring China's and Vietnam's claims there.

Organisational Structure

The area chosen could be governed by a robust Spratly Management Authority (SMA) complete with a Council, a Secretary-General, a Secretariat, and Technical and Financial Committees (Figure 11.11). The Council would be the decision-making body. The Secretary-General would be appointed by and responsible to the Council, implementing its decisions and managing the day-to-day affairs of the SMA. The Secretariat would consist of a small core staff of technical and financial experts serving the Secretary-General and through him or her the Technical and Financial Committees. The Technical and Financial Committees would be appointed by the Council on an equitable basis and would recommend action to the Council. At the other extreme, a loose Spratly Coordinating Agency (SCA) could coordinate and serve as a clearing house for separate joint development schemes managed by the particular claimants to a particular area. This approach might require only a Director and perhaps a small Secretariat. It is conceivable that the responsibilities of the intergovernmental Committee for Coordination of Joint Prospecting for Mineral Resources (CCOP) might be expanded to include the coordination/clearing house function since all claimants (except China and Brunei) are members.

The advantage of the loose SCA is that it allows maximum flexibility and essentially separate management for different areas involving only the claimants to each particular area. But it does not address the problems of transboundary fisheries and environmental management. The advantages of a robust authority are that all activities would be managed and all concerned parties would have a say in their management, thus building confidence through cooperation. It also provides the option of allocating meaningful positions within the SMA, including the Secretary-General position, to specific countries. It would also enable management of transboundary living resources and expand the possibilities for trade-offs.

Figure 11.11: Spratly Management Authority

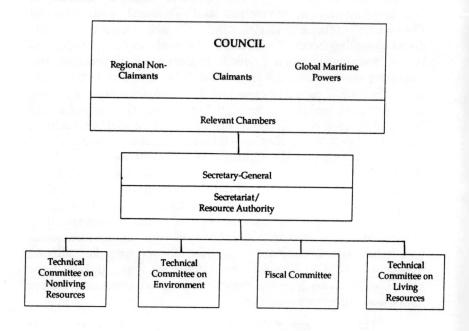

Sample Regimes and Allocation of Costs and Benefits

Having outlined the principles, objectives, critical elements and components of a South China Sea regime, we now outline several sample options.

(i) *A Robust Spratly Management Authority (SMA) Governing the Equidistant Area*

This approach would focus on development of resources, primarily hydrocarbons but also including the living resources, in the area within the line equidistant from the claimants' coasts and the Spratly islets (the 'core' area). All claimants would *set aside* (not give up) their claims to ocean space and resources there. Percentage shares of benefits and costs of operating the SMA could be allocated based on the extent of the original claims within the 'core' area (Figure 11.10) or, alternatively, on the length of coastline bordering the South China Sea. On the basis of extent of original claims, the largest share would fall to China and Taiwan, which claim the entire area, and, in descending percentages, smaller shares would be allocated to Vietnam,[29] the Philippines, Malaysia and Brunei.[30] The percentage accruing to China/Taiwan is 52 per cent, Vietnam 28 per cent, the Philippines 11 per cent, Malaysia 8 per cent and Brunei 1 per cent. China and Taiwan would have to work out between themselves the allocation of their shares and their respective roles in the functions of the SMA, which would administer the area within the

---

[29] Vietnam's share is based on its claim as interpreted from its petroleum block issued in the late 1980s. However Nyguen Binh, Vietnam's Director of Treaty and Legal Affairs, has stated to Van Dyke that none of the features which it claims should generate extended maritime zones or be used as basepoints for claims, and that Vietnam is in the process of adjusting its baselines to conform with the Convention and of finalising its EEZ and continental shelf claims, which will also conform to the Convention. In that case, Vietnam's share would be significantly less, or zero, and the other claimants' shares proportionately increased.

[30] The shares allocated to the various claimants were calculated in the following manner: first, the total area within the equidistant line - minus Scarborough Reef - was divided into twelve sub-zones, each claimed by a different combination of states (Figure 11.10). The percentage of the area of each sub-zone to total area was calculated and this percentage divided among the claimants to that sub-zone. These percentages were then totalled for each claimant. For example, although Brunei claims about 7 per cent of the area within the equidistant line, it

equidistance line and manage the exploration and exploitation of resources there. Giving China a symbolic majority might induce it to participate, but that might be unacceptable to the other claimants.

Finding a solution to the Vietnam/China dispute is the key to the solution to the larger Spratly problem. In addition to the core Spratly area, Vietnam and China have unresolved disputes on land, in the Gulf of Tonkin, in the Paracels, and in the Vanguard Bank/Wan'an Bei area. If Vietnam received a favourable settlement with China in the Tonkin Gulf and Vanguard Bank areas, it might consider settling for 28 per cent or less of the shares in an SMA that covers an area with less hydrocarbon potential. One possibility is that any gas to be found in the Vanguard Bank area could be converted to LNG by a plant sited in Vietnam or it could be used directly by Vietnam by tying into the pipeline to the Dai Hung field, perhaps with a share of the gas or proceeds going to China.

However, relying on the extent of original claims as a basis for share allocation raises several significant problems. First, the extent of China/Taiwan's and Vietnam's original claims is unclear, and second, countries would be tempted to argue that their original claims were more extensive than they actually were. Because of these difficulties, shares might be allocated based on the claimants' general directional coastline length on the South China Sea. Under this approach, China and Taiwan together would get about 31 per cent, Vietnam 26 per cent, the Philippines 21 per cent, Malaysia 20 per cent and Brunei 2 per cent. The major difference between this allocation and that based on the extent of original claims is that China's share is reduced from 52 per cent to 31 per cent while those of the Philippines and of Malaysia are sharply increased. Thus the incentive for China to participate or to make concessions to Vietnam elsewhere is greatly reduced.

Voting membership in the Council could be confined to the claimants, although other South China Sea countries and extra-regional maritime powers could have seats with a voice, but no vote. One problem with this approach is that it does not accommodate the resource access interests of other South China Sea countries or their

---

would receive only 1 per cent of the shares since its claim overlaps those of others.

frontage on the South China Sea - Indonesia, Singapore, Thailand, Cambodia, and land-locked Laos. But if they were each to receive a share equal even to that of the smallest of the claimants, namely Brunei (1 per cent), the percentage allotted to China/Taiwan under the allocation scheme based on the extent of original claims would fall below 50 per cent. China/Taiwan would thus not have a symbolic majority share in the organisation and might then not find this arrangement acceptable. Therefore these non-claimants should receive a few per cent of the profits 'off the top' in recognition of their interests as South China Sea countries, but they would have no vote in organisational decisions. The remaining shares would be recalculated to 100 per cent for purposes of allocation and voting. In any multilateral sharing scenario, special provision should be made for shares or the right of access to the surplus living resources of the area for the landlocked and geographically disadvantaged states - Laos and Singapore.

Consensus - the absence of formal objection - and compromise should be the norms in decision-making by the Authority's Council. But decisions by vote might be needed on the production-sharing system of the Authority, and on fisheries management and environmental management decisions. Suggested below are several alternatives, all of them fairly complicated in order to ensure fairness as well as to encourage compromise and consensus.

Weighted Voting with General and Weighted Votes

Regarding substantive matters affecting the Authority or the entire area, one method of decision making would be to allocate both general and special weights to each claimant following the examples of the International Coffee Organisation, the International Energy Agency and the Asian Development Bank. Each claimant-state would have five 'general weights' plus additional 'special weights' based on its claimed percentage of the area within the equidistant line or the length of its coastline on the South China Sea. If the 'special weights' were based on the current claims, total votes would be 125-57 for China/Taiwan, 33 for Vietnam, 16 for the Philippines, 13 for Malaysia and 6 for Brunei. If the 'special weights' were assigned based on coastline length, the total votes would still be

125-36 for China/Taiwan, 31 for Vietnam, 26 for the Philippines, 25 for Malaysia and 7 for Brunei. In both systems, China/Taiwan would not be able to pass or block decisions by itself, even in a simple majority vote, and would thus require the cooperation of at least one other claimant to do so. On the other hand, the other four claimants could not constitute a majority unless they all voted the same way. (In the coastline length system, Vietnam, Malaysia and the Philippines together could constitute a majority.) Procedural issues in the Council might require a simple majority of the voting shares. But a substantive Council decision affecting the entire area should require a two-thirds majority. In the system based on original claims, a China/Vietnam combination could pass any matter requiring a two-thirds majority (85 votes), but not a three-fourths majority (94 votes), which could also be made the decision threshold.

A Combined Chambered System

Perhaps a combined chambered system would be acceptable. In this system, decisions on matters affecting the entire regime or authority would be based on voting shares according to the extent of original claims or coastline lengths, while decisions concerning activities in a particular location or 'chamber', based on twelve separate geographic areas categorised by the pattern of overlapping claims (Figure 11.10), would have to be approved by both a majority of the overall votes and a majority of the claimants to that location or 'chamber'. Because China would be a member of every 'chamber', this provision would partially meet China's concern that issues should be resolved bilaterally or through the formation of multiple joint development arrangements each involving China. This approach would also require the parties to compromise to move forward.

This system is in itself a compromise, much like the recent agreement on mining of the international seabed, in which the dominant power allows participation and distribution of some benefits to smaller states while retaining considerable power. It also advantages the smaller powers by providing them with benefits and a strong voice in decisions affecting the specific areas they claim in common with others. By a 'gentlemen's agreement', a citizen of China/Taiwan might always be the Secretary-General of the SMA.

Allocation of Executive Positions

Perhaps as important as the process of decision making is the process of implementation, and for that process the composition of the administrative staff or 'executive branch' of the SMA becomes crucial. Many international organisations have a de facto - and sometimes *de jure* - system of allocating certain positions in the organisation to nationals of certain specified countries. This system works reasonably well in, for instance, the Asian Development Bank, where the President is traditionally a Japanese citizen and the General Counsel is traditionally a citizen of the United States. The existence of a similar system in the SMA could have the effect of reassuring member nations that their concerns would not be ignored. The Secretary-General might always be a Chinese citizen, perhaps with Deputy Secretary-Generals being identified with other member nations. Another approach would be to have a rotating system, whereby each country has a turn at the key positions.

Claims Set Aside, but Not Abandoned

It would have to be made crystal clear that *formal* sovereignty was not being surrendered and that the SMA is a body designed only to facilitate exploration and management of the resources, nothing more. In other words, jurisdiction would be de-coupled from resource management. Although *operational* sovereignty would be curtailed, *formal* sovereignty would be unaffected. The formal sovereignty issue would have to be decided by future generations. Nevertheless, China and Taiwan could argue that because they would be given the largest share in the SMA, the other claimants had recognised the validity of China/Taiwan's formal sovereignty claim to the features there. On the other hand, the other claimants could also argue that the agreement simply shelves the formal sovereignty claims and that they have not relinquished their own claims.

Demilitarisation of the Features

In conjunction with the establishment of the Authority, the core area could be declared a zone of peace as well as part of the

Southeast Asia Nuclear Weapon-Free Zone, thus providing a basis for building a larger Zone of Peace, Freedom and Neutrality (ZOPFAN) encompassing the whole of Southeast Asia, and thereby helping achieve one of ASEAN's (and China's) stated objectives: removing opportunities for great-power intervention and interference in regional affairs.

Other Elements and Functions

Under this cooperative regime, sovereignty claims would be frozen and the SMA would eliminate conflict, facilitate exploration and development of resources, manage fisheries and maintain environmental quality. Fisheries access to the core area would be equally available to all claimants. The legitimate passage of vessels would be allowed. The SMA would also promote international cooperation in scientific research and in protecting vulnerable ecosystems, including the possible designation of parts of the area as 'protected marine areas' as provided in the Law of the Sea Convention.

With the core area removed from contention, a few areas of overlapping claims would still need to be addressed by the claimants, perhaps by establishing joint development zones in, for example, the southwestern margin of the Spratlys claimed by Indonesia and Vietnam and the southern margin claimed by Brunei and Malaysia (Figure 11.2).

A company that has received a concession from one of the governments of the region at a location that has been historically recognised as within the claim of that nation and that has invested sufficiently in the exploration and/or exploitation of the resources at that location to render the concession as 'vested', would be provided with appropriate protection for its investments.

Eventually, sovereignty over the islands and rocks themselves might pass to the present occupants or, alternatively, be allocated on an equitable basis considering occupation, geographic proximity and the comparative lengths of South China Sea coastline. But the features should be entitled only to 500 m safety zones or, at the most, narrow territorial seas (for example, 3 nm), they could not be used for military purposes, and access for scientific research and to any resources they might harbour would be allowed for other claimants.

Because all parties have agreed to seek a peaceful solution, they have little justification for maintaining military forces on the islands.[31] The major problem with demilitarisation is 'how to get from here to there' without creating a power vacuum. To start the process, a communication committee could be established by the claimants. The committee would negotiate agreed rules for normal activities in the islands. The first might be a formal pact not to threaten or use force. Then the level of military activity could be limited by agreement and the size of forces frozen. The committee would be notified in advance troop exercises and movements, and would communicate this information to other interested governments. As mutual trust increased, the personnel on the Spratly Islands could change to non-combatants, such as engineering, construction and scientific units. Eventually, military units could be phased out completely and replaced by civilians. In this path to demilitarisation, no vacuum would be created and change would be gradual.

(ii) *The Equidistant Area and Multiple Joint Development Companies* (Figure 11.10)

If a less formal structure were desired, cooperation could be achieved through a looser set of relationships. A series of twelve joint development companies (JDCs) could be established, at least on paper, under a Spratly Coordinating Agency (SCA), based on the areas of overlap of the original claims. China/Taiwan would be a member of all joint development companies and Vietnam would be a member of all but the three that would cover areas it apparently does not claim. (If it does not claim any of the area it would not be a member of any joint development company.) Shares, benefits, costs and voice or vote in the operation of each joint development

---

31 At a press conference in Singapore on 13 August 1990, the visiting Chinese Premier Li Peng said that 'China is ready to join efforts with Southeast Asian countries to develop the [Spratly] Islands, while putting aside for the time being the question of sovereignty'. Under the proposal, Vietnam, China and the Philippines would withdraw their military units from the islands in favor of joint development of the area's seabed and marine resources.

company would be shared equally after allocating 5 per cent of the profits to the loose SCA, which would facilitate, coordinate and harmonise the operations of multiple joint development arrangements for resource exploitation within the core area. Perhaps another 5 per cent of the profits could be allotted to non-claimant South China Sea countries. Alternatively, the contributions could be the same as that stipulated in Article 82 of the Law of the Sea Convention for resource exploitation beyond 200 nm; that is, annual payments and contributions with respect to all production at a site after the first five years of production at that site. For the sixth year, the rate of payment or contribution is 1 per cent of the value or volume of production at the site. The rate increases by 1 per cent for each subsequent year until the twelfth year and remains at 7 per cent thereafter. In this formulation, production does not include resources used in connection with exploitation.[32]

Under this model, the SCA would have a Chinese as its head because of China/Taiwan's membership in every joint development company. Members would be drawn from each of the claimants. Although a joint development company would exist on paper for each of the 12 areas, it would become operational only when and if a simple majority of the claimants to that area agreed to operationalise it. This approach would go a considerable way towards satisfying China's demand that the issues be resolved between it and each of the claimants, while giving the claimants an opportunity for influencing decisions in areas they claim in common with others.

(iii) *The 'Archipelagic Option' with a Robust Spratly Management Authority* (Figure 11.10)

Another alternative is to create a robust SMA to administer hydrocarbon development and fisheries, but only in the smaller area enclosed by lines connecting the outermost drying reefs. If costs and benefits were allocated according to the extent of original claims to the area, the claimants would have the following percentage shares: China/Taiwan 37 per cent; the Philippines 28 per cent; Vietnam 20 per cent; Malaysia 14 per cent; and Brunei 1 per cent. If shares were allocated according to South China Sea coastline lengths, the shares

---

32   United Nations Convention on the Law of the Sea, Article 82(2).

would be: China/Taiwan 31 per cent; Vietnam 26 per cent, the Philippines 21 per cent, Malaysia 20 per cent and Brunei 2 per cent. Again, five per cent of the profits from mineral, hydrocarbon, and fisheries production in the enclosed area should be allocated to South China Sea non-claimants. Another five per cent from this area would go to meet the operating expenses of the SMA. The rest of the benefits and costs would be allocated according to the above percentages. The enclosed area would be managed by the robust SMA with substantive decisions requiring a three-fifths majority and each country having one vote (China and Taiwan would constitute one vote) or the required vote could be two-thirds - that is, four out of the six members, with China and Taiwan each having one vote. The organisational structure and treatment of territory could be the same as in Option (i), that is, the islands/features would have no or a very narrow territorial sea, would be demilitarised, and would be open to access by all claimants. Joint development of the areas outside the enclosed area would be negotiated between the claimants.

The disadvantage of this option is that it focuses on one of the smallest areas possible. Thus the potential for hydrocarbon discovery is diminished and the area to be negotiated by the claimants themselves greatly expands, leaving many issues unresolved including transboundary fisheries management and environmental protection. This illustration is useful in demonstrating that resolution of the controversy over the features *per se* will not resolve the disputes.

These alternatives are simply points along a continuum. There are many perturbations and these examples are illustrative only. We hope, however, they will stimulate constructive discussion on a comprehensive multilateral interim solution to these difficult and dangerous disputes.

It is almost always dangerous and difficult to predict the future of such international disputes. Nevertheless, some outcomes do seem more likely than others. Initially, a code of conduct may be established among all the claimants, including general principles of peaceful co-existence and specific measures for preventing fisheries conflicts or accidental military encounters. China will probably not be able to maintain or operationalise its claim to most of the South

China Sea. Moreover, it will probably be agreed that most, if not all, features in the region are not entitled to zones beyond a narrow territorial sea and possibly a contiguous zone, and should not affect the location of maritime boundaries. Instead they will probably be enclaved or otherwise provided with limited maritime areas. Geology and geomorphology will have little impact on the delimitations. Rather, the maritime boundary delimitations will be likely to be based primarily on the geography of the littoral states' mainland coastlines and the larger islands, and equidistance will play an important role in the initial positioning of these boundaries. But they also will be influenced by respective coastline lengths, resource development activities and, perhaps, other functional considerations. Finally, the entire area will probably wind up within the EEZs of the littoral states and navigation and overflight will be protected. Under this regime, the coastal states will have certain rights, including the right to exploit the living marine resources and the exclusive right to exploit the non-living resources of the seabed and subsoil in their sectors, as well as duties to protect the environment and manage the living and non-living resources. The result will be a complicated system of maritime boundaries which is not conducive to ecosystem and living resource management. Thus the littoral states are likely to eventually adopt cooperative management regimes at least for these purposes.

CHAPTER 12

MARITIME COOPERATION

I THE MIMA-SIPRI PROJECT ON ARMS TRADE TRANSPARENCY IN SOUTHEAST ASIA

Bates Gill and J.N. Mak

Introduction

The first steps for this project were taken in 1993 with the establishment of the Maritime Institute of Malaysia (MIMA), and its Centre for Maritime Security and Diplomacy.[1] Maritime arms procurement and holdings - a critical aspect of maritime security and diplomacy in Southeast Asia - became a key area of the Centre's research work. The project set out to collect, collate and analyse all arms procurement of the region, with special emphasis on defining, identifying and aggregating 'maritime armaments'.

To make the project more manageable and relevant, its work focused on Association of Southeast Asian Nations (ASEAN) arms acquisitions and their impact on stability or instability in the region. From the mid to late 1980s, ASEAN countries have been engaged in a significant arms modernisation drive, with a strong emphasis on maritime assets and capabilities. Analyses of these developments tended to focus narrowly on the question of whether or not an 'arms race' was unfolding in the region. However, using arms race theories to understand these developments in Southeast Asia could at best only explain why and if the region was involved in an arms race. The assessments could not answer the more conceptually challenging and practical question of whether and when regional acquisitions were stabilising or destabilising.

---

[1]   The other MIMA centres are the Centre for Economics and Ocean Industries; the Centre for Coastal Development, Marine Environment and Resources; and the Centre for Law and Ocean Policy.

264 The Seas Unite: Maritime Cooperation in the Asia Pacific Region

By exploring this latter question, researchers can develop 'sign posts' or early-warning indicators to prevent arms acquisitions from spiralling into a destabilising situation. Such an approach can help moderate arms build-ups by indicating when confidence-building measures should be adopted. Regional discussions of destabilising and stabilising arms acquisitions can in themselves also act as confidence-building measures among neighbours. Thus, in addition to collecting and analysing data, the project recognised the need to push forward the debate on arms trade transparency and discussions of how to use such data to help determine stabilising versus destabilising arms acquisitions.

MIMA-SIPRI Cooperation

MIMA's interests found resonance with the Stockholm International Peace Research Institute (SIPRI). The two institutes drew up a plan in June 1994 to jointly conduct a project which explores the notion of transparency in arms trade and defence policy for Southeast Asia. The project was well timed, coinciding with calls by the United Nations, the ASEAN Regional Forum (ARF) and several Southeast Asian governments to conduct such research and to help support ongoing first-track initiatives and policies on these issues.

The project has two initial objectives. The first was to combine carefully the efforts of SIPRI and MIMA to develop a de facto conventional arms trade register for ASEAN. The result was the publication of analysis and extensive data in August 1995 in the form of a volume entitled *ASEAN Arms Acquisitions: Developing Transparency*. This monograph captures all known and verified arms transfers to and within ASEAN from 1973 to 1995. Orders to the year 2001 are also included. The long time frame of the data captures the two major arms acquisitions periods for ASEAN and allows for more accurate analysis of long-term trends. It was hoped that such an effort would promote further thinking in the region as to the benefits and disadvantages of transparency in arms acquisitions.

The second major objective of the project was to move forward from the de facto register and develop further discussion and debate on the concept of transparency as a confidence-building measure and its relationship to security in Southeast Asia. This second step included the October 1995 MIMA-SIPRI workshop in Kuala Lumpur and the publication of the workshop papers in the form of an edited volume entitled *Arms Trade, Transparency, and Security in Southeast Asia*.[2]

The workshop included project researchers as well as a large number of officials and analysts concerned with arms trade and security issues drawn from Southeast Asia. The workshop reflected a quite alarming lack of understanding among analysts and practitioners of arms registers in general and the United Nations Register of Conventional Arms (UNROCA) in particular. More importantly, most participants expressed strong reservations, bordering on suspicion, about any formalised arms trade transparency measures such as a register. Participants tended to argue that little could be gained from such efforts, and that they might prove to be destabilising and counterproductive.

Based on the workshop discussions, the project's contributors revised their research for publication in the edited volume with the intention of improving regional understanding of transparency measures and their relationship to determining stabilising versus destabilising arms acquisitions. This volume draws together the work of eight experts on issues of arms trade, arms register and Asia Pacific security affairs to present conceptual frameworks, analysis and extensive data and information. It is intended to provide security analysts and policy-makers with the necessary tools to assist in their work concerning arms trade and defence policy transparency as an approach to confidence building in the region.

Looking Ahead

However, moving forward in implementing such an approach in the region is difficult. First, ASEAN's current defence planning, in the absence of any clear external threat, is based on contingency planning, and may not be conducive to such transparency and confidence-building measures.[3] Second, even if a wider consensus existed as to the need for such approaches, it remains very difficult to

---

2   Oxford University Press, forthcoming.
3   See J.N. Mak, 'The ASEAN Naval Build-Up: Implications for the Regional Order', *Pacific Review*, May 1995.

devise and implement effective models which satisfactorily define destabilising and stabilising acquisitions and create adequate multilateral mechanisms to deal with problematic build-ups.[4]

Bearing in mind these caveats, as well as the more general reservations evident in the region on the question of transparency, MIMA and SIPRI decided to focus their efforts on defence-related data sharing as a confidence-building measure. Data sharing is a more flexible and less formal concept of cooperation than arms trade transparency mechanisms, and can be conducted in a unilateral, bilateral and multilateral manner. Promoting further developments in this area may contribute to building greater confidence in the development of more formal arms trade and defence policy mechanisms for the future. The MIMA-SIPRI workshop scheduled for January 1997 will examine the role, limits and possibilities of data sharing in contributing towards a more stable security environment in Southeast Asia.

---

[4]   See Bates Gill, 'Enhancing National Military Capabilities in the Asia-Pacific Region: Debating Legitimate Needs versus Unwarranted Development', *10th Asia-Pacific Roundtable*, 8-9 June 1996, Kuala Lumpur.

II PROPOSAL FOR ANNUAL WORKSHOPS ON REGIONAL MARITIME ISSUES*

Introduction

The sea is important in the Asia Pacific region as a source of food, a medium for trade and a basis for longer term economic prosperity. Many regional countries are investing heavily in offshore resource development, expanding their merchant shipping fleets and developing the maritime capabilities of their defence forces. As Asia Pacific countries become more interdependent, maritime issues, particularly the sustainable development of coastal and marine areas, will become even more important. Regional seaborne trade stands to increase enormously in the future, particularly on the routes between Southeast and Northeast Asia.

Multidisciplinary education and training in marine and maritime affairs are an important element of capacity building for the integrated management and sustainable development of coastal and marine areas. When these activities are conducted at a regional level, they also constitute an important maritime confidence- and security-building measure, which enhances dialogue and cooperation between regional nations. Regional nations have a common interest in maritime issues, many of which are more effectively handled cooperatively rather than on a national basis.

The principal forum in the region concerned with peace and security, the ASEAN Regional Forum (ARF), has identified a list of prospective preventive diplomacy measures which could reduce tensions and the potential for conflict. These include numerous measures in the field of maritime cooperation, such as cooperative

---

* This proposal is an outline of a possible programme of cooperative workshops on regional maritime issues to be coordinated by the Council for Security Cooperation in Asia Pacific (CSCAP). It was endorsed by the Fifth CSCAP Steering Committee Meeting in Kuala Lumpur in June 1996. The proposed programme would foster regional maritime cooperation and provide a practical maritime confidence- and security-building measure (MCSBM) which would contribute both to regional security and to the sustainable development of regional countries.

approaches to sea lines of communication, joint marine scientific research, and conventions on the marine environment (dumping of toxic wastes and land-based sources of marine pollution).

Concept

- An annual workshop on regional maritime issues to be hosted each year by a different Asia Pacific country under the auspices of CSCAP.

- A maximum of 40 participants with a Director of Studies (a senior academic from the region involved in maritime affairs), Workshop Coordinator, approximately six resource persons, and administrative staff.

- The resource persons should be regional specialists in fields such as maritime security, law of the sea, shipping and ports, fisheries and marine environmental management.

- The workshop should be conducted over an intensive 5 to 6 day period.

- The workshop programme should include lectures, syndicate exercises and presentations and panel discussions.

Objectives

The objectives of the workshop should be to:

- develop greater awareness and knowledge of maritime issues within the Asia Pacific region and of their security implications;

- foster informal links and interaction between officers from different government departments and agencies with marine/maritime responsibilities, including defence forces (relevant links may extend both between regional countries and within individual countries);

- promote problem solving and cooperative approaches to the management of marine and maritime affairs in the region;

- identify and explore the security benefits of existing maritime cooperation through agencies such as the UNEP Regional Seas Programme, APEC Working Groups, Western Pacific Fisheries Consultative Committee (WPFCC), the South-East Programme in Ocean Law, Policy and Management (SEAPOL) and the Economic and Social Commission for Asia and the Pacific (ESCAP);

- contribute to regional maritime confidence- and security-building measures;

- contribute to comprehensive security in the Asia Pacific region by providing a bridge between the different elements of comprehensive security (for example, economics, environment, resources) and the various regional forums where such issues are discussed;

- acquaint specialists in one field of maritime activity with information on what is occurring in other fields; and

- provide a forum for the generation of initiatives for regional maritime cooperation.

Study Topics

The following are the proposed study topics (with an additional half-day to be allowed for things such as course administration):

- Law of the Sea (1-1/2 days)

  - introduction

  - maritime zones (territorial sea, EEZ, archipelagic waters, etc.)

  - navigational regimes (innocent passage, straits transit and archipelagic (sea lanes passage)

  - the resolution of overlapping claims and the delimitation of maritime boundaries

  - regime of islands, historic waters, straight baselines, etc.

- legal regimes for joint development zones and cooperative resource development
- Maritime Security (1 day)
  - regional security overview and developments
  - contemporary maritime strategy
  - regional maritime force developments
  - proposals for MCSBMs
  - maritime transparency, information exchange, etc.
  - piracy, drug smuggling, illegal migration and other unlawful activities at sea
  - maritime surveillance, regulation and enforcement
- Marine Environmental Management (1 day)
  - UNCED and *Agenda 21*
  - IMO Conventions
  - integrated coastal zone management
  - principles of oceans management and sustainable ocean development, including the importance of regional cooperation
  - prevention of marine pollution
  - marine scientific research, hydrography and oceanography
  - global warming and sea level rise
- Shipping and Ports (1 day)
  - trends in regional seaborne trade
  - regional port developments
  - port state control
  - marine safety issues
  - search and rescue

- security of sea lines of communication
- Other Marine Industries (1 day)
  - fishing
  - offshore oil and gas
  - shipbuilding
  - marine tourism
  - marine biotechnology
  - environmental management/consultancy
- Regional Maritime Cooperation (1/2 day)
  - dispute management and resolution
  - tri-regional linkages between Northeast and Southeast Asia and the South Pacific
  - scope for new initiatives

Syndicate Exercises

Typical syndicate exercises could include :

- development of a proposal for a cooperative regional maritime surveillance and safety regime;
- simulated negotiations to resolve difficulties associated with multiple use of a particular marine environment;
- simulated negotiations and game play to develop a proposal for a joint marine scientific research programme; and
- committee work to develop a proposal to government for a regional agreement on the avoidance of incidents at sea.

Who Should Attend?

The workshop is both an educational experience and a forum for the generation of ideas and problem solving. Attendees should be sufficiently senior that they are able to contribute ideas at the workshop while also gaining from the experience. For example:

- middle-ranking public servants from government departments and agencies in the region with marine/maritime responsibilities (for example, foreign affairs, shipping, fisheries, environmental management);

- security officials and officers from regional defence forces (primarily navies and air forces) of Commander/Captain (Lieutenant Colonel/Colonel) rank or equivalent;

- middle management executives from marine industries; and

- academics (including marine scientists) from regional institutions with teaching and research interests in relevant fields.

III THE WAY AHEAD

Sam Bateman and R.M. Sunardi

The informal objective of the CSCAP Working Group on Maritime Cooperation has been to move beyond the rhetoric of maritime cooperation and identify some practical measures and areas of cooperation which would help reduce the risks of maritime tension and promote a stable maritime regime in the Asia Pacific region. The Working Group has now met twice and made significant progress towards the identification of practical initiatives for regional maritime cooperation.

The Working Group has adopted a broad view of security with a range of non-conventional security issues, such as marine safety, resources conservation, coastal zone management and unlawful activities at sea (drug smuggling, illegal population movements and piracy) being considered, along with more conventional security issues, such as the security of sea lines of communication (SLOCs) and naval developments. We believe that Working Group meetings have confirmed the value of CSCAP establishing a working group on regional maritime cooperation. The sea and issues to do with the sea are high on the agenda of Asia Pacific countries and offer a host of opportunities for preventive diplomacy and confidence building. The nature of these opportunities is such that they are well suited for development through a 'second-track' process.

The papers presented at the first meeting of the Working Group[1] held in Kuala Lumpur in June 1995 provided a useful review of the extent of maritime security concerns in the region and confirmed the importance of pursuing regional maritime cooperation in the context of the comprehensive concept of security. This concept is well understood by the strategic community but this may not be the case with the other communities that look after the various elements of comprehensive security. People concerned with maritime security and

---

[1] The papers from the first Working Group meeting were published in Sam Bateman and Stephen Bates (eds), *Calming the Waters: Initiatives for Asia Pacific Maritime Cooperation*, Canberra Papers on Strategy and Defence No.114 (Strategic and Defence Studies Centre, Australian National University, Canberra, 1996).

national defence in a conventional sense may be uninterested in non-conventional defence issues, while those working on regional cooperation in fields such as shipping, marine scientific research, resource development or environmental protection do not necessarily appreciate the security implications and benefits of what they are doing.

Mark Valencia summed the situation up in his paper to the first meeting of the Working Group. Although he was speaking specifically about marine scientific research, his points are equally valid to the other communities dealing with marine issues:

> It is in this context that cooperation in this seemingly innocuous field can build confidence, dampen frontier tension and improve relations in this region so critical to world peace and prosperity. Indeed, successful cooperation in marine scientific research can build the confidence necessary for initiatives in other spheres, and establish the basis for a jump from tactical to complex learning.[2]

We also note that the process of second-track diplomacy in the Asia Pacific region appears to be better developed in the more theoretically sensitive areas of foreign policy and defence than it is in other, possibly less sensitive, areas at sea, such as the protection of the marine environment, marine safety, conservation of fish stocks, resource exploration and exploitation, and other transnational oceans management issues. These issues still tend to be handled by officials from specialist areas of government and are not necessarily placed in a broader strategic and political context. This means that the full value in contributing to a sense of regional community is not necessarily achieved from the dialogue and cooperation that does take place. Some second-track initiatives in the various dimensions of regional oceans management would demonstrate that comprehensive security encompasses both the 'concepts' and 'processes' of security (that is, both the issues discussed and the forums in which such issues are discussed).

In implementing the concept of comprehensive security in the Asia Pacific region, there is a need to ensure not only that the concept

---

2   Mark Valencia, 'Cooperation in Marine Scientific Research as a Confidence Building Measure' in ibid., p.139.

is understood by the strategic community, but also that the links are made with the other communities and forums dealing with the various aspects of the concept. There are numerous regional bodies where some aspect of comprehensive maritime security is considered including, for example, various Asia Pacific Economic Cooperation (APEC) working groups, the UNEP Regional Seas Programme, the Western Pacific Fisheries Consultative Committee (WPFCC), and the Economic and Social Commission for Asia and the Pacific (ESCAP). As a first step in making these links, two practising marine scientists were invited to participate in the second meeting of the Working Group.

This second meeting was held in Kuala Lumpur in April 1996. The agenda for this meeting reflected some greater focus on particular issues than was apparent at the first meeting. Sessions at the meeting covered regional naval cooperation, shipping and marine safety, marine scientific research and environmental issues, and the resolution of marine resource and boundary disputes. Deliberations during this meeting highlighted the importance of drawing some distinction between *naval cooperation*, which encompasses *all* military activities associated with the sea (recognising that in some regional countries, maritime aircraft are operated by the air force); and *maritime cooperation*, which is a broader concept in line with the theory of comprehensive security, encompassing the full range of activities and interests in the sea (for example, shipping, marine resources and environmental protection). Specialist matters of naval cooperation are generally being handled in the Western Pacific Naval Symposium (WPNS), while our CSCAP Working Group is concentrating on broader issues of maritime cooperation.

One major conclusion emerging from the activities of the Working Group to date is the extent to which regional security is severely compromised by the relative lack of agreed areas of maritime jurisdiction over the enclosed and semi-enclosed seas of East Asia.[3] It is not overstating the present situation to say that, to some extent, maritime disorder prevails in the region with unregulated pollution of

---

3   An 'enclosed or semi-enclosed sea' is defined by the UNCLOS Article 122 as 'a gulf, basin or sea surrounded by two or more States and connected to another sea or the ocean by a narrow outlet or consisting entirely or primarily of the territorial

the marine environment, overfishing, marine environmental degradation, widespread illegal activities at sea (for example, unlicensed fishing, piracy and drug smuggling), and relatively few agreed maritime boundaries. Disputation also arises between different activities at sea: shipping can cause pollution, overfishing depletes fish stocks, dumping and undersea mining degrade the marine environment, conservation clashes with development. Problems and difficulties will continue, with consequent risks to national security, unless new approaches are found to managing regional seas and oceans which are not based primarily on sovereignty, unilateral rights to resources and agreed maritime boundaries.

The new international law of the sea expressed in the 1982 UN Convention on the Law of the Sea (UNCLOS) sought to provide increased coastal state rights over the resources of adjacent waters, while also introducing a code of conduct for exploiting marine resources and preserving and protecting the marine environment. Unfortunately, it is becoming apparent that the regime of the Exclusive Economic Zone (EEZ), rather than helping to settle problems of maritime jurisdiction and to improve standards of marine environmental management, may in fact have produced greater insecurity and lower management standards, as a result of the incentive provided for opposite and adjacent countries to claim overlapping zones of jurisdiction. This is particularly the case in East Asian waters where, as the South Korean member of our Working Group has argued, the existence of EEZs has been 'more divisive than integrating'.[4]

While the conflicting claims to the Spratly Islands have attracted most attention in recent years, the problems of resolving maritime jurisdiction are not unique to the South China Sea but proliferate elsewhere throughout the marginal seas of East Asia. Despite the old adage that 'good fences make good neighbours', sometimes it is physically impossible, for a variety of reasons, to build good fences, particularly in the sea. This seems to be the situation

---

seas and exclusive economic zones of two or more coastal States'. Examples include the Gulf of Thailand, the South China Sea and the Yellow Sea.

[4] Jin-Hyun Paik, 'The Fisheries Regime in Northeast Asia', in Dalchoong Kim, Jiao Yongke, Jin-Hyun Paik and Chen Degong (eds), *Ocean Affairs in North-East Asia and Prospects for Korea-China Maritime Cooperation* (Institute of East-West Studies, Yonsei University, Seoul, 1994), p.86.

now with the East Asian seas where, until 1996, not one EEZ boundary has been delimited between opposite or adjacent countries.[5] The problem is a function of the peculiar geography of the region, with the offlying chain of archipelagoes enclosing a series of seas stretching from the Sea of Okhotsk in the north to the Timor and Arafura seas in the south. The problem is then further complicated by the various islands and island groups in the enclosed and semi-enclosed seas which are the subject of conflicting claims to sovereignty. As has been seen during 1996 with both the Takeshima/Tok-do Islands between the Korean peninsula and Japan, and the Senkaku/Diaoyutai Islands to the north-east of Taiwan, these issues have the potential to generate considerable nationalistic fervour.

Many maritime boundaries in the Asia Pacific region will not be agreed in the short term and it is necessary to find some other means of managing the area in dispute, and exploiting its resources, which is not based on unilateral jurisdiction and sole ownership of the resources. The development of these means is the key challenge of marine affairs in the region if territorial disputes are not to fester away as a destabilising element of regional security. The CSCAP Working Group on Maritime Cooperation sees itself as having some part to play in developing new ideas about managing the seas and ocean areas under dispute. The Working Group especially believes that an Asia-Pacific-wide approach to this issue has potential benefit in the utility of shared experiences from the various subregions (for example, Southeast Asia, Northeast Asia and the South Pacific).

The realisation of this major problem has led the Working Group to focus on three particular initiatives for its work programme in the immediate future. Specifically, the initiatives recognise the importance of the comprehensive approach to maritime security, the need to build links between the different forums and communities dealing with the various elements of maritime security (broadly defined), the importance of an integrated approach to the management of marine environments, and the confidence-building opportunities offered by activities in this field. The three initiatives are:

---

5   It was announced in September 1996 that an EEZ or water column boundary had been agreed between Australia and Indonesia in the Timor and Arafura seas.

- the development of draft Guidelines for Regional Maritime Cooperation;

- the conduct of regular Regional Maritime Issues Workshops; and

- focusing the next meeting of the Working Group specifically on 'Regional Oceans Management and Security'.

Guidelines for Regional Maritime Cooperation

This initiative started out as a proposal for a regional agreement, variously known as a Regional Agreement on the Avoidance of Incidents at Sea (INCSEA), Maritime Risk Reduction or Maritime Safety. The change of focus recognises the work already being carried out by the WPNS on a regional INCSEA, but whereas the WPNS is seeking practical (or 'sailor-made') solutions for naval cooperation, the Working Group has in mind a multilateral instrument with wider political and diplomatic implications for maritime cooperation. In fact this instrument may well provide the 'top cover' for any WPNS agreement.

The objective is to establish a regime aimed at enhancing maritime safety and cooperation in the region. In particular, the agreement should include the various items which have been identified by the ASEAN Regional Forum (ARF) in its lists of measures for preventive diplomacy and maritime cooperation.[6] The agreement should also provide clear support for the 1982 UN Convention on the Law of the Sea (UNCLOS) and *Agenda 21* Chapter 17: 'The Protection of the Oceans, All Kinds of Seas, Including Enclosed and Semi-enclosed Seas, and Coastal Areas and the Protection, Rational Use and Development of their Living Resources'.

The desirability of a regional agreement along these lines lies in the thought that, while the interests of regional countries in the sea often coincide, they can also conflict, particularly with regard to the

---

6   These lists are found in Annexes A and B to the 1995 ARF Concept Paper. See ASEAN Senior Officials, 'The ASEAN Regional Forum: A Concept Paper', May 1995, reproduced in Desmond Ball and Pauline Kerr, *Presumptive Engagement: Australia's Asia-Pacific Security Policy in the 1990s* (Allen & Unwin, Sydney, 1996), pp.111-19.

exploitation of marine resources, both living and non-living. Furthermore, waste disposal and other polluting effects of coastal, or even inland, developments in one country can be carried by sea and river to affect other countries. Or in the case of a maritime security consideration, many regional countries have a vested interest in the freedom of navigation through international straits and choke points, but the coastal states adjacent to these waters may feel that this freedom compromises their national security or the integrity of their marine environment, unless stricter procedures for navigation or marine safety are introduced. The draft agreement now circulating within the Working Group contains articles on matters such as respect for sovereignty and sovereign rights, law and order at sea, marine safety, marine scientific research and disaster mitigation.

Regional Maritime Issues Workshops

The detailed proposal for these workshops is included as Part II of this chapter. It has been developed in response to the idea that education and training for marine affairs is another area for worthwhile cooperation, particularly at the integrated policy level rather than in specific technical or vocational fields which are already relatively well covered.

The Working Group identified at its second meeting the need for increased regional maritime awareness - at all levels from an institutional or university level through the national and regional levels to an international level. There is a training and educational task involved in developing an environment conducive to regional maritime cooperation. Generally, people train in a single discipline under orthodox tertiary programmes, which are well established, in both national and overseas institutions. People in single disciplines talk with one another both at the national and regional levels, but there would be benefit now in training and educational programmes which bring together people from different disciplines and backgrounds to share experiences and values.

The concept of regional workshops on maritime issues was strongly supported by the Steering Committee of CSCAP at its meeting in June 1996. These workshops are seen by CSCAP as an achievable contribution to the fulfilment of the ideals and objectives of the ARF. Other benefits include:

- a significant contribution to maritime trust and security building in the Asia Pacific region;

- the fostering of further informal links between regional navies and defence forces, as well as with people from other organisations and institutions concerned with maritime issues in the region;

- the provision of a possible bridge between the security community of the region and other organisations and forums concerned with non-conventional aspects of maritime security in the region;

- the nomination of students to attend the workshop will be a demonstration of active engagement and commitment to regional security; and

- the provision of a forum in which further ideas for regional maritime confidence building may emerge.

If all goes to plan, the proposal to conduct these workshops will be put to the ARF during 1997 with a view towards the first workshop being conducted either in late 1997 or the first part of 1998. The likely venue for the first workshop will be somewhere in Southeast Asia.

Regional Oceans Management and Security

The next meeting of the full Working Group is planned for May-June 1997 on the theme 'Regional Oceans Management and Security'. The objective will be to turn the present lack of order, which exists in the region with regard to the management of regional oceans and seas, into opportunities for cooperation and dialogue, improved regional relations and confidence building. Sessions at the meeting will cover issues such as management regimes, conflict/dispute resolution, marine environmental management, and law and order and safety at sea, with a view to developing some ideas on building possible regional regimes to deal with these issues.

While 'oceans governance' is the term often used to describe the management of the oceans and seas of the world by national governments, regional organisations and international agencies, we have preferred to talk about 'oceans management' in the security context. The issue has received much attention in recent times due to the expansion of economic activities at sea, growing concern over the health of the world's oceans, overfishing, disputes over maritime boundaries, and tensions between different uses of coastal and marine areas (such as navigation, fishing, mining, disposal of waste, tourism and recreation). Clear understanding of rights and responsibilities of jurisdiction is essential for good management, although this does not have to be exclusive jurisdiction. The resolution of conflicting claims or, alternatively, the establishment of agreed administrative arrangements based on harmonious relationships is essential for the development of the region's marine resources and the maintenance of law and order at sea. If these conditions are not achieved, then maritime areas of the Asia Pacific region, particularly the seas of East Asia, will remain zones of tension and potential conflict.

The current system of marine resource exploitation in East Asia is based on national rights and obligations. It is ineffective because of the number of overlapping claims to maritime jurisdiction, the lack of agreed maritime boundaries, and countries acting largely in their own self-interest. Problems will continue, with consequent risks to national security, unless new approaches are found to the management of disputed areas of regional seas which are not based on sovereignty, unilateral rights and agreed maritime boundaries. These approaches may include some or all of the following:

- a functional approach to resource and environmental management, whereby sovereignty is set aside and resources and ecosystems are managed and exploited according to their own special demands, conservation needs and optimal utilisation;

- joint development of particular resources (such as the Timor Gap Treaty between Australia and Indonesia for developing the hydrocarbon resources of a disputed area in the Timor Sea);

- extension of the joint resource zone concept to possible joint EEZs, which would allow each country to participate in the economic benefits while spreading the costs of environmental management; and

- joint patrols for law and order and resource protection operations by neighbouring countries in areas of overlapping or adjacent jurisdiction.

This list is far from being exhaustive. We suggest that the development of fresh approaches needs a very different mind-set to the present one of trying to define boundaries between countries at sea in the same way as they are drawn on land. Pressing problems of resource management and environmental protection require resolution without the need to reach agreement on the underlying sovereignty and boundary issues, and nations must be able to pursue their maritime interests and manage their marine resources in an ecologically sustainable manner in accordance with agreed principles of international law. Regional cooperation and dialogue to develop the necessary regimes constitutes a significant confidence- and security-building measure and we see the CSCAP Working Group on Maritime Cooperation as continuing to play a useful role in generating new ideas and initiatives.

BIBLIOGRAPHY

BOOKS AND BOOK CHAPTERS, MONOGRAPHS

Abrahamse, Wayne, 'Developing Countries and Naval Diplomacy' in Greg Mills (ed.), *Maritime Policy for Developing Nations* (South African Institute of International Affairs, Johannesburg, 1995).

Ball, Desmond, 'Introduction' in Desmond Ball and Ross Babbage (eds), *Geographic Information Systems: Defence Applications* (Brassey's Australia, Sydney, 1989).

Ball, Desmond, 'The Post Cold War Maritime Strategic Environment in East Asia' in Dick Sherwood (ed.), *Maritime Power in the China Seas* (Australian Defence Studies Centre, Australian Defence Force Academy, Canberra, 1994).

Ball, Desmond, 'CSCAP: Its Future Place in the Regional Security Architecture' in Bunn Nagara and Cheah Siew Ean (eds), *Managing Security and Peace in the Asia-Pacific* (Institute for Strategic and International Studies (ISIS) Malaysia, Kuala Lumpur, 1996).

Ball, Desmond (ed.), *The Transformation of Security in the Asia/Pacific Region* (Frank Cass, London, 1996).

Bateman, Commodore Sam (Retd), 'Confidence and Security Building: An Australian View' in Jasjit Singh (ed.), *Maritime Security* (Institute for Defence Studies and Analyses, New Delhi, 1993).

Bateman, Sam, 'Maritime Cooperation and Dialogue' in Dick Sherwood (ed.), *Maritime Power in the China Seas: Capabilities and Rationale* (Australian Defence Studies Centre, Australian Defence Force Academy, Canberra, 1994).

Bateman, Sam and Anthony Bergin, 'Building Blocks for Maritime Security in the Indian Ocean: An Australian Perspective' in Major General Dipankar Banerjee (ed.), *Towards an Era of Cooperation: An Indo-Australian Dialogue* (Institute for Defence Studies and Analyses, New Delhi, 1995).

Bateman, Sam and Stephen Bates (eds), *Calming the Waters: Initiatives for Asia Pacific Maritime Cooperation* (Strategic and Defence Studies Centre, Australian National University, Canberra, 1996).

Bateman, Sam and Stephen Bates, 'Introduction' in Sam Bateman and Stephen Bates (eds), *Calming the Waters: Initiatives for Asia Pacific*

Maritime Cooperation (Strategic and Defence Studies Centre, Australian National University, Canberra, 1996).

Bhaskar, Captain C. Uday, 'India and the Indian Ocean: Post-Cold War Possibilities' in Major General Dipankar Banerjee (ed.), *Towards an Era of Cooperation: An Indo-Australian Dialogue* (Institute for Defence Studies and Analyses, New Delhi, 1995).

Bowett, D., *The Legal Regime of Islands in International Law* (Oceana Publications, Dobbs Ferry, New York, 1979).

Brown, Lester, 'An Untraditional View of National Security' in J. Reichart and S. Sturm (eds), *American Defence Policy* (John Hopkins University Press, Baltimore, 5th edn 1982).

Bull, Hedley, 'Sea Power and Political Influence' in Jonathan Alford (ed.), *Sea Power and Influence: Old Issues and New Challenges* (Gower, Farnborough, 1980).

Charney, J. and L. Alexander (eds), *International Maritime Boundaries*, Vols. I and II (Martinus Nijhoff, Dordrecht, 1993).

Clark, J.R., 'Annex C: Management of the Coastal Zone for Sustainable Development' in Dames & Moore International, Louis Berger International, Inc. and Institute for Development Anthropology, *Sustainable Natural Resources Assessment - Philippines* (United States Agency for International Development, Manila, 1989).

Daly, H.E., 'From Empty-World Economics to Full-World Economics' in R. Goodland *et al.* (eds), *Environmentally Sustainable Economic Development: Building on Brundtland* (UNESCO, Paris, 1991).

Davidson, M.A. and T.W. Kana, 'Future Sea Level Rise and Its Implications for Charleston, South Carolina' in M.H. Glantz (ed.), *Societal Responses to Regional Climatic Change: Forecasting by Analogy* (Westview Press, Boulder, Colo., 1988).

Defending Australia, Defence White Paper 1994 (Australian Government Publishing Service, Canberra, 1994).

Dixit, J.N., *Anatomy of a Flawed Inheritance: Indo-Pakistan Relations: 1970-1994* (Konark Publishers, Delhi, 1995).

Eberle, Admiral Sir James (Retd), 'Prospects for Regional Cooperation in Maritime Affairs' in *The Indian Ocean: Challenges and Opportunities* (Navy Foundation, Delhi, 1992).

Flemming, N.C., 'Analytical Report' in OECD, *Oceanography* (Megascience: The OECD Forum, OECD, Paris, 1994).

Fortes, M,D., 'Seagrass Resources of ASEAN' in C.R. Wilkinson (ed.), *Living Coastal Resources: Status and Management* (Australian Institute of Marine Science, North Queensland, 1994).

Foundation for Rural Economic Enterprise and Development, Inc. (FREED), *DENR Internal Assessment: Gearing the DENR* (Organization for Sustainable Development, Philippines, 1994).

Goodland, R. *et al.* (eds), *Environmentally Sustainable Economic Development: Building on Brundtland* (UNESCO, Paris, 1991).

Handl, Gunther, 'Environmental Security and Global Change: The Challenge to International Law' in *Yearbook of International Environmental Law*, Vol.1, 1990.

Hudson, Admiral M.W. (Retd), 'Australia's Naval Policy in the Twenty-First Century' in Jasjit Singh (ed.), *Maritime Security* (Institute for Defence Studies and Analyses, New Delhi, 1993).

International Tanker Owners Pollution Federation (ITOPF) Ltd., *Response to Marine Oil Spills* (ITOPF Ltd., London, 1986).

Japan Statistical Yearbook 1986 (published in Japanese by Management and Coordination Agency, Statistics Bureau, Tokyo, 1986).

Kumar, Satish (ed.), *Yearbook on India's Foreign Policy 1987-1988* (Tata McGraw-Hill, New Delhi, 1988).

Lean, G., D. Hinrichsen and A. Markham (eds), *World Wildlife Fund Atlas of the Environment* (Prentice Hall, New York, 1990).

Lynn-Jones, S.M., 'Agreements to Prevent Incidents at Sea and Dangerous Military Activities: Potential Applications in the Asia-Pacific Region' in A. Mack (ed.), *A Peaceful Ocean? Maritime Security in the Pacific in the Post-Cold War Era* (Allen & Unwin, Sydney, 1993).

Lyons, K.J., O.F. Moss and P. Perrett, 'Geographic Information Systems' in Desmond Ball and Ross Babbage (eds), *Geographic Information Systems: Defence Applications* (Brassey's Australia, Sydney, 1989).

Mahathir bin Mohamad, '"Tak Kenal Maka Tak Cinta"' in *Asia-Pacific in the 1980s: Toward Greater Symmetry in Economic Independence* (Centre for Strategic and International Studies, Jakarta, May 1980).

Meconis, C.A., 'Naval Arms Control in the Asia-Pacific Region after the Cold War' in Elisabeth Borgese and Norton Ginsburg (eds), *Ocean Yearbook 11* (International Ocean Institute/University of Chicago Press, Chicago, 1994).

Meconis, Charles A. and Commander Stanley B. Weeks (Retd), *Cooperative Maritime Security in the Asia-Pacific Region: A Strategic and Arms Control Agreement* (Institute for Global Security Studies, Seattle, 1995).

Meng, Qing Nan, *Land-based Marine Pollution: International Law Development* (Graham and Trotman, London, 1987).

Menon, Rear-Admiral K.R., 'Maritime Developments and Opportunities in South Asia' in Sam Bateman and Dick Sherwood (eds), *Australia's Maritime Bridge Into Asia* (Allen & Unwin, Sydney, 1995).

Mitchell, Ronald, 'Intentional Oil Pollution of the Oceans' in Peter M. Haas, Robert O. Keohane and Marc A. Levy (eds), *Institutions for the Earth: Sources of Effective Environmental Protection* (MIT Press, Cambridge, Mass., 1993).

Organisation for Economic Cooperation and Development (OECD), *Oceanography* (Megascience: The OECD Forum, OECD, Paris, 1994).

Paik, Jin-Hyun, 'The Fisheries Regime in Northeast Asia' in Dalchoong Kim, Jiao Yongke, Jin-Hyun Paik and Chen Degong (eds), *Ocean Affairs in North-East Asia and Prospects for Korea-China Maritime Cooperation* (Institute of East-West Studies, Yonsei University, Seoul, 1994).

Pederson, Susan and Stanley Weeks, 'A Survey of Confidence Building Measures' in Ralph Cossa (ed.), *Asia Pacific Confidence and Security Building Measures* (Center for Strategic and International Studies, Washington DC, 1995).

Roy, Vice-Admiral Mihir (Retd), 'Maritime Cooperation in the Indian Ocean' in Greg Mills (ed.), *Maritime Policy for Developing Nations* (South African Institute of International Affairs, Johannesburg, 1995).

Roy-Chaudhury, Rahul, *Sea Power and Indian Security* (Brassey's, London, 1995).

Soedibyo, Brigadier General (Retd), 'Regional Security and Military Cooperation: An Indonesian Perception' in *The Indian Ocean: Challenges and Opportunities* (Navy Foundation, Delhi, 1992).

Sprout, H. and M. Sprout, *The Ecological Perspective on Human Affairs: With Special Reference to International Politics* (Greenwood Press, Westport, Conn., 1965).

Thayer, G.W., S.M. Adams and M.W. La Croix, 'Structural and Functional Aspects of a Recently Established *Zostera Marina* Community' in L.E. Cronin (ed.), *Estuarine Research*, Vol.I (Academic Press, New York, 1975).

Townsend-Gault, Ian, 'Petroleum Development Offshore: Legal and Contractual Issues' in N.D. Beredjick and Thomas Walde (eds), *Third World Petroleum Investment Policies for the 1990s* (Graham and Trotman, London, 1989).

Townsend-Gault, Ian and William G. Stormont, 'Offshore Petroleum Joint Development Arrangements: Functional Instrument? Compromise? Obligation?' in Gerald H. Blake *et al.* (eds), *The Peaceful Management of Transboundary Resources* (Graham and Trotman/Martinus Nijhoff, London and Boston, 1995).

'Treaty between Australia and the Independent State of Papua New Guinea Concerning Sovereignty and Maritime Boundaries in the area between the two Countries including the area known as Torres Strait, and Related Matters' in *New Directions in the Law of the Sea*, compiled and edited by Myron Nordquist, S. Houston Lay and Kenneth Simmonds, Vol.8 (Oceana Publications, London, 1980).

United Nations, *The Law of the Sea: Official Text on the Convention on the Law of the Sea*, UN Doc A/CONF. 62/122, UN Sales No.E.83.v.5, 1983.

United Nations Environment Programme (UNEP), *The Convention for the Prevention of Marine Pollution from Land-Based Sources* (UNEP, Nairobi, 1974).

United Nations Environment Programme (UNEP), *Global Programme of Action for the Protection of the Marine Environment from Land-Based Activities* (UNEP, Nairobi, 1995).

Valencia, Mark J., *South-East Asian Seas: Oil under Troubled Waters: Hydrocarbon Potential, Jurisdictional Issues, and International Relations* (Oxford University Press, Singapore and Oxford, 1985).

Valencia, Mark J., 'Cooperation in Marine Scientific Research as a Confidence-Building Measure' in Sam Bateman and Stephen Bates (eds), *Calming the Waters: Initiatives for Asia Pacific Maritime Cooperation* (Strategic and Defence Studies Centre, Australian National University, Canberra, 1996).

Vallega, Adalberto, *Sea Management: A Theoretical Approach* (Elsevier Applied Science, London and New York, 1992).

Van Dyke, Jon M. and Dale L. Bennett, 'Islands and the Delimitation of Ocean Space in the South China Sea' in Elisabeth Borgese and Norton Ginsburg (eds), *Ocean Yearbook* 10 (University of Chicago Press, Chicago, 1993).

Vinogradov, Sergei, 'International Environmental Security: The Concept and Its Implementation' in A. Carty and G. Danilenko (eds), *Perestroika and International Law: Current Anglo-Soviet Approaches to International Law* (Edinburgh University Press, Edinburgh, 1990).

Weeks, Stanley, 'Measures to Prevent Major Incidents at Sea' in J. Goldblat (ed.), *Maritime Security: The Building of Confidence* (United Nations, New York, 1992).

Woods, Lawrence T., *Asia-Pacific Diplomacy: Nongovernmental Organizations and International Relations* (University of British Columbia Press, Vancouver, 1993).

Young, Oran R. and Gail Osherenko, 'International Regime Formation: Findings, Research Priorities and Applications' in Oran R. Young and Gail Osherenko (eds), *Polar Politics: Creating International Environmental Regimes* (Cornell University Press, Ithaca and London, 1993).

JOURNAL ARTICLES

Ball, Desmond, 'A New Era in Confidence Building: The Second Track Process in the Asia/Pacific Region', *Security Dialogue*, Vol.25, No.2, June 1994.

'Beagle Channel Arbitration, Report and Decision of the Court of Arbitration', *International Legal Materials*, Vol.17, 1978.

Bhaskar, Captain C. Uday, 'Regional Naval Cooperation', *Strategic Analysis*, November 1992.

Bradbury, Roger, 'Marine Informatics: A New Discipline Emerges', *Maritime Studies*, No.80, January/February 1995.

Brown, E.D., 'Rockall and the Limits of National Jurisdiction of the UK: Part 2', *Marine Policy*, Vol.2, 1978.

Calhoun, Martin, 'The Big Green Military Machine', *Business and Society Review*, No.92, Winter 1995.

Deudney, Daniel, 'Muddled Thinking', *Bulletin of the Atomic Scientists*, Vol.47, No.3, April 1991.

Dimri, Lt Cdr B.M., 'Naval Diplomacy and UNCLOS III', *Strategic Analysis*, April 1994.

Fallon, L.A. and T.-E. Chua, 'Towards Strengthening Policy and Strategic Orientation for Fisheries Resources Management: The Role of Coastal Area Management', *Tropical Coastal Area Management*, Vol.5, No.3, 1990.

Frederick, Michel, 'La securité environmentale: éléments de définition', *Etudes Internationales*, Vol.24, No.4, December 1993.

Gleick, Peter, 'Enviroment and Security: Clear Connections', *Bulletin of the Atomic Scientists*, Vol.47, No.3, April 1991.

Gleick, Peter, 'Water and Conflict: Fresh Water Resources and International Security', *International Security*, Vol.18, No.1, Summer 1993.

Hills, Ann, 'Conservation: Britain's Defence Ministry Fights back', *Geographical Magazine*, Vol.63, No.5, May 1991.

Hodgson, R.D. and R.W. Smith, 'The Informal Single Negotiating Text (Committee II): A Geographical Perspective', *Ocean Development and International Law*, Vol.3, 1976.

Irwin, P., 'Settlement of Maritime Boundary Disputes: An Analysis of the Law of the Sea Negotiations', *Ocean Development and International Law*, Vol.8, 1980.

'Joint Force To Fight Pirates', *Asian Defence Journal*, March 1992.

Karl, D., 'Islands and the Delimitation of the Continental Shelf: A Framework for Analysis', *American Journal of International Law*, Vol.71, 1977.

Kimball, Lee, 'International Law and Institutions: The Oceans and Beyond', *Ocean Development and International Law*, Vol.20, 1989.

'KL, Singapore, Jakarta Study Surveillance System in Strait', *Asian Defence Journal*, April 1993.

Leifer, Michael, 'The Maritime Regime and Regional Security in East Asia', *The Pacific Review* , Vol.4, No.2, 1992.

Lok, J.J., 'Partnership With Potential', *Jane's Navy International*, Vol.101, No.3, April 1996.

Lukas, R., E. Firing, P. Hacker, P.L. Richardson, C.A. Collins, R. Fine and R. Gammon, 'Observations of the Mindanao Current during the Western Equatorial Pacific Ocean Circulation Study', *Journal of Geophysical Research*, Vol.96, 1991.

Lynn-Jones, S.M., 'A Quiet Success for Arms Control: Preventing Incidents at Sea', *International Security*, Vol.9, No.4, Spring 1985.

Macintyre, A.D., 'Environmental Monitoring of the Oceans', *Marine Policy*, Vol.19, No.6, 1995.

Maddock, R.T., 'Environmental Security in East Asia', *Contemporary Southeast Asia*, Vol.17, No.1, June 1995.

Mak, J.N., The ASEAN Naval Build-Up: Implications for the Regional Order', *Pacific Review*, May 1995.

Mathews, Jessica, 'Redefining Security', *Foreign Affairs*, Vol.68, No.2, 1989.

McManus, J.W, 'Coral Reefs of the ASEAN Region: Status and Management', *Ambio*, Vol.17, No.3, 1988.

Menon, Rear-Admiral K.R. (Retd), 'Maritime Conflict Resolution and Confidence-Building in South Asia', *Indian Defence Review*, October-December 1995.

Mookerjee, Vice-Admiral S. (Retd), 'Joint Naval Exercises: Overdue Change of Course', *United Services Institute of India Journal*, April-June 1992.

Myers, Norman, 'Environment and Security', *Foreign Policy*, No.74, 1989.

O'Brien, Terence, 'Track Two: Creating a Meltingpot', *New Zealand International Review*, Vol.20, No.4, July/August 1995.

Phillips, R.C., 'Seagrasses and Coastal Marine Environment', *Oceanus*, Vol.21, No.3, 1978.

Pillai, Rear-Admiral Sampath, 'Somalia-Indian Navy in the Land of Punt', *Quarter Deck*, 94, 1994.

Roy, Vice-Admiral Mihir (Retd), 'From Confrontation to Cooperation: A New Agenda for the Indian Navy', *United Services Institute of India Journal*, January-March 1993.

Roy-Chaudhury, Rahul, 'Indian Naval Diplomacy', *Indian Defence Review*, January-March 1995.

Roy-Chaudhury, Rahul, 'India's Defence Shipyards', *Maritime International*, March 1995.

Roy-Chaudhury, Rahul, 'Showing the Flag', *Maritime International*, February 1996.

Smith, Hance D., 'The Environmental Management of Shipping', *Marine Policy*, Vol.19, No.6, 1995.

Sorensen, Jens, 'The International Proliferation of Integrated Coastal Zone Management Efforts', *Ocean and Coastal Management*, Vol.21, No.1/3, 1993.

Steinberg, Barry P., 'The Hidden Costs of Closing Military Bases', *Public Management*, Vol.73, No.5, May 1991.

Symmons, C.R., 'The Canadian 200 Mile Fishery Limit and the Delimitation of Maritime Zones around St. Pierre and Miquelon', *Ottawa Law Review*, Vol.12, 1980.

'The United Nations Register of Conventional Arms - Whence? Whether? ... and Why?', *Disarmament*, Vol.XVII, No.1, 1994.

Timoshenko, Alexandre, 'Ecological Security: Global Change Paradigm', *Colorado Journal of International Environmental Law and Policy*, Vol.1, No.1, 1990.

Ullman, Richard, 'Redefining Security', *International Security*, Vol.8, No.1, Summer 1983.

United States Department of State, Bureau of Intelligence and Research, Office of the Geographer, 'Continental Shelf Boundary: Iran-Saudi Arabia', *Limits in the Seas*, No.24, 6 July 1970.

United States Department of State, Bureau of Intelligence and Research, Office of the Geographer, 'Continental Shelf Boundary: Iran-Qatar', *Limits in the Seas*, No.25, 9 July 1970.

United States Department of State, Bureau of Intelligence and Research, Office of the Geographer, 'Continental Shelf Boundary: Argentina-Uruguay', *Limits in the Seas*, No.64, 24 October 1975.

United States Department of State, Bureau of Intelligence and Research, Office of the Geographer, 'Historic Water Boundary: India-Sri Lanka', *Limits in the Seas*, No.66, 12 December 1975.

United States Department of State, Bureau of Intelligence and Research, Office of the Geographer, 'Continental Shelf Boundary: Canada-Greenland', *Limits in the Seas*, No.72, 4 August 1976.

United States Department of State, Bureau of Intelligence and Research, Office of the Geographer, 'Maritime Boundaries: Colombia-Panama', *Limits in the Seas*, No.79, 3 November 1978.

van der Kroef, Justus, 'The South China Sea Problem: Some Future Scenarios', *The American Asian Review*, Vol.12, No.4, Winter 1994.

Watson, R.A., R.G. Coles and W.J. Lee Long, 'Simulation Estimates of Annual Yield and Landed Value for Commercial Penaeid Prawns from a Tropical Seagrass Habitat, Northern

Queensland, Australia', *Australian Journal of Marine and Freshwater Resources*, Vol.44, 1993.

Westing, Arthur, 'The Environmental Component of Comprehensive Security', *Bulletin of Peace Proposals*, Vol.20, No.2, June 1989.

Woods, Lawrence T., 'Non-governmental Organizations and Pacific Cooperation: Back to the Future?', *The Pacific Review*, Vol.4, No.4, 1991.

PRESS AND NEWSLETTER REPORTS

'Anti-piracy centre "to be set up in Malaysia"', *Straits Times*, 28 February 1992.

'ASEAN and the ASEAN Regional Forum', *Pacific Research*, August 1995.

Baum, Julian and Matt Forney, 'Strait of uncertainty', *Far Eastern Economic Review*, 8 February 1996.

Chanda, Nayan, 'Long shadow', *Far Eastern Economic Review*, 28 December 1995 and 4 January 1996.

'China agrees to discuss Spratlys "code of conduct"', *Reuters*, 10 May 1995.

'China is firm on Taiwan, Spratlys ahead of ASEAN meeting in Brunei', *Japan Times*, 22 July 1995.

'China seen defusing tension in South China Sea', *Reuters*, 2 August 1995.

'China stands firm on Spratlys, Harry Wu', *Reuters*, 30 July 1995.

Ching, Frank, 'Vietnam: a challenge to ASEAN', *Far Eastern Economic Review*, 3 November 1994.

FBIS, Daily Report: East Asia, 2 July 1992.

Hiebert, Murray, 'Comforting noises', *Far Eastern Economic Review*, 10 August 1995.

Lague, David, 'ASEAN: China flexes its muscles', *Sydney Morning Herald*, 2 July 1994.

Lee Lai To, *CALS Newsletter*, Vol.1, No.2, September 1994.

'Li Teng-hui proposes South China Sea development', FBIS–CHI-95-072, 14 April 1995.

'Manila sees China as threat despite assurances', *Reuters*, 27 October 1995.

'Ministers endorse security forum', *Canberra Times*, 24 July 1993.

Murdoch, Lindsay, 'Jakarta mounts crackdown on Asian pirates', *Age*, 9 July 1992.

'Naval hydrography charting new courses' (Interview with Commodore K.R.Srinivasan, the Chief Hydrographer of the Indian Navy), *Times of India*, 4 October 1995.

'Paper: Beijing planning naval games in Spratlys', *Honolulu Advertiser*, 25 July 1995.

'Passage to India', *Far Eastern Economic Review*, 19 January 1995.

'Philippines, Vietnam agree on Spratlys pact', *Honolulu Advertiser*, 9 November 1995.

Pieth, Reto, 'Toxic Military', *The Nation*, Vol.254, No.2, 8 June 1992.

Powers, Mary B., 'DOD's Gary Vest speaks out on its new global cleanup links', *Engineering News-Record*, 6 March 1995.

'PRC limits claim', FBIS-EAS-95-094, 16 May 1995.

'Qian views Spratlys with Vietnamese counterpart', FBIS-CHI-95-096, 18 May 1995.

'Ramos' preference for diplomacy, dialogue noted', FBIS-EAS-95-068, 10 April 1995.

'Regional Briefing', *Far Eastern Economic Review*, 22 September 1994.

Richardson, Michael, 'China takes softer stand in dispute on Spratly isles', *International Herald Tribune*, 31 July 1995.

Schwarz, Adam, 'Where oil and water mix', *Far Eastern Economic Review*, 16 March 1995.

'Spratly joint venture', *Indochina Digest*, 24 December 1993.

'Spratlys: China wants in on development', *Straits Times*, 1 June 1995.

Taira, Keisuke, 'Message From Chairman', *WESTPAC Information*, No.4, May 1996.

'The Jane's Interview', *Jane's Defence Weekly*, 19 February 1994.

Tiglao, Rigoberto, 'Remote control', *Far Eastern Economic Review*, 1 June 1995.

Vallega, Aldaberto, 'ICCOPS International Workshop on Regional Seas towards Sustainable Development - Challenges for Research and Policy' in Aldaberto Vallega *et al.* (eds), *Special Issue of ICCOPS Newsletter*, 1995.

Vatikiotis, Michael, 'Uncharted waters', *Far Eastern Economic Review*, 5 August 1993.

ADDRESSES, PAPERS, REPORTS, PROCEEDINGS

Agenda 21, United Nations Conference on Environment and Development, Rio de Janeiro, 3-14 June 1992.

Ball, Desmond and Commodore Sam Bateman, RAN, *An Australian Perspective on Maritime CSBMs in the Asia-Pacific Region*, Working Paper No.234 (Strategic and Defence Studies Centre, Australian National University, Canberra, August 1991).

Bilney, The Hon. Gordon, Minister for Defence Science and Personnel, 'Address at the Regional Defence Cooperation Conference', Sydney, 4 November 1991.

'Case concerning delimitation of continental shelf between the United Kingdom of Great Britain and Northern Ireland, and the French Republic', *Reports of International Arbitral Awards*, Vol.18 [1978].

'Chairman's Statement of the Second ASEAN Regional Forum (ARF)', Bandar Seri Begawan, August 1995.

'Chairman's Statement, ASEAN Post-Ministerial Conferences, Senior Officials Meeting', Singapore, 20-21 May 1993.

Chia Lin Sien, 'Alternative routes to the Straits of Malacca for oil tankers: a financial, technical and economic analysis', paper presented at the Workshop on the Straits of Malacca, Kuala Lumpur, 24-25 January 1995.

Chircop *et al.*, 'Conflict and cooperation in regional seas: a background paper', Oceans Institute of Canada, Halifax, July 1994.

Chou, L.M. (ed.), *Implications of Expected Climate Changes in the East Asian Seas Region: An Overview*, RCU/EAS Technical Report Series No.2, United Nations Environment Programme, 1994.

Chua, T.-E., 'Asian Fisheries towards the Year 2000: A Challenge to Fisheries Scientists' in *Proceedings of the Third Asian Fisheries Forum, Singapore* (The Asian Fisheries Society, Manila, 1994).

Chua, T.-E., 'Managing Coastal Resources for Sustainable Development: The ASEAN Initiative' in T.-E. Chua and L. F. Scura (eds), *Managing ASEAN Coastal Resources for Sustainable Development: Roles of Policy Makers, Scientists, Donors, Media and Communities* (ICLARM Conference Proceedings, Manila, 1991).

Coenen, R., 'Presentation notes on the London Convention 1972', presented at the *Seminar on Prevention of Marine Pollution: The Implementation of Marpol 73/78 and the London Convention 1972*, Kuala Lumpur, 4 April 1996.

'Continental Shelf (Libyan Arab Jamahiriya/Malta), Judgment', *International Court of Justice Reports 1985.*

'Continental Shelf (Tunisia/Libyan Arab Jamahiriya), (Diss. Op. Oda)', *International Court of Justice Reports 1982.*

CSCAP Pro-tem Committee, *The Security of the Asia Pacific Region*, Memorandum No.1, Council for Security Cooperation in the Asia Pacific, April 1994.

'Delimitation of the Maritime Boundary in the Gulf of Maine Area, Judgment', *International Court of Justice Reports 1984.*

Estacion, J. and A.C. Alcala, 'Associated Fisheries and Aquatic Resources of Seagrasses' in *Proceedings of the First National Conference on Seagrass Management, Research and Development* (National Environmental Protection Council, Diliman, Quezon City, 1986).

Evans, Gareth and Paul Dibb, *Australian Paper on Practical Proposals for Security Cooperation in the Asia Pacific Region*, paper commissioned by the 1993 ASEAN PMC SOM and submitted to the ARF SOM, Bangkok, April 1994, published by the Strategic and Defence Studies Centre, Australian National University, Canberra, January 1995.

Food and Agriculture Organisation of the United Nations (FAO), Living Marine Resources Research Paper No.5, commissioned by the United Nations Conference on Environment and Development (UNCED), Rome, 1991.

Fortes, M.D., *Seagrasses of East Asia: Environmental and Management Perspectives*, RCU/EAS Technical Report Series No.6, United Nations Environment Programme, 1995.

Fortes, M.D., *Seagrasses: A Resource Unknown in the ASEAN Region*, ICLARM Education Series No.5 (International Centre for Living Aquatic Resources Management, Manila, 1989).

Gill, Bates, 'Enhancing National Military Capabilities in the Asia-Pacific Region: Debating Legitimate Needs versus Unwarranted Development', *10th Asia-Pacific Roundtable*, Kuala Lumpur, 8-9 June 1996.

Gomez, E.D., P.M. Aliño, W.R.Y. Licuanan and H.T. Yap, 'Status Report on Coral Reefs of the Philippines 1994' in C. Wilkinson, S. Sudara and L.M. Chou (eds), *Proceedings of the Third ASEAN-Australia Symposium on Living Coastal Resources*, Vol.1: *Status Reviews* (AIMS, Townsville, Australia, 1994).

Hilton, R.P., 'A Confidence-Building Measure at Work: The 1972 United States-USSR Incidents At Sea Agreement' in *Naval Confidence Building Measures*, Disarmament Topical Papers No.4 (United Nations, New York, 1990).

Hodgson, R.D., 'Islands: Normal and Special Circumstances' in John King Gamble, Jr and Guilio Pontecorvo (eds), *Law of the Sea: The Emerging Regime of the Oceans*, Proceedings of the Law of the Sea Institute Eighth Annual Conference (Ballinger Publishing Company, Cambridge, Mass., 1974).

Joint Communique of the Twenty-Fourth ASEAN Ministerial Meeting, Kuala Lumpur, 19-20 July 1991.

Joint Communique of the Twenty-Sixth ASEAN Ministerial Meeting, Singapore, 23-24 July 1993, Press Release, 26th ASEAN Ministerial Meeting/Post Ministerial Conferences, Singapore, 23-28 July 1993.

Jones, Peter, 'Maritime security cooperation and CBMs in the Asia-Pacific: applying maritime CBMs in regional contexts', paper prepared for the *Fourth Asia-Pacific Dialogue on Maritime Security*, Nakorn Pathom, Thailand, 8-9 August 1994.

Jones, Peter, 'Maritime confidence-building measures in the Middle East', paper prepared for the conference, *From Cooperative Security to Multinational Peacekeeping: The Role of Medium Power Navies in the New Century*, University of British Columbia, 23-25 February 1995.

Lacanilao, F., 'Research and development problems of Philippines fisheries', lecture presented at the *Scientific Symposium on Sustainable Development of Fisheries Resources*, National Research Council of the Philippines, University of the Philippines, Diliman, 22 November 1995.

Lee, H.B. and J. Low, 'The Enhancement of Fish Community in the Singapore River through the Use of Artificial Seagrass' in L.S Chia and L.M Chou (eds), *Urban Coastal Area Management: The Experience of Singapore* (ICLARM Conference Proceedings, Manila, 1991).

Lennon, G.W., 'ROD and the significance of the ASEAN seas', Proceedings of the symposium on *The Seas of South East Asia - The Key to Regional Climate Patterns*, Lombok, Indonesia, June 1995.

MacDougall, Vice Admiral I.D.G., Chief of Naval Staff (CNS), 'CNS presentation to WPNS III on the Inaugural Western Pacific Naval Symposium Workshop', Sydney, 9-10 July 1992.

Morgan, Joseph R., *Porpoises among the Whales: Small Navies in Asia and the Pacific*, East-West Center Special Report No.2, March 1994.

'North Sea Continental Shelf, Judgment', *International Court of Justice Reports 1969*.

Ono, Akio, 'Japan's Contribution to the Safety of Navigation and Pollution Mitigation Efforts in the Straits of Malacca', paper presented at the Workshop on the Straits of Malacca, Kuala Lumpur, 24-25 January 1995.

Poole, A., 'Electronics and instrumentation CME', Proceedings of the symposium on *The Seas of South East Asia - The Key to Regional Climate Patterns*, Lombok, Indonesia, June 1995.

Prescott, Victor, 'Sharpening the geographical and legal focus on the potential regional conflict in the Spratly Islands', paper presented at the ISEAS Workshop on *The Spratly Islands: A Potential Regional Conflict*, Singapore, 8-9 December 1993.

Raja Malik Saripulazan Raja Kamarulzaman, 'ASEAN-OSRAP: strengthening regional capabilities', paper presented at *1995 International Oil Spill Conference*, Long Beach, California, 27 February-2 March 1995.

Razak, Dato' Sri Mohd Najib bin Tun Haji Abdul, Keynote Address at MIMA seminar on *CBMs at Sea in the Asia Pacific Region: Meeting the Challenges of the 21st Century*, Kuala Lumpur, 2-3 August 1994.

Regional Security Dialogue: A Calendar of Asia Pacific Events, July 1995-June 1996, prepared jointly by the Regional Security Section, Department of Foreign Affairs and Trade, Canberra, and the Strategic and Defence Studies Centre, Australian National University, Canberra, 5th edn, July 1995.

Sherwood, Commander Dick, RAN, 'The Australian experience with regional maritime cooperation', paper delivered to the *Anatalya Round of the Middle East Peace Process Multilateral Working Group on Arms Control and Regional Security*, Anatalya, Turkey, 21 March 1994.

Swinnerton, Russ and Desmond Ball, *A Regional Regime for Maritime Surveillance, Safety, and Information Exchanges*, Working Paper

No.278 (Strategic and Defence Studies Centre, Australian National University, Canberra, 1993).

'The ASEAN Regional Forum - A Concept Paper', May 1995, reproduced in Desmond Ball and Pauline Kerr, *Presumptive Engagement: Australia's Asia-Pacific Security Policy in the 1990s* (Allen & Unwin, Sydney, 1996).

United Nations Convention on the Law of the Sea, 10 December 1982, UN Doc.A/Conf.62/121, reprinted in *International Legal Materials,* No.21, 1982.

United Nations Educational, Scientific and Cultural Organisation (UNESCO), 'Year 2000 challenges for marine science training and education worldwide', *UNESCO Reports in Marine Science,* No.52, Paris, 1989.

United Nations Environment Programme (UNEP), *Programme of Action to Control Land-based Sources of Pollution in the East Asian Seas Region - Regional Report* (UNEP, Bangkok, 1994).

Wong, T.M., 'Currents in the Singapore Main Straits', Port of Singapore Authority internal report, 1995.

OTHER MATERIAL

Davison, Geoffrey, Project Director, World Wide Fund for Nature Malaysia, pers. comm.

Ocean Rescue 2000, *Australian Marine Data Inventory - An Interim Guide to the Supporting Information,* Document 3, Version 2.0 dated August 1995.

STRATEGIC AND DEFENCE STUDIES CENTRE

The aim of the Strategic and Defence Studies Centre, which is located in the Research School of Pacific and Asian Studies in the Australian National University, is to advance the study of strategic problems, especially those relating to the general region of Asia and the Pacific. The Centre gives particular attention to Australia's strategic neighbourhood of Southeast Asia and the Southwest Pacific. Participation in the Centre's activities is not limited to members of the University, but includes other interested professional, diplomatic and parliamentary groups. Research includes military, political, economic, scientific and technological aspects of strategic developments. Strategy, for the purpose of the Centre, is defined in the broadest sense of embracing not only the control and application of military force, but also the peaceful settlement of disputes which could cause violence.

This is the leading academic body in Australia specialising in these studies. Centre members give frequent lectures and seminars for other departments within the ANU and other universities, as well as to various government departments. Regular seminars and conferences on topics of current importance to the Centre's research are held, and the major defence training institutions, the Joint Services Staff College and the Navy, Army and RAAF Staff Colleges, are heavily dependent upon SDSC assistance with the strategic studies sections of their courses. Members of the Centre provide advice and training courses in strategic affairs to the Department of Defence and the Department of Foreign Affairs and Trade.

Since its inception in 1966, the Centre has supported a number of Visiting and Research Fellows, who have undertaken a wide variety of investigations. Recently the emphasis of the Centre's work has been on problems of security and confidence building in Australia's neighbourhood; the defence of Australia; arms proliferation and arms control; policy advice to the higher levels of the Australian Defence Department; and the strategic implications of developments in Southeast Asia, the Indian Ocean and the Southwest Pacific.

The Centre runs a Graduate Programme in Strategic Studies, which includes both Graduate Diploma and Masters programmes. It maintains a comprehensive collection of reference materials on strategic issues, particularly from the press, learned journals and government publications. Its Publications Programme, which includes the Canberra Papers on Strategy and Defence and SDSC

Working Papers, produces more than two dozen publications a year on strategic and defence issues.

CANBERRA PAPERS ON STRATEGY AND DEFENCE:

NEW SERIES

NO.	TITLE	$A
CP43	Australia's Secret Space Programs by **Desmond Ball**	15.00
CP44	High Personnel Turnover: The ADF is not a Limited Liability Company by **Cathy Downes**	15.00
CP45	Should Australia Plan to Defend Christmas and Cocos Islands? by **Ross Babbage** Out of Print	15.00
CP46	US Bases in the Philippines: Issues and Implications by **Desmond Ball** (ed.)	15.00
CP47	Soviet Signals Intelligence (SIGINT) by **Desmond Ball**	20.00
CP48	The Vietnam People's Army: Regularization of Command 1975-1988 by **D.M. FitzGerald**	15.00
CP49	Australia and the Global Strategic Balance by **Desmond Ball**	15.00
CP50	Organising an Army: the Australian Experience 1957-1965 by **J.C. Blaxland**	20.00
CP51	The Evolving World Economy: Some Alternative Security Question for Australia by **Richard A. Higgott**	15.00
CP52	Defending the Northern Gateway by **Peter Donovan**	20.00
CP53	Soviet Signals Intelligence (SIGINT): Intercepting Satellite Communications by **Desmond Ball**	20.00
CP54	Breaking the American Alliance: An Independent National Security Policy for Australia by **Gary Brown**	20.00
CP55	Senior Officer Professional Development in the Australian Defence Force: Constant Study to Prepare by **Cathy Downes**	20.00
CP56	Code 777: Australia and the US Defense Satellite Communications System (DSCS) by **Desmond Ball**	22.50
CP57	China's Crisis: The International Implications by **Gary Klintworth** (ed.)	17.00
CP58	Index to Parliamentary Questions on Defence by **Gary Brown**	20.00
CP59	Controlling Civil Maritime Activities in a Defence Contingency by **W.A.G. Dovers**	17.00
CP60	The Security of Oceania in the 1990s. Vol.I, Views from the Region by **David Hegarty** and **Peter Polomka** (eds)	15.00
CP61	The Strategic Significance of Torres Strait by **Ross Babbage**	30.00
CP62	The Leading Edge: Air Power in Australia's Unique Environment by **P.J. Criss** and **D.J. Schubert**	22.50